D1712840

THE DASHING KANSAN

THE DASHING KANSAN

Lewis Lindsay Dyche

The Amazing Adventures
of a Nineteenth-Century
Naturalist and Explorer

William Sharp and Peggy Sullivan

HARROW BOOKS

in association with

THE MUSEUM OF
NATURAL HISTORY
The University of Kansas

The Dashing Kansan
The Amazing Adventures of a Nineteenth-Century Naturalist and Explorer

First Printing: November, 1990

Harrow Books
Kansas City, Missouri

ISBN Number: 0-916455-06-8
Library of Congress Catalogue Card Number: 90-083791

Printed in the United States of America

To Chester, Phil, and David

CONTENTS

PREFACE

When the authors asked me several years ago whether the Museum of Natural History would be interested in publishing a biography of Lewis Lindsay Dyche, my immediate reaction was an enthusiastic "yes." Why? The reasons are abundant and diverse.

Some of the more obvious ones include the fact that Dyche is one of the three most important and influential figures in the development of the natural history collections at the University of Kansas as well as its Museum of Natural History, the other two being Francis Huntington Snow, a member of the original faculty at KU, and E. Raymond Hall, Director of the Museum of Natural History from 1944 to 1967. Dyche's work and influence were largely responsible for persuading the Kansas legislature to appropriate funds to construct a new museum building, completed in 1903 and eventually named Dyche Hall.

During his association (1877–1915) with KU, first as an enthusiastic and talented student and then, starting in 1888, as professor of anatomy and physiology, taxidermist, and curator of mammals, birds, and fishes, Dyche's extraordinary abilities evolved dramatically. While still an undergraduate, he was appointed an instructor in natural history in 1882. As time went on, Dyche increasingly attracted public notice as an adventuresome explorer, gifted taxidermist, and flamboyant showman on the lecture circuit.

Dyche's significance as a public figure, a P. T. Barnum of natural history if you will, is perhaps best appreciated by contemplating the late nineteenth and early twentieth centuries from the standpoint of the communications and public entertainment media of the day. Radio as a means of mass communications did not come into its own until after World War I. Movies did not become a widespread form of popular entertainment until the early twentieth century, and television did not blossom until half a century later. It was in this context, a time when sources of public entertainment and edification were considerably fewer than they are today, that Dyche's talents as a naturalist, explorer, scientific collector, taxidermist, and showman had such enormous impact. Artfully constructed exhibits of lifelike mammals in their natural habitats provided realistic glimpses of inaccessible wild places that we encounter readily on movie and television screens. The enthralled public could see Dyche (often in the native costumes of faraway places) at first hand, in person, as he told fascinating stories, illustrated with lantern slides, about "Wild North American Animals and Their Haunts" or "The Land of the Midnight Sun."

Dyche made his mark—and it was a significant one—in natural history, scientific exploration and collecting, taxidermy, wildlife conservation, and the development of the KU Museum of Natural History. But perhaps his most significant contribution was in promoting public understanding and appreciation of nature. Snow, Dyche, and Hall, during the first century of the university, created and promoted museums of natural history at KU that to this day continue the tradition of scientific inquiry and public education that has characterized them since the founding of the University of Kansas.

Philip S. Humphrey
Director
Museum of Natural History
The University of Kansas
May 23, 1990

FOREWORD

The career of Lewis Lindsay Dyche provides us with an example of one of the more dramatic ironies in the evolution of modern natural history exploration. To the casual reader of that history, there may appear to be an unfathomable contradiction between the objectives of the gatherer of animal specimens for taxidermic displays and the ideals of wildlife conservation.

As a nineteenth-century pioneer in that field, a vital figure in the early development of the Museum of Natural History at the University of Kansas, and the man responsible for the creation of the wildlife panorama at the 1893 Chicago world's fair, Dyche enthusiastically set out to kill and preserve animal specimens. In an age denied the more benign intrusion of film and television cameras into a natural habitat, it remained for biologists to preserve species samples in museum panoramas approximating various environments.

These scientific collectors were not indiscriminate killers of animals, but men who — unlike many hunters and poachers — were acutely aware of the status of the animals they studied and were among the most ardent supporters of protective measures. Dyche's career was influenced, in part at least, by fortunate timing. If the roots of modern organismic biology and natural history explorations in the United States are traced, a convenient milepost for these endeavors is 1850. In that year a young college-trained biologist, Spencer Fullerton Baird, came to the Smithsonian Institution as Assistant Secretary with responsibility for the newly established U.S. National Museum. Seven years later, Dyche was born.

Unlike Dyche, Baird was born into a comfortable middle-class family, and received an excellent formal education. Such education stressed classical learning rather than subjects considered germane to appropriate training for a biologist. American scientists such as Baird found "The West" more accessible after the California gold rush of 1849. Previous government surveys and expeditions had charted maps and returned to Washington with all manner of collections. Among the first of these forays was the Expedition to the Pacific Ocean and the South Seas led by Wilkes, which returned to Washington in 1842. It was the fruits of these expeditions and surveys which led the Smithsonian's first Secretary, Joseph Henry, to realize the importance of scientific exploration and biological inventory of the West and the need to establish a National Museum within the Smithsonian. This was by no means the first public museum in America, that honor belonging to Charles Willson Peale who founded a private museum in 1785. However, Henry's vision, later brought to reality by Baird, did not include displays of nature's wonders and oddities for public entertainment, but rather a museum to house scientific collections.

The 15 years that ended with the commencement of the Civil War saw 20 different expeditions sent out from Washington, each staffed by biologists, geologists, and medical doctors as well as military surveyors. At the center of an informal network of these professional explorers were Baird and the National Museum. Nor was the West the only destination. In 1859 Robert Kennicott, twenty-six years old and a Smithsonian volunteer, began the first of a series of northern explorations that led him eventually to Russian America and the Bering

Strait; in 1867 the United States purchased what we now call Alaska from Czar Alexander II.

It was against this background of scientific exploration, which continued unabated after the Civil War, that Dyche spent his boyhood. He apparently was a regular visitor in the Indian village near his childhood home. Refusing to attend school, he helped his father on the farm, hunted and trapped, and in general lived a life comparable to that of the Indian children his own age. He was fully conversant with the natural history of the Wakarusa Valley and became a crack rifleman.

What diverted Dyche from this wilderness idyll is uncertain, but at the age of 17, still virtually illiterate, he suddenly decided to take the considerable savings he had accumulated in farming and trapping and enroll in school. The story of the "learned stranger" who encountered Dyche and recognized the self-taught natural historian has an apocryphal ring, but may be true. Whatever the reason, this presumed meeting was a turning point in Dyche's life. During his three years at Kansas State Normal School he met Professor F. H. Snow, an eminent biologist at the the University of Kansas, where Dyche resolved to continue his education. His course was thus set for a career in biology, natural history, and eventually wildlife conservation.

Dyche's professional career can be said to have commenced in earnest in the fall of 1882 when he was appointed an instructor in the Natural History Department, even though he was still an undergraduate. Four years later the university had a new natural history building, Snow Hall, which in addition to classrooms and laboratories also contained the museum, Dyche's particular responsibility. Three years later he went to Washington, D. C., to study with William T. Hornaday, who although only three years older than Dyche, was already chief taxidermist at the U. S. National Museum. In addition to learning from Hornaday modern methods of mounting museum specimens, Dyche probably received an indoctrination into the then-fledgling field of wildlife conservation, of which Hornaday went on to become a leading American proponent. His new mentor also seemed to have instilled in Dyche an appreciation of the value of publicity, which was to serve Dyche exceedingly well later in life.

The object of the Hornaday-Dyche collaboration were specimens of wild American bison collected in Montana by Hornaday and an assistant of Dyche's, William H. Brown. Hornaday, both biologist and conservationist, justified the shooting of some of the last wild bison in the United States on the grounds that they soon would be exterminated in any case and that scientific specimens needed to be preserved. Hornaday's bison group, mounted in the National Museum for many years, was eventually broken up and specimens returned to several institutions in the State of Montana, where efforts are even now being made to bring them together again in a single display. The two animals on which Dyche worked remain on display in the University of Kansas Museum of Natural History. And in a high-tech twist to the story, these last individual wild bison to have been collected now provide an opportunity for modern biologists to assess the amount of genetic variation that occurred in the vast herds of wild bison that once roamed the Western Plains. Small fragments of tissue adhering to the specimens still contain DNA and can be used, through the magic of modern biochemistry, to produce samples sufficiently large for analysis of the genetic characteristics of each individual. Thus, Hornaday's rationalization concerning the scientific importance of those collections proves to be true, and the specimens may contribute once again to the continued existence and health of the bison.

Dyche, like his contemporary Hornaday and his younger colleague Joseph Grinnell of California (founder of the University of California's Museum of Vertebrate Zoology), was a member of a small fraternity of field and museum biologists who laid the foundations for today's modern museums of natural history. Judged by modern sensibilities, their emphasis on collecting and preserving large numbers of individual organisms may to some be off-putting. However, it must be remembered that they were working at a time when, although some species such as the Passenger Pigeon and and Labrador Duck had become extinct in the wild, and others such as the bison were severely threatened, the biological diversity of the North American continent was still largely intact, although fraying about the edges. Dyche himself was a product of the Darwinian revolution in thought and a convinced evolutionist, as were his colleagues. They recognized the importance of understanding the nature of variation in species and the necessity of having large samples from multiple areas in order to chart and interpret this variation. A legendary story about Grinnell will illustrate this. One day a visiting legislator, upon seeing the large numbers of cabinets filled with prepared specimens of California Quail (the state bird), asked Grinnell when he would have enough specimens. Grinnell is reported to have replied, "When I have them all." This is not to be taken literally, of course, but the scientific imperative of the day dictated extensive field collecting, and Dyche played an important role in this activity. At the same time, he and his colleagues were beginning to see the effects of untrammeled habitat destruction and overharvest on some species of birds and mammals, and it is natural that they should have begun to express their concerns.

Dyche's career has been paralleled by that of many of the naturalists-scholars who followed him. An initial, seemingly innate, responsiveness to the natural world, often involving childhood collections of snakes, insects, or other organisms, is followed by an often fortuitous discovery of (or by) a mentor who nurtures the budding scientist to begin to see the scholarly underpinnings of his or her emotional response. Those who continue the study of biology as a profession (if not sidetracked into more lucrative substitutes such as medical practice or biomedical research) often become, in addition to scientists, advocates for the earth. Most of us never achieve the prominence that Dyche gained in his lifetime. Baird, Hornaday, Dyche, Grinnell, Seton, Aldo Leopold, and many others built the foundations of the modern wildlife conservation movement. This in turn has led to recent public awareness of the importance of global biological diversity and the increasingly critical nature of threats to the planetary environment and its inhabitants stemming from the activities of an ever-increasing number of human beings on a finite sphere and the ever-increasing demands they put upon its life support systems. Were Dyche alive today, he would be in the forefront of the movement to arrest and reverse global and environmental change and deterioration.

Robert S. Hoffmann
Assistant Secretary for Research
Smithsonian Institution
Washington, D.C.
March 31, 1990

Lane's Fort on Mount Oread, near Lawrence. This etching of an ox-drawn covered wagon, much like the one that carried the infant Lewis Lindsay Dyche and his parents to the Kansas Territory, was first published in Harper's Weekly *June 6, 1857, the year that the Dyche family homesteaded. (Kansas Collection, University of Kansas Spencer Research Library)*

1 Prairie Dreams

The telegrams had poured in from all corners from those who wished to attend, so many that the house on Massachusetts Street could not hold them when they arrived in Lawrence from Washington, Chicago, and New York. The shocked procession of statesmen, scientists, students, and dear ones instead had streamed through the carved portal of the Museum of Natural History. They gathered in the main room on the first floor, unaware of the effect growing beneath the vaulted ceiling, of the tableau forming in the dim light. As their eyes adjusted to the surroundings, the embrace of the Great Panorama wrapped the guests in a sweep of grandeur and stillness. Encircled by the motionless bison, wolves, sea lions, and bighorn sheep, the casket of Lewis Lindsay Dyche rested under the sightless gaze of his great achievements. This atmosphere of time halted offered onlookers the chance to speculate that in this his final sleep, the Professor's Dream was spinning again, perhaps onto another perilous expedition or colossal world's fair. Free at last of politics and human greed, but perhaps not of a bit of danger . . .

Lewis Lindsay Dyche was born on March 20, 1857, to Alexander and Mary Ann Dyche in the Blue Ridge Mountain town of Bath, Virginia (called Berkeley Springs, West Virginia, following the Civil War). German on his father's side of the family and Irish on his mother's, Alexander Boyle Dyche was employed in a wool mill. His father was a blacksmith and wheelwright. Dyches had lived at Bath for several generations. The ancestral origins of Mary, or "Molly" as she was

called, are uncertain. Her parents, Hiram and Elizabeth Reilly, owned a
wool mill close to Bath.

Shortly after the birth of Lewis, Alexander and Mary Dyche brought their
new baby to the Kansas Territory, traveling by steamboat as far as St. Joseph,
Missouri, and then by ox-drawn covered wagon over the Santa Fe Trail to a place
near the Wakarusa and Osage Rivers where the town of Ridgeway was forming
(just north of present-day Overbrook). Accounts vary, but the family apparently
arrived in late April of 1857. Alexander had arranged to purchase 160 acres of land
in the Kansas Territory (probably from the U.S. Land Office) for about $150, with
payment to be made after one year of homesteading. Mary Dyche was ill, and
while she recuperated from the journey the baby Lewis was cared for by women in
a nearby camp of Sauk and Fox Indians. Alexander built a log cabin on their claim
near Elk Creek and began farming the prairie.

The earliest settlers to the area had arrived in 1855, but 1857 was the boom
year for the community of Ridgeway. Corn and wheat were the principal cash
crops, and most trading took place in Lawrence, to the northeast. Although
farming remained his occupation, in 1858 Alexander Dyche was elected one of
three constables of the Wakarusa Township in Shawnee County.[1] By 1859
Ridgeway's cluster of buildings included a general store, a tavern, a blacksmith
shop, and a post office. Mail arrived twice a month on the Santa Fe stage, drawn
by "six Mexican mules." A log schoolhouse, District #11, was built in 1859, and it
served as a church on Sundays.

Mary's parents established a farm adjacent to the Dyche property in 1858, as
did her brother, John. Alexander's brother Lewis and sister-in-law Harriet bought
land near Ridgeway in 1859, but they stayed only one year. A letter from Mary
Dyche, written to a sister and brother in Bath, describes these early days on Elk
Creek:

Ridgeway, Shawnee County
Kansas Territory
July 30, 1859

Dear Sister and Brother,

I will write a few lines to you this evening to let you know how we are
getting along. We are all well at this time. We have had our health very good
since we have been here. We get the ague sometimes but it does not last long. I
reckon you think we have forgotten you as we never write, but we have not. . . .
Sally, I think if you and Mr. Thompson would come out to see us you would never
go back for it is a beautiful country. It don't look much like old Morgan [County],
but there are a great many persons here who don't like it. They like the country
very well; some say wood is scarce and some say water is too scarce and some
don't like the houses. I think there is plenty of wood and water to last as long as
Kansas and the people last. That is my opinion.

Some of them want fine houses to live in as soon as they come here. They don't think about it being a new country till they get here. I did not like it much when I first came here but I like it very well now, for it is not so lonesome. There are so many people coming in and every person trying to get along. There is a great deal of farming going on in the neighborhood. Some of the beautifulest corn fields you ever looked at. One man has eighty acres in one field and it is all in corn. It is very pretty to look at. There will be a great deal of corn raised in Kansas this year. We will have, I think, two thousand bushels if we get one more good rain next month. It has been a very good season so far. We have very good potatoes. I have a garden and plenty of watermelons, very long ones. I wish you had some of them for I never saw any in Morgan. . . . I must bring my letter to a close. Little Wilson is crying, he is a very fine child. Lewis looks like Reilly only he has light hair. He can talk. . . .[2]

The Dyche family home in Berkeley Springs, West Virginia, in 1883. Lewis Lindsay Dyche, age 30, stands on the porch. (University of Kansas Archives)

In 1860 the region suffered a severe drought from June to November. Many settlers left. Those who remained survived largely due to provisions sent to them by eastern aid societies. For three weeks in January 1861, as Kansas was being admitted to the Union as the thirty-fourth state, provisions failed to reach Ridgeway due to drifting snow following one of the worst snowstorms in the state's history.

The Civil War came in the spring of that year. Alexander Dyche and John Reilly enlisted as privates in the Osage County Battalion of the state militia, and in 1864 their company helped repel Confederate forces at the Battle of Westport. After the war's end, Alexander Dyche purchased land near Auburn, fifteen miles west of Ridgeway, and moved his family there, probably as a result of a devastating grasshopper invasion on September 15, 1866. Like Ridgeway, Auburn was settled in the mid-1850s. The town lay at the headwaters of the Wakarusa River (*Wakarusa* is the Kaw Indian word meaning "river of big weeds"). Auburn vaunted a log-house hotel, a church, a brickyard, a sawmill, a blacksmith shop, and a two-story concrete schoolhouse. Although Alexander Dyche bought and sold land over the years, moving his family on several occasions, the family remained in or near Auburn as Lewis grew up.

Details of Lewis's childhood are not known, but life in the pioneer family undoubtedly was hard. His mother bore twelve children: Hiram and Frederick died in infancy, William succumbed to lockjaw, and Elliot was killed by a fall into the cistern. A "German grandmother," as Lewis called her (presumably Mary's mother), helped to care for the children. Lewis remembered his grandmother as a severe disciplinarian. In an early draft for his hunting memoirs[3] he alleged that she "had been taught in the days when children were classed with dumb brutes."[4] Mary Dyche and the Reillys were Spiritualists, as were many settlers in the area, believing that the dead survived as spirits that could communicate with the living, especially through mediums. Alexander Dyche abhorred such beliefs, however, and insisted that the children be brought up as Presbyterians.

Lewis recollected that "Indians were camped near my father's farm in Osage County, Kansas, and I did not think much about Indians being different from other people. We used to go to the Indian camps and I ate about everything that could be put on an Indian bill-of-fare. I ate turtles roasted in the fire, muskrats, and I am not sure but that I ate snakes and many other things I did not know much about."[5] He recalled a prairie fire that threatened the Dyche family farm: "The whole country was swept clean at one burning. We all stood in mortal terror of that dreadful day when the country would 'burn off,' as the phrase went. On one occasion, I remember seeing father fight fire until I thought he would drop dead. Of course farms and houses were protected by plowing around them and burning wide fire 'breaks' as they were called. But the high wind would sometimes carry the fire by blowing, burning, tumbling weeds, etc. incredible distances. It was on an occasion of this kind when father fought so hard to save his fences and hay. At the last moment the fire broke over near the wheat stacks. Father hastened to the spot, dragging me with him, as well as a piece of old wet blanket. He made a last desperate effort to save his wheat. He moved me two or three times to keep me out of the fire. I can see him yet pounding the fire with that old blanket. He finally conquered the flames but the fire burnt up to the very edge of the stack. Father (who is a large man, over six feet tall and who never had a sick day, and never knew his real strength) was soaking wet with perspiration and so completely exhausted by the heat of the fire and that of over exertion that he could not stand up. It was a dreadful hour for me. I have been in a cyclone, but its phenomena could not begin to compare with those of that occasion."[6]

The oldest of the Dyche children, Lewis did not attend the district school. While still a young boy he worked horses at a sorghum mill. He shocked corn. He saved his money. He hunted and trapped animals along the banks of the nearby Wakarusa River: muskrats, beaver, skunks, minks, badgers, and raccoons. By the age of twelve he had made enough money from his fur business to purchase a calf, and the following year he bought another. William Allen White reminisced, "The earth around about us then was new to the white man. . . . The prairie sod, much of it, was unturned . . . and Kansas boys in those days roamed like other wild young mammals through the woods and prairies."[7]

"As I look back," Lewis recalled, "it seems to me that some of the happiest days of my boyhood life were spent in Shawnee county south of Topeka on the banks of the Wakarusa, fishing. . . . Those were the happy days when the streams seemed to be full of fish and it was possible for almost any one with pole and line and a can of worms and a few live minnows to catch a good string of fish."[8] Lewis enjoyed hunting as well. "I remember a day," he mused, "when the ground was covered with snow and ice. The trees were all heavy with frozen mist and frost. Many prairie chickens were on the trees. I went hunting with a small muzzle-loading rifle and killed fifteen chickens in one day. . . . It was the first gun I ever owned and the first I ever killed anything with. I used to shoot it to kill. I knew that I did not have but one shot and that it would take some time to load. This made me careful, and I did not take many chances at too long range, and usually killed a bird every shot."[9]

The plains were full of game, although wildlife was becoming scarcer each year as fences went up, railroad track was laid, and the state's population increased. On one winter morning Alexander Dyche shot two dozen prairie chickens and wild turkeys out of elm trees near his house. In 1868, when Lewis was eleven years old, bison were so numerous on the western Kansas plains that William F. Cody supplied buffalo meat to crews building the Kansas Pacific Railroad to Denver. During a span of eighteen months Cody is said to have killed 4,280 bison.

The Auburn village school was close enough to the Dyche farm that Lewis could have attended, but by his thirteenth birthday he was reluctant to attend school with children younger than himself. One summer he attended a short term in a school two and a half miles away, but the appeal of an education was not strong enough to entice him to return the following year. At sixteen Lewis was lean and strong, though not particularly tall, and he could work as hard and as long as a man. He was a good shot with his rifle, and he was skillful at cleaning the game he killed. But he was virtually illiterate.

In 1874 Lewis decided to turn his small herd of cows into cash. When he combined that profit with his other savings, he had amassed over six hundred dollars. He decided to invest the money in his education, and he enrolled in the Kansas State Normal

Tintype of Lewis L. Dyche, age 19. (University of Kansas Archives)

School in Emporia for the fall semester. Lewis's sudden willingness to submit to book learning is a mystery. By one account he "became angered upon being twitted of his ignorance."[10] Another explanation involves a mysterious "learned stranger." According to the story, the young Lewis shot birds unlike those that the other boys shot, and he was laughed at for collecting and dissecting useless birds. One day he shot a bird that no one recognized, and it became "the talk of the countryside." At that point "a learned stranger came by and the people told him of Lewis Dyche's strange bird." The stranger asked Lewis if he knew what kind of bird he had killed. Lewis told him he did not know its proper name, but he correctly identified the species. The stranger asked him how he knew, and Lewis replied that he had studied its bone structure and recognized its similarity to other birds of that species. Impressed by the boy's resourcefulness, the learned stranger purportedly outlined a course of study for him.[11]

On a dare by some Auburn friends, Lewis arrived at Emporia wearing a black silk stovepipe hat; consequently everyone soon knew him. Lewis found his classwork more difficult than making acquaintances, however. One of Lewis's teachers, Abigail P. Morse, recalled his first semester at Emporia:

"Personally, I first met Mr. Dyche when he was assigned to my class in grammar. He made himself prominent during the first week by his peculiarities in language and manners. Early in the term, as the class was passing from the room, he stopped at my desk and informed me, quite decidedly, that he did not like grammar, and did not see the use of it. He was told that his indifference had been observed; that the use of good English I considered of prime importance to him, personally, and the only way for him to secure it was by a conscientious study of grammar. An appointment was made, that we might talk the matter over more fully. He came promptly at the appointed hour, and he had the appearance of one bristling with arguments. I began to realize that this was no common mind with

An 1896 portrait of Francis Huntington Snow, one of the original three faculty of the University of Kansas and Dyche's lifelong mentor. (University of Kansas Archives)

which I had to deal. I stated some facts, and his expression changed to one of serious thought. I said, 'One may be lacking in mathematics or in science and yet conceal the fact, but he could not converse or recite without showing a lack of knowledge of the English language—if there was a lack.' These facts were enforced by repeating some of the grievous mistakes in his recitations.

"After a brief space, he said, 'Well, then, I must study grammar, must I?'

"After this interview, our life-long friendship began. He came to me often for advice, and we discussed a large range of subjects. . . . Mr. Dyche became interested in a religious life during his last year in our school, and entered into its duties with all the fervor and intensity of his nature."[12]

Lewis's sudden interest in "a religious life" could be attributed in part to another student, the pious Ophelia Axtell, whom he was courting.

Sometimes it was Lewis's task to take visitors on a tour of the school, which is how he came to meet a short, compact man with long sideburns and piercing, yet kindly, gray eyes. The man was Francis Huntington Snow, one of the three original faculty members at the University of Kansas in Lawrence. Professor Snow made a considerable impression on the young Dyche. He was the most educated man Lewis had ever met, a man who had been raised in the more refined world of Fitchburg, Massachusetts, and who had served as a member of the Christian Commission during the Civil War. Yet, like Dyche, Snow was a man exhilarated by nature and the outdoors. On graduating from the normal school in June 1877, Lewis had resolved to follow Professor Snow to Lawrence and enroll at the University of Kansas. And he vowed that he "intended to take every course offered before he accepted a diploma."[13]

The country bumpkin rides his pony to Kansas University, but before he can pass through the diploma gate he must master the subjects fencing him out. The new University Building (renamed Fraser Hall in 1897) stands in the background. From the 1883 Kansas Cyclone *(a student yearbook). (University of Kansas Archives)*

2 The Camp Below the Bluffs

Early in September 1877, Lewis Dyche and an anonymous Auburn friend drove a covered wagon east to Lawrence. Their landmark was Mount Oread and the twin towers of the new University Building. Three hundred trees had been planted on the campus that spring, but none were large enough to be seen from a distance. The boys saw, against the sky, the most magnificent building in the state, its red roofs gleaming on the hilltop.

Lewis and his companion set up camp at the base of the bluffs on which the university buildings stood. Their camp lay near the site of the present-day Spencer Museum of Art (directly behind Dyche Hall). At night the boys slept in the wagon; they cooked meals over an open fire. By some accounts they spent most of the semester outdoors, renting a room in the city only when cold weather drove them inside, while other accounts indicate they may have camped as briefly as several days.

Lawrence had been settled in 1854, a few years before Lewis's birth, by a party from the New England Emigrant Aid Company. Headed by Charles Robinson of Fitchburg, Massachusetts (Francis H. Snow's hometown), the settlers were abolitionists, determined to bring Kansas into the Union as a free state. In his history of the University of Kansas, Clifford S. Griffin noted that many of the town founders thought of Lawrence "as a bit of New England transplanted to the prairies." The first citizens of Lawrence hoped to build a university atop the ridge later known as Mount Oread, but it was not until February 20, 1863, that the governor of the newly admitted state of Kansas signed a bill authorizing a university to be located in Lawrence. When the institution finally opened in 1866, it consisted of a chancellor, three faculty members, and fifty-five students: "Twenty-six young ladies and twenty-nine gentlemen."

By the time Lewis Dyche and his friend arrived eleven years later, the number of faculty had grown to twelve members, and 361 students were registered for the fall term. The new University Building was to be dedicated in November. Later named Fraser Hall, it was constructed of native limestone and contained fifty-four classrooms. The university advertised that it offered "an ample course of study in Ancient and Modern Languages, Mathematics, Metaphysics, Natural Sciences, English Literature, Engineering and Normal Instruction. Vocal Music in Normal Classes free. Piano and Organ at Reasonable rates. A cordial welcome to all who desire an education and are willing to work for it. Others not invited."[1]

The twenty-year-old Lewis was admitted to the university's Preparatory Department, where the majority of students were enrolled; of the 361 registered, only 110 students were of a college level. Professor Snow explained the preparatory system in a letter to his fiancé: "You wonder that so few are ready for the college course, but must remember that our standard is as high as at Harvard, and that it takes at least three years to get an ordinary preparation in the eastern academics, six in the Boston Latin School. There are no high schools in the state outside of the cities, and even in the latter places they teach very little—if any—Latin or Greek, so we must wait for our excellent school system to develop. Kansas is in her infancy."[2] Compelled to adapt to its time and place, the University of Kansas resembled a secondary school more than it did a university. Not until 1885 would it enroll more college than preparatory students.

Clifford Griffin noted that during its early years the university was widely criticized in the state for "offering to an elite class advantages unknown to most of the people."[3] Although no tuition was levied (there was a five-dollar contingent fee per session), living costs could prohibit children from poorer families from attending the university. According to Lewis, however, virtually all of his fellow students were "farmer boys who earned with their own hands most if not all the money which kept them at the university."[4] And Lewis Dyche belonged to no "elite class." In fact, when he brought a classmate, Will C. Stevens, home with him to visit the family farm, Stevens was astonished by the setting, which reminded him of a "wild Indian camp," with dogs and children running everywhere.[5]

Lewis Dyche was a rare bird, and he was quickly taken under Professor Snow's protective wing. Lewis excelled at collecting insects for Professor Snow, and Snow was impressed with his enthusiasm. An acquaintance later recalled Lewis's early days at the university: "Snow was a great Entomologist and working especially in Coleoptera and . . . he offered the Lawrence boys $1.00 each for any new species they might bring him. . . . Dyche, then a boy of 19 [he was actually 20], clothed like an Indian, brought the Chancellor so many new species of Coleoptera and earned so many dollars [that] Chancellor Snow took an interest in him and finally sent him out to his house with a note to his wife to tog him out with proper clothes and later put him to work for the University."[6] Lewis had found in Professor Snow a true mentor.

Snow's teaching method emphasized the direct study of nature as a means of cultivating the faculties of observation and comparison in students. "These faculties can be trained only by being exercised upon appropriate objects," Snow explained in his yearly report to the university regents. "Accordingly, students in botany daily furnish themselves with fresh plants from the forest and the prairie for dissection, description, and classification. The plant takes precedence of the text-book in the apparatus of instruction. The eye of the pupil is used to detect the peculiarities of the specimen in hand rather than to read from a text-book what some other observer has seen. . . . Familiarity with the terms employed in describing plants, and the requisite tables for classification, are obtained from some botanical text-book. Students are taught not only to observe the peculiarities of the plant before them, but also to make a careful record of their observations."[7] Snow applied the same technique to the teaching of zoology, employing as objects for study the insects, fishes, birds, and mammals of the vicinity. The second floor of the new University Building was filled with cabinets of insects and birds collected by the professor and his students. Due largely to Snow's influence within the university, all students, regardless of their course of study, were required to devote an entire semester to botany and zoology, and as part of that requirement, each student prepared "a small herbarium, representing at least forty indigenous species of the neighboring region, well preserved, and carefully 'mounted.'"[8]

During the years 1876 to 1907 Professor Snow organized twenty-six scientific collecting expeditions to sites in Kansas, Colorado, New Mexico, Texas, and Arizona. Several of the students who accompanied him on those expeditions became distinguished scientists and collectors. In the summer of 1878 Snow organized an expedition to Gove County, Kansas. Lewis Dyche, with two semesters of preparatory work under his belt, was invited to join. Members of the party included one other student (Richard Foster), a guide, and Benjamin F. Mudge, who had been collecting fossils in the western states for decades. Years earlier, when Mudge was a professor at the Kansas State Agricultural College in Manhattan, he and Snow agreed to divide between themselves, for the purposes of study, the kingdoms of the living and the dead: Mudge assumed responsibility for the fossil forms of the state and Snow for the living forms. (Snow's biographer, Clyde Kenneth Hyder, remarked that "theirs was the boldness of the early gods.")[9] The 1870s encompassed years of competitive efforts to collect fossils for America's major museums. O. C. Marsh of Yale and Edward Drinker Cope, editor and owner of the *American Naturalist,* financed numerous expeditions to collect extinct invertebrates in western Kansas (Professor Mudge had collected fossil specimens for Cope on many occasions). One location rich in specimens was the chalk exposures at the mouth of Hackberry Creek in eastern Gove County, the site of Snow's 1878 expedition.

Calling themselves "the bug hunters," Snow's party collected insects and reptiles as well as fossils. Lewis, who intended to concentrate on classical literature once he began college-level studies, composed descriptive essays and mailed them back to the *Lawrence Republican Daily Journal.* "Everything went well until about two o'clock in the morning," he wrote a few days after their arrival in western Kansas, "when I was wakened by Professor Snow, who was stumbling about in the tent looking as he said for boots and hat. He had some plants and other specimens out of doors that needed care. Prof. Mudge (who had been sleeping outside) had just stepped in and said it was raining. The Professors were soon quieted and were quite asleep, when all at once the wind began to blow at a fearful rate. The rain was falling fast when our body guard . . . made his appearance at the door of the tent with pantaloons on one arm, and wet blankets on the other, while his nightly linen seemed to be flying loose about his head. . . . The wind blew harder, the thunder made the earth shake, and the air was alive with lightning. The dashing rain and powerful wind forced our tent open at the door, when Prof. Snow sprang to his feet exclaiming 'Ho! ho!!' and was attempting to hold it shut when the ridge pole broke and down came the tent. Well, now we were in a fix. If any of you have ever camped out of doors in a wind and rain storm, without much or any shelter, you will have some idea of what we had to put up with. We did the best we could under the circumstances, that is, we stayed under the remains of the old tent and took it 'cold and heavy.' I heard Prof. Snow rejoicing that he had his 'bugs' in a safe place at a time when I was thinking of things of more importance, such as the uncertainty of life."[10]

"The buffalo are gone," Lewis recorded in his next report to the *Journal*. "We only know they have been here from the skeletons scattered over the prairie and the old trails leading to the watering places. Antelope are quite plentiful, usually one, two, or three in a place; saw a herd of ten last week, and managed to kill one of them, shooting a distance of over 200 paces. . . . After dressing the antelope, leaving the hide on, I proceeded towards camp. Had a mile and a half to go with about fifty pounds of antelope. Found myself pretty well 'tuckered' when I got there, yet the sport highly paid for the labor. The professors were somewhat surprised and highly pleased to think we would have antelope meat for a few days."[11]

The day before Lewis posted the preceding story, Professor Snow had caused considerable excitement in camp. Snow had captured a small rattlesnake and wished to preserve it in a bottle of alcohol. As he struggled to put the snake into the long, small-necked bottle, tail first, the snake bit him sharply on the middle finger of his right hand. "By George, he has bitten me," Snow exclaimed. He dropped the snake, held it with his foot, put his finger to his mouth, and began to suck. He expressed gratification at the opportunity to observe the effects of a rattlesnake bite, while admitting that the pain was the worst he had ever felt. Lewis tied a bootlace around Snow's finger to isolate the venom, then lanced the wound twice with a pocket knife and bled it. Aching replaced the intense pain, and members of the party took turns sucking the wound, while Snow studied his symptoms. He recorded swelling, discoloration, and blood pressure changes. He quickly recovered, though, and by lunchtime felt well enough to eat. In fact, he ate so heartily that someone suggested that a few more snakebites would completely exhaust the food supply. The bite occurred at mid-morning and by the afternoon Snow was out collecting again.[12]

When Snow wrote his wife about the incident, he assured her, "I promise you I will not handle them alive any more, so you need not fear for the future."[13] But in his next story for the *Lawrence Republican Daily Journal,* Lewis revealed that Professor Snow had not given up snake handling entirely: Snow apparently put on a "snake show" for a passing wagon train, running his arm into a sack of live snakes, pulling out six, and draping them about his body, to the delight

Lewis Dyche utilizes Professor Snow's "snake show" to scare tramps away from camp. This posed studio photograph was originally taken for Clarence Edwords's Camp-Fires of a Naturalist, *but was not used in the book. (University of Kansas Archives)*

of the onlookers.

After three weeks of collecting, Professor Mudge left the party. The expedition moved to a site near the town of Sheridan, home formerly to seven or eight hundred inhabitants while the Kansas Pacific Railroad was under construction but that since had literally up and moved on: The frame houses simply were placed on flatcars and transported west. "The number of inhabitants varies according to the number of tramps present at any given time," Lewis reported. "Only three new ones have made their appearance in the past fifteen minutes."[14] One member of the party remained in camp at all times to guard the expedition's goods against the drifters. During his shift on watch, Lewis employed Professor Snow's snake-show performance to good effect. With tramps encroaching the camp, Lewis took an armful of snakes from the snake bag and adorned himself with them. So successful was the display, he reported, that from then on whenever tramps came too near all one needed to do was bring out the snake bag.

The Kansas Pacific Railroad sometimes gave Snow, his expeditions, and their collections free transportation, and toward the end of July Snow took back to Lawrence two thousand pounds of specimens: birds, mammals, reptiles, rocks, plants, and insects. When Snow rejoined his party, they moved to Platte Canyon, Colorado, partly to avoid the inconvenience of having to continuously guard their camp against drifters. In the mountains near Pike's Peak, Lewis was overcome by the view and put his youthful excitement to paper. When finished, he termed his literary creation a "derangement of mind," but mailed it to the Lawrence newspaper nevertheless: "O ye mountains with peak upon peak rising in the heavens, you are sublime. . . . You stretch your snowy white arms and raise your hoary locks to the clouds. . . . Your garments are excelled by none; you are continually changing the form and color of your raiment. To do this you make use of the rain drop and the sunbeam, take advantage of the laws of light, and proudly throw the coat of many and changing colors about you in all manner of shapes. Lightning is your eye, and you see most sharply; thunder your voice, and you speak most loudly. The tempest that sweeps the plains and rules the waters of the sea is hushed and made your slave. . . ."[15]

Lewis's literary ambitions diminished, and he abandoned his reportage of the next two summers' expeditions: Chicago Creek Canyon, Colorado (near Idaho Springs), in 1879, and Santa Fe Canyon, New Mexico (north of Santa Fe), in 1880. In the fall of 1879 Lewis entered the Collegiate Department of the university, studying the traditional classical curriculum, a course of study "fashioned for candidates of the learned professions." The following year he changed his field of study from the classical course to the scientific course, a curriculum intended to prepare students for "the skilled industries."[16] Not satisfied with this arrangement, he finally decided to combine the classical course of study with the scientific course, thus nearly fulfilling his vow to take every course the university offered.

The most dramatic of Snow's summer expeditions took place in 1881. Snow, Herbert S. Smith (a professor of physics), Snow's twelve-year-old son, Will, and Dyche set up a camp in Water Canyon, about twenty-five miles west of Socorro, New Mexico. One morning while Lewis was hunting deer he heard gunshots in the direction of Socorro. He did not attach any significance to the shots until later in the day when two Socorro men rode into camp. Lewis quickly ran to Professor Snow with their news. "Professor, do you know where we are?" he asked Snow. "Well the Apaches have killed seven men two miles from camp and are coming after us tonight!"[17] Such a chill came over Snow that, despite the arid climate, he put on his overcoat.

A small band of Apache warriors, led by the chief Nana, had crossed the Rio Grande to steal horses and to avenge the death of the chief Victorio, killed the previous year. They had attacked freight wagons on the road between Snow's camp and Socorro. Snow, who had bought a Winchester rifle in Boston that spring, gathered his party together. About thirty nearby miners joined Snow's small band, and they organized into armed squads, posting ten men on duty at all times. At three in the morning they heard dogs barking down the canyon, and they were convinced that the Indians were coming. Snow's party and the miners slipped into a miner's cabin where they could better defend themselves. They remained there for three days, posting picket guards at night and sending men out to scout the area during the day. They found fresh footprints near their camp, and at the top of the canyon, fifteen hundred feet above them, they saw Indians peering down at them. Snow's party and about a dozen miners decided to try to hike to Socorro. Despite urgings from the others to carry only the necessities, Snow took thirteen cigar boxes filled with insects, tied together in such a way that he could carry them with one hand, leaving the other hand free for his rifle. He walked along the right flank of the column with his son clinging to his sleeve.

On the road to Socorro they came across the scene of the attack on the freight wagons. The bodies had been removed, but they saw the looted wagons (including the one that had transported their party a few days earlier) and patches of blood-stained earth. Five men had been killed, including the teamster who had delivered the Snow party. Only one man escaped, receiving during his flight a bullet hole through the crown of his hat. A posse met Snow's party on the road and escorted them out of the canyon. In Lawrence, due to distressing telegraph messages from Socorro, newspapers had reported that the Snow party was believed to have been massacred.

As a result of Snow's summer expeditions and the perpetual collecting around Lawrence during the school year, the university's collection of sundry objects of natural history was growing rapidly. In November 1881, the Board of Regents authorized the Building and Grounds Committee to provide additional cabinet cases to display the collections. These collections were referred to as the university's "cabinet of natural history," hearkening back to earlier days when the university's entire natural history collection was contained in a few glass-front display cabinets in the North College building.

Collecting such specimens for study was a necessary part of the methodology of scientific investigation, which required that one *gather data* on a selected problem according to a coherent plan in which accurate observations could be made. Observations could be made with the human senses, assisted at times by instruments of precision, but they had to be recorded in definite terms. The next step was to *classify and organize the data* on the basis of similarities, variations, processes, causes, results, and so on. Then one could *generalize* in order to formulate tentative principles and theories. One then attempted to *verify* these generalizations through controlled experiments and by gathering additional data. The final step was to *report* on the research, thereby subjecting the results to criticism and verification by others.

The field collecting conducted by Snow and his students was part of the first stage of the scientific method, gathering data, the data in this case being the objects themselves. The objects were collected rather than simply observed *in situ* in order to make possible the next step, classification and organization. To dissect objects, examine and measure them with the use of laboratory instruments, and compare and contrast them with other objects, it was necessary to procure them.

By the summer of 1882 Dyche had decided to collect mammals for scientific study. Throughout his boyhood and during Snow's summer collecting expeditions, he had enjoyed hunting—and he was good at it. Now, in addition to hunting for food, he intended to hunt for science.

On Professor Snow's 1882 summer expedition to Gallinas Canyon near Las Vegas Hot Springs, New Mexico, Lewis and a fellow student, Walter Russ, separated from the main party to collect on their own further down the Gallinas River. "I had nothing to do with the camp any more than to send my man down with venison," Dyche noted cockily.[18] Lewis and Russ made their way up a mountain to a place known as "Harvey's Ranch." H. A. Harvey, the owner, referred to the setting as "Paradise Valley." A Boston merchant who had gone bankrupt, Harvey had homesteaded in "Paradise Valley" the previous year. According to *Camp-Fires of a Naturalist*, Lewis told Harvey the following (in dialogue typical of the book): "We have come up here to collect insects and plants and perhaps to kill animals. We did not come up to inflict ourselves on you or to bother you in any way, unless it might be to get a little milk from that cow now and then."[19] Welcoming the company, Harvey and his wife invited the young men to stay at the ranch and collect specimens in relative comfort. Lewis and Russ gathered insects and plants for several days, and then Russ returned to the Snow party at the foot of the mountain, taking with him what they had collected. Lewis stayed at Harvey's Ranch, and over the next several weeks he killed seven Virginia (white-tailed) deer, each with a single shot from his Winchester rifle. He gave some of the venison to Snow's party and the rest to his hosts, the Harveys. The skins and skeletons he brought back to Lawrence.

That fall, on Professor Snow's recommendation, Lewis was given an instructor's position in the Natural History Department while retaining his place in the junior class. That same semester he helped launch a student newspaper, the *University Courier,* serving as its science editor. The second issue of the newspaper recorded that Dyche took a first prize of forty dollars at a Topeka fair for his entomological collection. Later in the year, Lewis wrote the following in his column: "The other night about 8 o'clock as we were passing from the north gate to the University building we stumbled over some sort of a beast which immediately showed fight. It was raining and very dark and we could only hear the threatening grunts and hisses of the animal. After a short skirmish in which our only weapon was an umbrella, we secured the stranger by the end of the tail. Then we ran for light and assistance, meanwhile whirling the thing around vigorously, fearing that it might be a dangerous or biting beast. It proved to be a very fine specimen of an opossum, which may now be seen in the Upper Natural History Room, in the attitude of surprising a very dignified and self-important squirrel."[20]

Over Christmas vacation, Lewis and Professor David H. Robinson departed for Indian Territory to hunt American wild turkey. Along with Snow, Professor Robinson had been one of the university's original three faculty members. A professor of Latin, Robinson was a veteran quail and rabbit hunter. At Caldwell, Kansas, a border town at the end of the railroad line, the two men engaged a wagon and two ponies. In Indian Territory near Pond Creek, they came across a ranch where a cowboy dance had been in progress for over twenty-four hours. Due to a lack of women, some of the cowboys had put on dresses, to the evident satisfaction of the participants ("They were good ones too," Lewis observed). A six-foot four-inch Arkansan called "Short" ("on account of his size") played a reckless fiddle accompaniment. The music and merriment was a such a high pitch that a deputy sheriff who happened by en route to Caldwell got so caught up in the dancing that he forgot about his prisoner, who slipped away unnoticed. "Some of the boys got a little too much," Lewis noted, "but everything went off real pleasant."[21]

Lewis and Robinson had elected to spend the night at the ranch house, but the fiddle music and general noise of the dance permitted them no sleep. They left at four o'clock the following morning, riding south in their light wagon. The cowboys had told them of a ranch at the mouth of Turkey Creek that might serve as a suitable headquarters for their hunts. Their destination, Thompson's Ranch, turned out to be merely a dugout, a man-made cave in an earthen bank with a door in front but no windows. There Lewis and Robinson were again confronted with rough cowboy habits: While their new hosts were proficient in caring for the ponies and provided the two tired men with hot food, they smoked pipes incessantly, and the two nonsmokers repeatedly had to step out of the unventilated room for fresh air.

The Thompson's Ranch cowboys proved to be poor hunting guides: They preferred to shoot before their clients, and they shot from horseback without bothering to take careful aim, which resulted in wounded game, dispersed animals, and hard feelings. On the first day out Lewis and Robinson, hunting separately, were abandoned by their cowboy guides and left to find their way back to the ranch. "The miserable fellow went off while I was after a bunch of turkeys," Robinson complained to Lewis as he straggled in after midnight.[22] Lewis gave the exhausted Robinson his blankets and went out alone to hunt, taking with him his big shotgun (which he called "Old Vesuvius"). In the dim starlight Lewis stalked more by sound than sight. Hearing claws scrambling across the ice of Turkey Creek, he fired his shotgun at a black object. A lighted match revealed an otter, a good specimen. He strung it from a tree branch and continued the hunt. Hours later he spotted a large bird near the top of a cottonwood tree. He waited a while, listening, watching, and decided it was a wild turkey. He hit it with a load of shot. A golden eagle fell to the ground. The following evening, after a day of solo hunting, Lewis heard scores of shots near the ranch. Approaching the sounds on

horseback, he found a group of cowboys firing their rifles pell-mell at a wildcat they had trapped in a small ravine. Lewis headed the cat off and fired a running shot as it broke for the trees. A piece of shot hit the animal near the spine and it sat down, growling. Lewis removed all but a dozen pieces of shot from a cartridge so as not to damage the hide excessively and then killed the wildcat with a close shot to the neck.

A rare "trophy" photograph of Dyche beside a dead wildcat. This was the only such photograph found from among the hundreds in Dyche's collection, indicating, perhaps, an early aversion to trophy killing. (University of Kansas Archives)

Having had such success during only three days of hunting, the twenty-six-year-old Dyche returned to the Indian Territory a year later, in December 1883. He had obtained a letter of introduction to Colonel John D. Miles, the Indian agent in Fort Reno, 115 miles south of Caldwell, and he made Fort Reno his destination. In Caldwell he found three men traveling to Fort Reno who were willing to let him accompany them. After the first day's ride they set up a camp and one of the men, an Indian named John, cooked several meadowlarks he had killed that day. Dyche enjoyed the meal, admiring the skill with which the birds had been prepared, but when the men began passing around a small brown jug and smoking pipes, Dyche withdrew and busied himself cutting grass and arranging it under his sleeping bag.

Dyche was especially proud of the sleeping bag he had devised for this trip: He had folded a wool blanket in half and sewed it into a bag, and then sewed waterproof canvas around it. "It was always clean & dry," he recorded, "and the bottom of it was a splendid place to carry extra woolen clothing. Moreover I always had my own bed—did not—in fact could not put my blankets in with this that & the other fellow who wanted to join me with him . . . ." The others made sport of this camping innovation, dubbing Dyche's bag a "sleeping poke" and asking how he managed to get into "the consarned thing," but in the cold December nights Dyche was pleased at how warm he slept.[23]

The third day out of Caldwell a strong blizzard overtook the party. They knew they were close to the Cimarron River, the banks of which would provide shelter to build a fire, but the wind and snow stopped them. They blanketed the horses and employed the wagon as a crude windbreak. John tried to find the river on foot but returned in a matter of minutes. Building a fire was impossible. There was nothing to do but wait out the storm. The men made a crude windbreak of boxes and oat sacks and ate a dinner of dry bread and raw bacon. Brushing the snow from his clothing as best he could, Dyche crawled into his sleeping bag and pulled his coat over his head. The only sound he could hear was the wind blowing through the grasses around his bed. He did not sleep for some time, half fearing that if he did he would not wake up. Then it was morning and John was peering down at him, asking, "You no freeze last night?" The storm had passed.

By ten o'clock that morning they reached the Cimarron River, and the following day they arrived in Fort Reno. There Colonel Miles put Dyche up for the night and filled him in on game conditions in the area. On Miles's recommendation, Dyche took a mail wagon to Cantonment, sixty miles to the northwest on the Canadian River. At some point, in the midst of a hard wagon ride, Dyche was handed a leg of turkey and a chunk of corn pone by "an old crusty piece of humanity" at a mule changing station, and he ate his Christmas dinner riding on the buckboard.

At Cantonment Dyche met Sam Horton, foreman of the Dickey Brothers Cattle Ranch, a fifty-square-mile tract to the west of Cantonment leased from the Cheyenne Indians. Such ranches existed in the Indian Territory due to a program established by Colonel Miles to improve the financial situation of the Cheyenne. Horton offered to provide Dyche with room and board and to serve as guide on his hunts. When they arrived at the main ranch house, they found most of the hands gone. An elderly French cook informed them that "the squaw humpers gone to the Injun dance."[24] About a half mile from the ranch was the winter camp of a Cheyenne tribe. Horton escorted Dyche there, approaching the camp with club in hand to fend off the dogs, which were kept so hungry that one had to beat them away.

Horton introduced Dyche to the Cheyenne chief and advised him to buy a pair of moccasins from each of the chief's two daughters. Although Dyche referred to the chief as "Old Chief Coho," it is possible that the man he met was Cohoe, a Cheyenne chief only a few years older than himself. Cohoe had been imprisoned for three years at Fort Marion, Florida, as punishment for leading a series of raids against white settlers and surveyors in 1874. After receiving an education at a Negro agricultural and industrial school in Virginia, he had returned to Colonel Miles's Cheyenne and Arapaho Agency in 1880.[25]

Except for his moccasins, Cohoe was dressed as a white man, in buckskin leggings and a woolen shirt, as were the other Indians attending the dance. A blanket was drawn around his shoulders instead of a coat, and he wore a high plug hat. The setting for the dance was a large teepee, where about twenty-five Cheyenne women and a smaller number of men were seated on rolled up blankets pushed against the sides of the teepee. A drum, "about the size of a half kerosene barrel," was beaten by five men who sang a prolonged, guttural melody, while the women placed the tips of their fingers against their front teeth to produce a rhythmical succession of notes.

The women were dressed in pink calico dresses with red-striped shawls covering their heads and shoulders. A woman would pick a cowboy she was willing to be kissed by and throw her shawl over his head—provided he gave her twenty-five cents. "This seemed exorbitant to a fellow who had just come from a country where he could occasionally kiss his best girl for the mere fun of the thing," Dyche remarked. Dyche tried his luck at dancing, and noted later, "I do not think the indians are through laughing even to this day over my efforts at that run around the five crow hop dance."[26] After each hour of dancing came an intermission, during which the drummer passed the hat for donations, a practice learned from Methodist missionaries, according to the cowboys.

During the third intermission Sam Horton decided to have fun at young Dyche's expense. He gave one girl a dollar to put her shawl around Dyche's head, and her sister fifty cents to help. One of the girls promptly struck up a conversation about the dance with Dyche in broken English. "I was a little bit suspicious of that big red shawl," Dyche recorded, "but knew nothing of the deep laid plot. . . . All at once she gave the shawl a swing & partly caught me, but I slipped out in fine shape. I was now caught by the second squaw & [she] succeeded in throwing her shawl over my head. . . . Both cowboys & Indians were whooping like . . . a mob at a football game . . . . After a five minute scuffle the two proved too much for me & one succeeded in kissing me all over my left ear."[27] After the dance a large kettle of soup and boiled meat was brought into the teepee, but Dyche left early, vowing to attend no more Indian dances.

During the following days Dyche killed wild turkeys and examined the contents of their crops to see what the birds found to eat in the long winter. "It was cold weather," Dyche recorded, "the birds were drawn—a little dry hay placed in them & then sewn up in as small a package as possible in thin muslin. The mouth & nostrils & shot holes were filled with cotton. Head & neck placed under wing. In this shape they were allowed to freeze solid."[28] Dyche had opportunities to observe several flocks of turkeys as well as to hunt them. The cowboys showed him old roosting spots where they had once seen thousands of birds. Dyche was convinced that the wild turkey would be extinct within a few years. He had, however, secured numerous specimens for study and to preserve through taxidermy.

Mammals that Dyche and other students collected for the university often were preserved for study through taxidermy, but the Natural History Department commissioned the taxidermy work outside of the university. In the fall of 1882 Dyche's column in the *Courier* noted that Frank Dixon, a Kansas City taxidermist, was mounting a deer family for the university. Dyche had collected part of the group near Harvey's Ranch the previous year. When completed, the group was to occupy one of the new cabinets in the third floor natural history room of the

University Building. Dyche later described Dixon's work: "The family of deer, consisting of a buck, doe and two beautifully spotted little fawns, is a valuable and handsome addition. The group is represented as standing on the side of a ledge of grey moss-covered rocks. The buck has just been shot and is falling back dead. The doe has a frightened but very natural appearance. The fawns look innocent but create as much disturbance among visitors and students as did Mary's lamb at school."[29]

The group was a shining example of two themes commonly found in taxidermy at that time: the sentimental family portrait, and the dramatic death struggle. Partly to make subjects interesting to the casual viewer, partly to demonstrate their skills in the craft, taxidermists frequently went beyond mounting a specimen merely for scientific study. Such taxidermy was disparagingly referred to as "ornamental" by those taxidermists who advocated preserving a specimen as accurately as possible without embellishment. Nevertheless, "ornamental taxidermy" was popular and had found its way even into scientific collections, including the natural history cabinets of the University of Kansas. Lewis Dyche was not above being drawn to the dramatic or the sentimental, as is apparent in his description of another of the university exhibits: "One of the cutest things we have ever seen in the line of taxidermy was secured last week. It is a little baby pointer dog in the attitude of 'pointing' a bird. The bird is cunningly hid in the grass a short distance from the dog's nose. It is worth seeing."[30]

Dyche was trying his hand at taxidermy during his junior year, and by the spring term of 1883 he had mounted three wild turkeys and the golden eagle he had collected in the Indian Territory. They were placed on display in the cabinets of the University Building. The editor of the *University Courier* remarked that Dyche's work in taxidermy was "in many respects superior to any previously done for the University."[31]

A further scientific note in the *Courier* recorded that the Natural History Department's resident Gila monster, collected live by Snow in New Mexico, appeared to have fallen into a state of hibernation. Professor Snow had been performing experiments to determine whether or not the Gila monster's bite was poisonous. Dyche wrote that the reptile had bitten a number of Lawrence cats without effect.[32]

"Dyche the Ripper on his Rounds." The 1883 KU yearbook Helianthus *shows Dyche in pursuit of a Lawrence cat. Dyche paid a bounty of fifteen cents apiece for cats, which his anatomy classes used for dissection. (University of Kansas Archives)*

Lawrence cats were utilized often by the Natural History Department, and Dyche's zoology classes dissected them. The *Courier* noted, "Prof. Dyche has offered fifteen cents a piece for cats. The Lawrence small boy threatens to flood the market; if they do we will put up a dyke against them."[33] There was also a market for dogs in laboratory classes, as evidenced by a solicitation in Dyche's column: "More kittens, cats, puppies and dogs wanted, at from fifteen to twenty-five cents."[34] Approximately fifty cats and a dozen dogs were dissected during the twenty-week anatomy class of 1882.

The last issue of the *Courier* to which Dyche contributed reported that he objected "to his students spending so much time after Kats." That same issue also provided gossip concerning a recent trip Dyche had made to Chicago, "where he went to get married, but he didn't get."[35] Dyche was still courting the girl he had met in Emporia, Ophelia Axtell, who was now attending the Congregational College at Wheaton, Illinois. Dyche was beginning to reach a level within the university where he was secure enough to consider marriage. Professor Snow was pleased with the progress of his protégé and arranged for Dyche to be his assistant for the next term, salaried at six hundred dollars per year.

A poster promoting an 1894 Dyche lecture. (University of Kansas Archives)

3 Nimrod

Lewis Dyche graduated from the University of Kansas on June 4, 1884, receiving both the Bachelor of Arts and Bachelor of Science degrees. He was twenty-seven years old, and his was the twelfth class to graduate from the university. Commencement was held in the chapel of University Hall. Red, white, and blue bunting draped a stage embellished with flowers and evergreen boughs. A black banner read, in Greek, "The End Crowns the Work." The chapel was filled to capacity.

Dyche was one of several graduating students to deliver an oration. His topic, "The Last Quarter Century in Science," probably was suggested to him by Professor Snow: "Too much steeping in Roman fable, too much lullaby in Grecian dream, too much fetish worship in religion has at last produced a revolution in thought," he began. "The change wrought in the ideas of men during the last quarter century is without parallel. . . . The appearance, in 1859, just twenty-five years ago, of Darwin's *Origin of Species,* and the almost simultaneous announce-ment of Herbert Spencer that 'evolution is a universal principle,' marked the beginning of an impulse given to thought and investigation, the most splendid of the nineteenth century."[1]

Dyche took his enthusiasm for Darwin's theory from Professor Snow. Clyde Kenneth Hyder has noted that Snow incorporated evolution "into a point of view that remained essentially religious."[2] Dyche, too, reconciled the theory of evolu-tion with religion, ending his oration with the benediction, "All honor, again, to the men who have done so much to dispel the imp and nymph of the ancient, the superstitions and dogmas of our fathers, and are at last bringing man face to face with his brother and that great Reformer who died eighteen hundred years ago upon the Cross."[3]   The *Topeka Daily Capital* reported that "Mr. Dyche's production was one of the best on the programme, being exceedingly practical in its character, unlike the average college oration. With a pleasant delivery and an eloquent voice he held the close attention of the audience throughout."[4]

Harvey's Ranch, located in New Mexico's Pecos high country. (University of Kansas Archives)

Professor Snow's annual summer expedition returned to New Mexico in 1884, encamping twelve miles north of Silver City. The previous year Snow's party had worked in Gallinas Canyon, where Dyche and a fellow student, William Harvey Brown, had separated from the main group to work in the vicinity of Harvey's Ranch. The 1884 expedition followed a similar pattern: Dyche and Brown reached Harvey's Ranch in June, while Snow's group arrived in the area in August. Dyche and Brown were on their own, calling themselves "The Wildcat Division of the K.S.U.[5] Scientific Expedition."[6]

The twenty-two-year-old Brown was admitted to the university in 1879 and, like Dyche, spent a few years in the Preparatory Department. He was a popular student, a member of the Phi Gamma Delta fraternity and president of his freshman class. He accompanied Dyche to the Harvey's Ranch area with the intention of collecting butterflies, but soon was tempted by Dyche's mission: collecting grizzly bears.

Since their last visit to the ranch, Harvey had built a new log house with a shingle roof, had added a milk-house, and was in the process of constructing a log barn. He had plowed several acres of mountainside for potatoes, wheat, and oats. Furniture and a cooking range had been hauled up the mountain on burro-back. Despite those signs of civilization, Dyche noted, "Yet there was an air and flavor of wildness & freshness to everything, and I was delighted to get back on the old stomping grounds."[7]

No deer had been killed in Dyche's absence, although mica prospectors, especially George Beatty, had hunted them, but within hours of his arrival Dyche killed a doe. He noted, "Harvey told me afterwards that he would not have had me miss that deer for fifty dollars after the way he had been bragging on me to Beaty & the other hunters . . . . However, I was loaded for bear this year & had no time to spend at the ranch."[8]

Taking ranch burros with them, Dyche and Brown began their bear hunt. As they entered the mountain woods the wind rose, and dead spruce trees proved dangerous. "The tall dead trees would be hurled to the ground with the wildest kind of creaking, cracking, crashing & mashing noises," Dyche wrote. "We could not sleep that night for fear of some accident. . . . it seemed as though the world was just about to come to some kind (or unkind) of an end."[9]

The following morning they fled "Camp Falling Timber," slowed by having to cut through fallen spruces while managing burros that Dyche declared were "born contrary to reason." One burro, Reuben, was especially troublesome, though both men later recalled him with affection. "We dared not leave him loose about camp," Brown recorded, "on account of his ravenous appetite for sugar, bacon, flour, tin cans, meat rinds, soap, dish cloths, etc. One day while we were both absent he slipped his halter, and when we returned to camp he was eating a loaf of hot bread out of the bake kettle."[10]

The men eventually arrived at a place honeycombed with trails worn by years of grizzly bear traffic. Their objective seemed assured. They named the place "Camp Bear Trail" and settled in. Convinced that an encounter was imminent, they brought the burros into camp each night and passed up shots at deer so as not to frighten away bears. "We talked about bear all day & dreamed about bear at night," Dyche recalled,[11] but after a few days with no bear sightings, the men changed their diet from cold bacon to fresh venison. Dyche surprised a herd of nine deer and fired four shots from his Sharp's rifle, his "bear gun." When he reached the deer he found that he had killed six, one bullet having passed through three animals. Brown later boasted in the *University Courier* that "the professor can scarcely be excelled as a marksman."[12] But in his notes for *Camp-Fires of a Naturalist,* Dyche regretted his reckless shooting, writing that he considered giving up hunting altogether after the incident. Dyche and Brown took time out from their bear hunt to save all the meat and skins of the deer, and Brown transported them the considerable distance back to Harvey's Ranch.

Despite being unnerved by his slaughter of the deer, Dyche resumed his bear hunt as soon as Brown left for Harvey's Ranch. Since the bears would not come to him no matter how inconspicuously he positioned himself, Dyche decided to stalk them. He followed a set of tracks, each print as big as "a peck measure," for fifteen miles. At nightfall he stopped to build a small fire on a flat rock. Then he scooted the coals aside and put spruce boughs on the warm spot, covering them with his rubber blanket. He dozed, frequently awakened by the low-burning fire and "a horrible dream about a bear."[13]

When he returned to the main camp the following day, he found that a bear had poked through the camp and had wallowed in the spring from which Dyche took his drinking water. "I was not only disgusted & mortified," he recorded, "but mad & resolved that something must be done & that right early about this bear business."[14] When Brown returned, he and Dyche built a hunting platform in a nearby tree. For three nights they perched above a venison bait. On the third morning, stiff and tired, Dyche unhitched himself from his safety strap and went into camp for a hot breakfast Brown had prepared. Returning to the platform five minutes later, Dyche saw that the venison was gone; bear tracks were everywhere, and a bear had wallowed in the nearby spring. "Fire & Brimstone," Dyche wrote. "I was tired and weary from the loss of a nights sleep, but I could not stand the pressure of such insolence. I determined to follow that bear if it was the last bear act of my life."[15]   But the bear traveled quickly, and Dyche could not catch sight of it.

The next day he found a place where the bear's trail crossed and mixed with other trails. He saw earth that was freshly picked, rooted, and dug up. Logs had been rolled aside and rocks were overturned. Following the main trail, he came upon a choke-cherry patch and saw that the bushes were torn and stripped with their tops chewed off. He forded a stream and climbed a hill, expecting every second to see a bear. The bear's trail of destruction was easy to follow. Ant hills were torn to bits, stumps and huge rotten trees were turned over. As he crossed an open green park onto a mesa, flanked on one side by the forest and on the other by a granite-ledge dropoff, Dyche found his bear: "Suddenly there came out of the forest, directly to the west of me and not over seventy yards away, a huge grizzly bear. Before I could realize what had happened, out came another, then a third, a fourth, a fifth, a sixth and a seventh. Just think of it, seven big bears in sight all at once! I think there were four more which I saw, making eleven in all in that band. I knew I was in a most desperate situation. On one hand was a bottomless preci-pice and on the other a herd of the most ferocious animals which range the mountains. How the sweat did roll off of my face! There was only one thing to do, and I did it to perfection. That was to stand perfectly still and let those bears go about their business. I was hunting bears, but not these particular bears."[16] Dyche later attempted to let off a shot at the bears from the relative safety of the woods, but they "unintentionally outwitted" him, going up a ridge while he waited for them by the stream.

Back in camp, Dyche and Brown decided that if they were going to collect a single bear, a trap was the answer. Brown left the next morning for Las Vegas to purchase supplies and a steel trap. Dyche set out stalking again. He came across a fresh trail near the spot where he had encountered the bear herd the previous day. "All at once to my great astonishment a monster of a grizzly stepped out into the opening made by the little stream. Fortune alive what a monster he was—as big as a cow. The wind was in his favor & he got scent of me. He immediately threw his front feet on a log & stood facing me. . . . The old gun had always seemed too big & heavy, but now I longed for a cannon. . . . The old gun belched forth a tremen-dous blast, & with the dying roar of its report there was another roar—a bellowing roar on the other side of the willow patch. And there was a bear rolling & tum-bling, jumping & falling—roaring & bellowing. It was an awful sight."[17] Dyche left the animal where it had fallen and returned to camp, spending a restless night filled with dreams about the group of bears he had seen the previous day and the bellowing bear he had just killed.

Early the next morning Dyche returned to the bear and began the long process of measuring and skinning it. He discovered two other bullets in the body of the old bear. His own bullet had passed through the animal. At the end of the day he carried the meat, skin, and head to a snow bank and buried them. The succeeding days were spent dressing the skin and salting it, removing traces of fat and flesh, and cleaning bones.

Eight days later Brown returned with a fifty-pound bear trap. Dyche, having spotted him coming up the mountain, had prepared dinner: bear steaks. Brown complained that the meat was tough and asked Dyche if he had cooked one of the burros. He was dumbfounded to learn that Dyche had, by himself, killed, skinned, and transported a grizzly bear. Upon realizing what he was eating, Brown remarked that the bear "must have been the one old Noah had in the ark."[18]

Within a few days the new steel trap snared a silver-tipped grizzly bear, which tore apart a log pen around the trap, tossing whole logs twenty feet, and dragged away the trap, its chain, and a twenty-five-foot pole fastened to the chain. The catch-pole caught in the underbrush and rocks. Alerted by the bear's bellowing, Dyche and Brown pursued it through the woods. Brown's war hoops blended with the cries of the bear, which had managed to drag its shackles 225 yards before a shot from Dyche's rifle slowed it. Brown was yelling at the top of his lungs, "Give it to him! Give it to him! Give him another!" After three more shots the bear was rolling in its death throes. Dyche and Brown were hysterical with relief, grabbing each other's hands and performing "a regular war dance." Dyche estimated that their prize weighed six to eight hundred pounds.

The issue of the *University Courier* that carried Brown's accounts of the "Wildcat" expedition also included reports on the progress of Lewis Dyche's romance with Ophelia Axtell. "Prof. Dyche captured one dear after his return," read one item. "Some of his stories bear a bare resemblance to poetry," read another. "He no longer goes it alone."[19] Dyche had announced his engagement to Ophelia Axtell.

Born in 1859, Ophelia moved with her family, from Monmouth, Illinois, to Kansas in 1874—the year of the great grasshopper invasion. While on the road to Kansas, Ophelia recalled people saying to her father, "You're going the wrong way. Better turn around and go back." Her father established a farm in Rice County near Peace (later named Sterling), founded by members of the Society of Friends. Pliny Fiske Axtell's farm prospered, and he acquired a good deal of land that he eventually donated for the site of Sterling College. Ophelia attended the State Normal School for two years, where she met Lewis Dyche. She attended the fundamentalist Wheaton College in Illinois for four additional years, pausing to teach school at Sterling. Lewis and Ophelia graduated from their respective institutions in 1884, and were married at the Axtell family home in Sterling on October 4.

Their honeymoon was delayed. Married life necessarily revolved around the university calendar, and the fall semester was underway. In fact, during their thirty-one years of marriage the couple had very little time strictly for themselves. From September to June, Dyche worked at instruction, class preparation, grading, laboratory work, and study. He assisted Professor Snow in teaching comparative anatomy, and he directed special students in natural history. From June to September Dyche was in the field, collecting.

In the summer of 1885, however, he orchestrated a honeymoon, taking Mrs. Dyche to Harvey's Ranch. A student, E. D. Eames, accompanied them. Dyche resolved to hunt no large game, devoting his time to mounting birds in the field and vacationing with his wife. Time spent with the Harveys was pleasant: Harvey made improvements every year, and he earned more money by boarding hunters and sightseers than he did by ranching or farming. Dyche and Eames prepared 115 birds, and Mrs. Dyche, on this her first visit to the mountains, enjoyed the spruces, white-barked aspens, and mountain meadows surrounding the ranch.

After a month at Harvey's Ranch, George Beatty, the mica prospector, convinced the Dyches that they should come to his cabin, promising them "the best hunting and fishing in the country." Dyche thought his bride might enjoy the rustic excursion, and he hired donkeys from Harvey for a three-day trip. Ophelia borrowed a pair of trousers from one of the teenaged Harvey boys and was given old Reuben to ride, the donkey that, according to Harvey, ate eggs and young chickens. "If you and Brown had killed him for a specimen . . . it would have saved me much trouble and bad temper," Harvey told Dyche.[20] En route to Beatty's cabin, all semblance of a trail disappeared. Beatty led the way, telling bear stories, with Ophelia Dyche on Reuben and Lewis following behind to "drive Reuben & help Mrs. D. on whenever she falls off."[21]

On the second night the burros disturbed a grouse hen as the excursionists prepared to camp. The mother bird flew up and disappeared. In the quiet, chick grouse could be heard in the tall grass. Their chirping continued until Mrs. Dyche decided that her husband should catch them for the night to ensure their safety. Lewis went into the neck-high grass and spent an hour on his knees stalking baby grouse, while Ophelia assured him that she would be unable to sleep until every one of the young birds was found. "I crawled, scrambled over logs & brush on my hands and knees for an hour or two & finally secured every one of the little

George Beatty and his bear knives "long enough to reach a bear's heart." A posed studio photograph originally published in Clarence Edwords's Camp-Fires of a Naturalist. *(University of Kansas Archives)*

squeakers," Dyche recorded.[22] Ophelia nestled the birds under a blanket and soon they quieted down. Early in the morning, when the hen's call was heard, Mrs. Dyche released her flock from under the blanket.

As the party went farther into the mountains, George Beatty pointed out, to

Mrs. Dyche's distress, several places where he had encountered grizzly bears. He showed her his buckhorn-handled "bear knives," which he had made from finely ground drill bits. Each knife was twelve inches long, "long enough to sure reach a bear's heart."[23] He boasted that he had once stood off four bears "when they saw [he] was sure ready for them."[24]

Beatty's two-room cabin stood on a flat, grassy piece of land between the main fork and the Rito del Padre fork of the Pecos River. Bear tracks could be seen all about the cabin, and vegetables had been clawed up from the garden. Upon unlocking his cabin door, the pleasant raconteur suddenly roared, "I've sure been robbed!" As Beatty cursed, Mrs. Dyche retreated to the edge of the woods, preferring an encounter with a bear to the miner's oaths. Dyche tried unsuccessfully to quiet Beatty, but the longer Beatty searched his cabin the more he discovered was missing. His fury grew as he described what would happen to the thieves once he had caught them. "I am sure a bad man when I am mad!" he declared. That night Beatty's intermittent outbursts prevented the weary honeymooners from getting any rest, and at daybreak Beatty strapped on his bear knives and left, vowing, "I will sure have every one of them." Beatty eventually discovered that a friend had sent a boy to watch over his cabin while Beatty was away. Frightened by the appearance of several bears, the boy had placed Beatty's guns, supplies, and equipment under the cabin floor for safekeeping and had then fled the mountain.[25]

The Dyches quickly packed and retreated from the cabin, spending the following night at Mora Flats, a mountain valley at the junction of Mora and Valdez creeks. From there Dyche took his wife to "Camp Bear Trail," where they spent several days. Finding abundant trout and venison, Dyche finally was able to share Arcadian camp life with his wife.

Whether Ophelia was perturbed by the insolent burro, the profane miner, or camping among grizzly bears, or whether Lewis found it a nuisance to spend hours on his hands and knees collecting grouse chicks, this expedition proved to be the only wilderness collecting trip that husband and wife shared. And Dyche never returned to Harvey's Ranch, which the Boston entrepreneur subsequently renamed "Harvey's Resort." Harvey built a carriage house at the base of the mountain, and visitors rode burro-back up to his "Paradise Valley." The resort became popular, and its success prompted Harvey to build a road up the mountain, eliminating the need for the seven-mile burro ride. The road, ironically, marked the downfall of the resort: Harvey's guests evidently found the long burro-back ride part of the romance of his wilderness paradise.

Professor Snow's ambition to erect a museum building was achieved in 1886 with the completion of the Snow Hall of Natural History. The state legislature appropriated fifty thousand dollars for the new building, an exorbitant sum considering that the Chemistry Building had been erected at a cost of twelve thousand dollars in 1883 (and the legislature had provided only eight thousand dollars toward its construction). The Regents allowed Snow to choose the location of the new building, and he selected a site west of University Hall (in front of the present-day Watson Library).

The building had two main stories, each sixteen feet high. *Science* magazine praised the basement and attic for being "so commodious and well lighted as to make the structure practically four stories in height."[26] The collections belonging to each department were placed on the same floor as the classrooms and laboratories of that department and thus were readily accessible for study. Professor Snow intended to generate printed labels for every specimen, an ambitious undertaking considering the scope of the collections.

A characteristic feature of the natural history collections was that they had been gathered and prepared by the professors and students. Professor Snow, while superintending the entire work, took direct charge of the collection of plants and insects. Dyche had killed and mounted many of the cabinet's mammals and birds. Judge E. P. West had collected, prepared, and classified thousands of plant and animal fossils. William Harvey Brown had prepared skeletons of reptiles, birds, and mammals. Many other students and graduates also had contributed to the collections. The Natural History Department had thus assembled extensive collections at little expense to the state or to the university, yet they were among the most valuable of the university's possessions—from a monetary as well as an educational perspective.

Among the most noteworthy additions to the university collections were two bison procured by Dyche's sometime hunting companion, William Harvey Brown, and they had a profound impact on Dyche's career. Professor Snow had arranged for Brown to spend the summer of 1886 as a volunteer assistant at the National Museum in Washington, D.C., working for the museum's chief taxidermist, William Temple Hornaday. Pleased with Brown's work in osteology, Hornaday arranged for Brown to accompany him on an expedition to Montana that fall to collect twenty to thirty bison skins and skeletons. Hornaday had organized the expedition upon the realization that bison specimens literally might not be available in another few years. Although it was later learned that a herd of about 550 bison existed in a remote region near Great Slave Lake in Canada, Hornaday was convinced at the time that there were no more than 300 extant. In fact, he dramatically referred to the Smithsonian Institution's expedition as "The Last Buffalo Hunt."[27]

Hornaday's objective was paradoxical: to kill individuals of an endangered species in order to preserve a taxidermic record of the species. He conceded the irony four decades later: "To all of us the idea of killing a score or more of the last survivors of the bison millions was exceedingly unpleasant; but we believed that our refraining from collecting the specimens we imperatively needed would not prolong the existence of the bison species by a single day. Subsequent events proved the absolute correctness of that belief. The three bison remnants then alive in Montana, Colorado and Texas all were utterly exterminated by hide-hunters, reckless cowboys and poachers, by the end of 1887 [the year after the hunt]. . . . At that time there was not the slightest reason for either the belief or the hope that the bison species could or would be brought back and SAVED to the world by breeding in captivity."[28]

As part of the arrangement for William Harvey Brown to accompany Hornaday, Professor Snow personally contributed one hundred dollars to the expedition with the understanding that the University of Kansas would receive one good bison skin, skeleton, and skull. Arriving at Miles City, Montana, on September 24, 1896, Hornaday and Brown, accompanied by three cowboy guides and two soldiers, spent three months tracking and killing bison. A large bison bull that eventually was given to the University of Kansas was killed on October 14. Brown proved himself invaluable, according to Hornaday: "He displayed the utmost zeal and intelligence, not only in the more agreeable kinds of work and sport incident to the hunt, but also in the disagreeable drudgery, such as team-driving and working on half-frozen specimens in bitter cold weather." In all, the expedition procured twenty-two bison skins and eleven skeletons. "Nearly every adult bull we took carried old bullets in his body," Hornaday noted.[29]

Brown was rewarded for his volunteer work with a bison cow. A bull was sent to the University of Kansas as per the arrangement with Professor Snow, but the cow (the second largest collected on the expedition) was given to Brown. Hornaday advised Brown to use the skin to his best advantage, suggesting that he take no less than fifty dollars for it. Whatever the financial arrangement may have been, the bison cow as well as the bull was added to the university collections. Hornaday also provided Snow with list of field measurements for use by the university taxidermist, Lewis L. Dyche.

Brown returned to Lawrence in the spring semester to resume his studies, working in the afternoons as Dyche's assistant in the Natural History Department. The two bison specimens were due to arrive in the Snow Hall workrooms in March. It is understandable if Dyche was intimidated by the task that lay ahead of him; he had mounted large animals previously, including mule deer and grizzly bears, but the bison specimens were immense. More importantly, they were rare and remarkable.

From Brown, Dyche heard tales of the buffalo hunt and of William T. Hornaday. It would be difficult to exaggerate the impression Hornaday had made on Brown. Years later Brown would confide to Hornaday, "Ever since the time (when in Washington preparing for the buffalo trip) that I purchased a pair of trousers many sizes too large for me in order to have them of the same color and material of yours, you have been the model after which I have endeavored to pattern. In fact, you have little conception of the influence that you have exerted in moulding my ideas and the course of my life. . . . In order to improve, it is necessary for one to have an ideal to attain to, and of all the men I have yet met, none can compare with you for manly qualities."[30]

Dyche resolved that before he attempted to mount the bison he would go to Washington and study under Hornaday, the nation's leading taxidermist. Hornaday had stated firmly that he would not accept students, considering them to be nuisances, but in January 1887, a Lawrence newspaper reported that "Prof. Dyche will go to Washington next summer and take special instruction from Hornaday in taxidermy and then will permanently mount the [bison] skin."[31] This brash "leak" to the press undoubtedly came from Dyche himself.

Dyche preparing a hide in the field. (University of Kansas Archives)

4 In a Taxidermy Shop

Dyche's boyhood on the Wakarusa River had provided him with experience in skinning and cleaning animals he had killed, but he first attempted taxidermy in 1883, his junior year at the University of Kansas, mounting eagles, turkeys, and other large birds. By 1885 he had mounted Virginia deer and grizzly bear. Those specimens became popular attractions in the university's natural history collections, and Professor Snow encouraged Dyche's endeavors in taxidermy.

Taxidermy in America was experiencing a rennassiance in the 1880s. Prior to 1880, Montagu Browne, a British taxidermist, placed the United States last on his "world taxidermy list," behind Germany, France, and England. But he noted that taxidermy at Ward's Natural Science Establishment in Rochester, New York, showed promise due to the importation of "clever foreign artists" who were also gradually educating Americans in the craft.[1] Numerous men who would become prominent taxidermists and museum preparators began their careers at Ward's, including Frederic Lucas, who went to the American Museum of Natural History in New York; Carl Akeley, who would revolutionize taxidermy at the Milwaukee Public Museum, the Chicago Field Museum, and the American Museum of Natural History; and William T. Hornaday, who became chief taxidermist at the National Museum.

Founded by Professor Henry A. Ward, Ward's Natural Science Establishment provided American museums and colleges with natural history specimens, such as fossils, skeletons, and mounted animals, for study and display. By later standards taxidermy performed at Ward's was crude. Carl Akeley claimed that

"Our Taxidermists at Work." This drawing by Frederic Lucas depicting the taxidermists of Ward's Natural Science Establishment in Rochester, New York, was originally published in Ward's Natural Science Bulletin, *January 1, 1883.*

Ward's taxidermists merely filled "a raw skin with the greasy bones of the legs and skull and stuffed the body out with straw, excelsior, old rags, and the like."[2] Nevertheless, Ward's served as a gateway for European techniques of taxidermy.

Such techniques were disclosed reluctantly, however. Taxidermists tended to keep their methods to themselves. Montagu Browne remarked that there were no brothers in the art of taxidermy—only rivals. Even at Ward's a French preparator, Charles Roch, was so secretive about his methods that he would cover his work in progress when Professor Ward entered the shop. The Society of American Taxidermists was formed in 1880 partly as an attempt to forestall such "absurd jealousies and closet secrets," as William T. Hornaday termed them.

But for Lewis Dyche, working at a young university in distant Kansas, the innovative "secrets" of taxidermy remained secret. The university's two bison specimens collected by William T. Hornaday's Smithsonian expedition to Montana arrived in Lawrence on March 22, 1887, and Dyche spent long days on the skins, scraping, poisoning, and tanning them. In the evenings Mrs. Dyche read aloud from *Two Years in the Jungle,* Hornaday's chronicle of mammal-collecting expeditions to India, Ceylon, the Malay Peninsula, and Borneo. To many (and certainly to William Harvey Brown), Hornaday was America's leading taxidermist, and Dyche resolved to learn what he could from him. Dyche had induced Brown to write Hornaday on his behalf, asking if Hornaday would be willing to instruct him on how to mount the bison. Hornaday's reply to Brown was hardly encouraging: "I am pretty certain no one would care to pay what I would consider it worth. I could not give anyone a thorough course in mammal mounting without taking a two weeks vacation without pay, and I am pretty certain no taxidermist could be willing to pay the $200 I would consider it worth. As to taking anyone in to work here with me in the regular course of my work I would not take anyone at any price."[3]

Undaunted, Dyche gamely drafted another letter to Hornaday:

Dear Sir,

I take this opportunity to address you a few lines upon the subject of taxidermy. . . . I have been trying for a few years past to mount specimens of birds and mammals. I have prepared for the University Museum 500 birds and a few mammals (eight deer—two bears and about fifty smaller animals). I have heard so much from Mr. Brown and others of your fine work that I have determined to visit the Nat[ional] Museum this coming spring and to receive some instruction from yourself if I can make satisfactory arrangements with you. I have no opportunity to learn anything about the art in this western country. There is a taxidermist (not a good one) at Kansas City but he works by *magic* and *secrets known to no one but himself* and I cannot learn anything from him.

Prof. Ward of Rochester visited our institution last year. He saw the results of my efforts and asked me through Prof. Snow to visit his establishment. He told Prof. Snow it would do me a great deal of good to spend some time there. . . . But Dr. Bessey[4] put me out of the notion of going to Ward's at least until after I had visited Mr. Hornaday, "one of my old pupils" as he termed you. Indeed he spoke of you and your work in such flattering terms that I have been all in a humor to visit the Nat[ional] Museum ever since.

Mr. Brown told me recently that you would give me a short series of lessons in mammal mounting for a consideration of two hundred dollars ($200). I will be glad to receive them. I would like very much to see you mount a Buffalo and would be willing to pay reasonably for the privilege. . . .

Hoping to hear from you favorably,

I am sincerely yours,

L. L. Dyche[5]

William Temple Hornaday, taxidermist, builder of zoos, conservationist. This inscribed portrait was given to Dyche by Hornaday in 1892, five years after Dyche studied under Hornaday at the Smithsonian Institution. (University of Kansas Archives)

Hornaday replied to Dyche's entreaty within the week, inviting Dyche to come to Washington. Dyche left immediately. Hornaday had mounted all but one of the Smithsonian's Montana bison already, and he urged Dyche to come at once in order to observe the preparation of the last specimen.

Hornaday took Dyche into his workshop at the Smithsonian on April 12. Though only two years older than Dyche, Hornaday, with vast experience in their shared field, assumed a fatherly attitude toward Dyche. Dyche possessed the experience and observational skills of a good field scientist, and Hornaday built on that experience. He took Dyche step by step through the mounting of a bison bull. To Hornaday, the ideal taxidermist was "a combination of modeller and anatomist, naturalist, carpenter, blacksmith, and painter. He must have the eye of an artist, the back of a hod-carrier, the touch of a wood-chopper one day, and of an engraver the next."[6]

Dyche spent his first day making wooden bones (used to replace lost originals or when the actual bones were used to make up a separate study skeleton). Then he worked at shaping the iron rods for the legs. He was shown how to cut a paper outline of a freshly killed specimen and how to record a copious series of skinned body and limb measurements. Dyche spent one day sketching the buffalo. Then, for the next several weeks, he observed Hornaday mount the bison bull.

While working at Ward's, Hornaday had learned from Johannes Martens, a German taxidermist, a method of constructing a central body board with attached iron legs that formed a rough model on which a specimen could be mounted. This technique produced a specimen eminently more lifelike than those produced by the common practice of simply "stuffing" a skin with hay or tow. The more complete the model inside the skin, the less the stuffing tended to look like loose material in an empty bag. At the National Museum, Hornaday had improved on that technique by using a clay-covered hollow statue, or manikin, to mount large mammals. Hornaday's manikin counterfeited the form and size of the entire living animal and thus required of the taxidermist a thorough knowledge of the specimen's anatomy as well as the skills of a sculptor.[7] Hornaday had developed the technique only a few years earlier, in 1882. What Dyche observed was truly the latest in the craft of taxidermy.

In addition to Hornaday's clay-covered manikin method, Dyche learned the techniques of smaller details such as how to cover skulls with clay and how to prepare ears, noses, and mouths. He made lead ears and sewed them into the skin. He learned to sculpt facial detail with papier-maché, and he learned how to paint eyes and noses.

Outside of the taxidermy shop, Dyche attended concerts and church meetings with Hornaday and his wife. One Saturday he helped Hornaday lay a carpet at his home. Hornaday introduced Dyche to prominent men, galleries, and clubs. On several occasions they shot targets at the Soldier's Home. Ophelia Dyche joined her husband on May 21, and the two couples often dined together. One evening the Horndays introduced the Dyches to a new card game, "Hearts."

When Hornaday had nearly finished the bison bull, he and Dyche progressed to other specimens. Dyche assisted with a wolf and an antelope, and he received a seal-mounting lesson. In the basement of the Smithsonian he practiced making plaster casts and painted fish and snakes. An entry in his diary reported, "Worked at laboratory all day upon the antelope head. Mr. Hornaday said I did splendidly and had reason to feel proud *which of course I do*."[8] Hornaday ultimately decided not to charge Dyche for the taxidermy lessons; Dyche was officially accounted for in the National Museum's annual report as "an unsalaried volunteer in the department for the sake of the experience acquired."[9]

Dyche kept a notebook during his stay in Washington and made drawings, notes, and comments on the exhibits and works in progress. Observing Hornaday's bison group in the National Museum, he noted: "Exageration. Remember to make animals thin. But it is frequently necessary to make muscles larger than they really are or they will not show at all; vice a versa; It is frequently necessary to make a depression deeper than it really is."[10] Dyche noted the value of groundwork and how proper placement of specimens clarified the point of the exhibit. He wrote, "Animals do not look good standing at random. Should be placed in a group. Each group should be an object lesson and the object should be apparent."[11] An outsider to Eastern museums, it seemed perfectly natural to Dyche that mounted specimens be displayed in groups, but, in fact, group displays often were considered too sensational for the purpose of scientific study, and their inclusion in established museum and university collections was controversial. The first group exhibit displayed at the American Museum of Natural History, for example, depicted an Arabian courier riding a camel being attacked by lions.

Hornaday, however, was an advocate of group displays. In 1879, while at Ward's, he mounted a group of orangutans he had collected in Borneo, which aroused the interest of taxidermists around the world both for its exotic subject and its technical excellence. Hornaday himself described the group, titled "A Battle in the Tree-Tops," as "a trifle sensational," with "immense and hideously ugly male orang utans fighting furiously while they hung suspended in the tree-tops. The father of an interesting family was evidently being assailed by a rival for the affection of the female orang utan, who, with a small infant clinging to her breast, had hastily quitted her nest of green branches, and was seeking taller timber." Hornaday maintained that the element of combat "was introduced for the specific purpose of attracting attention to the group and inviting discussion."[12] The background setting for the group was also noteworthy. As the orangutan battle was fought aloft, Hornaday had reproduced the upper heights of a Bornean forest: trees, leaves, orchids, pepper vines, mosses, vegetation, and an accurate reconstruction of an orangutan nest. Although Hornaday popularized his orangutans, he had taken care to represent them in their natural habitat.

"A Battle in the Tree-Tops" won a special medal at a competition sponsored by the newly formed Society of American Taxidermists. But at that same exhibition second place was awarded to a single wood duck, mounted traditionally on a small wooden stand, which discouraged Hornaday greatly because the wood duck's taxidermist, Frederic Webster of Ward's, also had submitted a large group of flamingos. Hornaday viewed the circumvention of the flamingo group as a rejection by the judges of the group-display concept.

The resistance of many taxidermists to group exhibits was understandable: They wished to maintain a clear distinction between specimens mounted for scientific study and popular or "ornamental" taxidermy. Taxidermy was becoming a popular hobby, and amateur and even professional taxidermists were mounting animal specimens in distinctly unscientific attitudes. Rowland Ward outlined in his *Sportsman's Handbook* a procedure for transforming an elephant's foot into a liquor stand. Montagu Browne, in *Practical Taxidermy,* described how to mount hummingbird heads as brooches. Small birds were pressed, preserved, and made into medallions. Dogs were turned into footstools, puppies into ink blotters, and kittens into paperweights. After leaving Ward's, the French taxidermist Jules Bailly was known for mounting groups of frogs playing billiards, dueling, electioneering, making love, getting drunk, smoking, dancing, and fishing.

Of course there was a world of difference between an accurately prepared display group of mammals and mounted frogs playing billiards, and Hornaday perceived taxidermists and museum curators who opposed group displays and background settings as "too conservative by half."[13]

Lewis Dyche left Washington filled not only with Hornaday's innovative techniques for mounting mammals, but also with his concepts for displaying them. Before returning to Kansas, the Dyches took a tour of the Northeast, stopping in Berkeley Springs, West Virginia, to visit Dyche's birthplace and relatives. In Philadelphia Dyche met several independent taxidermists. He studied briefly at the Agassiz Museum at Cambridge, and in Boston he paid a call on Kate Stephens, a former faculty member at the University of Kansas. He also became acquainted with Frank Webster, considered the country's finest bird taxidermist. The Dyches spent several weeks in New York City, where Dyche inspected exhibits at the American Museum of Natural History. Then they visited Ward's Natural Science Establishment in Rochester. Fresh from Hornaday's tutelage, Dyche found the state of taxidermy in the Eastern museums to be far below his expectations.

On August 25 the Dyches arrived in Lawrence. Dyche eagerly set to work on the bison. Hornaday considered the bison cow given to William Harvey Brown to be the second largest and finest cow taken on the hunt. The bull, the first killed on the hunt, was also one of the largest collected, weighing sixteen to seventeen hundred pounds and measuring over ten feet long. He stood six feet high from hoof to the top of his hump. Old buffalo hunters, including one of the university regents, considered the bull to be as large as any they had seen on the plains. Dyche started with the bull.

In describing his procedure, Dyche noted that the skin "should be thoroughly tanned. In order that this may be accomplished, all fat and flesh should be carefully removed from it. It should also be shaved down, if thick like that of a moose or buffalo skin, to an even thickness all over. A draw shave and sharp knives used by tanners have been productive of the best results . . . ."[14]

Ideally, the animal to be mounted should have been studied in life before it was killed and skinned. When that was not possible, as with the bison, it was advisable to study living representatives of the species. To that end Dyche frequently visited Bismarck Grove, a park north of Lawrence where eight live bison were kept. The animals roamed freely, penned only during picnics and fairs. On one occasion Dyche was chased by a bison bull, "a mean rascal," and he spent four hours observing the bison from the branch of an apple tree.[15] Dyche wrote, "The operator must know his animal before he can hope to produce its form in the shape of a statue. In order to facilitate his work he should have at hand a complete series of notes and measurements, giving all diameters, circumferences and anatomical characteristics of the animal. Drawings, sketches and photographs of dead and live animals are always of great value. Aside from all this, the operator should know his animal in another way. He should know it so well that he could produce a good sketch or small clay model of it from memory."[16]

The next step was to create the manikin, or core of the statue. A thick body board was placed in the center, roughly representing the vertical and longitudinal section of the body, extending from the base of the neck to the back part of the pelvis. To the sides of it were bolted L-shaped angle irons, made of heavy scrap iron. Leg irons were attached to the angle irons and bent into shape. The bones of the animal's legs were fastened to the leg irons with cord and wire. The skull, pelvis, and shoulder blades were put into place using stout rods. Perpendicular side strips were fastened to the body board, and lathing then was nailed to them. The result was a hollow image of the animal.

What Dyche termed the "development of the statue proper" came next. Excelsior was wound and sewn onto the manikin. A statue wrapped in wood fiber should be solid, he observed, yet it should spring when the hand is pressed against it. There should be no soft places. The manikin thus became a rough statue of the animal, with the body surface contours depicted obscurely.

Modeling clay then was applied, the first coat being put on as a thin paste rubbed into the excelsior. Additional clay was applied and built up in much the same way a sculptor composes. "Without anatomical knowledge and skill," Dyche remarked, "the operator cannot hope for much success either with the rough statue or the finished clay model."[17] Sometimes in the evening Lewis and Ophelia would stroll up the hill to the Snow Hall workroom so that she could observe her husband's progress on the bison bull.

Preparation of the bison was time-consuming, and Dyche complained to Hornaday by letter that so much of his time was necessarily devoted to teaching. Hornaday replied, "Am *sorry* you have to do *any* teaching while mounting those buffaloes. It is all wrong, unfair to them and to you. They will need your *undivided attention,* more than anything else you will be called upon to mount in some time." Hornaday encouraged Dyche to take on an assistant: "In a few days you could teach a raw hand to clean skins, and do no end of rough work, which would save that much of your time. But the mischief of it is, every such assistant always expects, nay *demands* unlimited instruction, of the highest class, & if they are not put to *mounting* in the course of a couple of months (leaving the boss to hew his own wood and draw his own water, of course), why then they feel injured. . . . Students who come to work 'for what they can learn' are an unmitigated nuisance, and I would always rather pay them to stay away than work on such terms."[18] (Hornaday had seemingly forgotten how Dyche had approached *him.*) Seldom coy with his opinions, Hornaday easily assumed the role of Dyche's mentor, and further advised him to submit articles to scientific periodicals to "*make people familiar*" with his name.

Dyche did receive help in the form of student assistants and from his other longtime mentor, Professor Snow. In order to relieve Dyche's teaching load while he worked on the bison, Snow taught eight of Dyche's ten classes that school year. "The result has been a degree of physical and mental exhaustion which ought not to be repeated," Snow later reported to the Board of Regents.[19]

When the skin of the bull was finally installed on its manikin, the event was attended by a number of onlookers and reporters. Then it took six days to sew on the skin, which had been kept in tannin to make it flexible and soft. Dyche and his assistants sewed into the evening hours in their race against shrinkage. Six more days were devoted to the head, three days to the eyes, and two to the nose. Finally, after nearly five months of work, the bull was finished.

Once the local newspapers began to write about the university's new buffalo, there was no limit to their praise. "Professor L. L. Dyche has just completed the mounting of the best of the buffalo skins secured by Brown, giving the university, perhaps, the finest specimens of taxidermy in the world," reported the *Weekly Capital and Farmer's Journal*.[20] A student newspaper at the State Agricultural College called it "the finest mounted specimen of the American bison in existence."[21]

In Washington, Hornaday followed the local media attention given to Dyche's work with wily approval: "Today came the two column account of the great beast. I am glad to see he is properly 'whooped up,' for beyond all question that sort of thing does count. The more you have of that sort the better, for in the end it will put money in thy purse. No matter about their calling it the finest buffalo on this earth. That will do you good, and will do me no harm. But, man alive, you miss it by not setting forth in large letters early and often that you have journeyed to the distant East and taken a thorough course of study under the Chief Taxidermist of the Smithsonian Institution, and learned all the latest and most important methods and principles. It will be of great benefit to you with everyone."[22] Dyche heeded Hornaday's advice—the next reporter to write about Dyche's buffaloes mentioned Hornaday prominently.

In April Hornaday wrote to offer his "tenderest congratulations upon the safe and prompt arrival of your new assistant . . . ." The Dyches' second child,[23] Walter Snow Dyche, had arrived. Hornaday also commented on the "various newspaper clippings about your buffalo bull. Of course the cow when finished will also be like the bull, 'the finest in the world,' to which from all accounts, ours is not a circumstance. Now, I believe in putting it on pretty thick myself, but you Kansas folks are too many for me, by half."[24]

Work on the bison cow went quickly, and by April 15 it was completed. As Hornaday had predicted, it too was judged to be "the finest in the world." That

spring Dyche was awarded a Master of Science degree for special work in the natural sciences.

Proud of his work, Dyche sent Hornaday stereoscopic photographs of the bison, and on July 12, Hornaday wrote to thank him for the pictures. Of the two bison, Hornaday liked the cow the best, finding it "most like a live buffalo, wide

Dyche's bison bull after he deferred to William T. Hornaday's criticisms. The earlier version was, according to Hornaday; "really poor *in flesh." (University of Kansas Archives)*

awake and breathing." The bull, on the other hand, Hornaday found to be "really *poor* in flesh." Dyche had made the animal thin and had exaggerated the muscles so that they would be visible to the viewer. "While I recognize the fact that this was quite intentional," Hornaday wrote, "I think it hardly does the animal justice. The typical buffalo must be a well-fed animal, though not necessarily *fat* by any

Dyche's completed bison group. (University of Kansas Archives)

means." Hornaday also pointed out that Dyche had positioned the bison's pelvis too far forward. He advised Dyche, "By the powers, I would coax the old bull off into a quiet corner during this very vacation, soften the skin on that region, cut it open and change that even now! It is too bad that you did not have a picture made of the manikin and send it to me before the final act in the drama. I think I see exactly how it happened. You got so interested in the development of the muscular anatomy you forgot the osteological side of the problem. Go to, young man! Are you another John L. Sullivan that you should so run to muscle?"[25]

Dyche deferred to Hornaday's criticism. He altered the hindquarters and refashioned the bull into a stouter, better fed animal, a more accurate representative of a healthy American bison bull. Virtually all wild Kansas bison had been exterminated by 1879, but a few survived into the 1880s. The last single wild bison in Kansas was seen near the southwest corner of the state in the fall of 1888, the same year Dyche completed his pair for the University of Kansas.

In his yearly report to the Board of Regents, Professor Snow summarized Dyche's work: "In addition to the instruction of the classes in Comparative Anatomy and Osteology, my regular assistant, Mr. L. L. Dyche, has during the past year completed the mounting of the two specimens of American buffalo obtained for the University through Mr. W. H. Brown's connection with the Smithsonian hunting expedition of 1886. Mr. Dyche's knowledge of anatomy, combined with his indomitable energy and his extraordinary power of imitating natural attitudes, has enabled him to produce what I consider to be the best specimens of taxidermic art as yet produced in America. I most heartily recommend his promotion to a full professorship. The University of Kansas should permanently retain the services of such a man, by making it more desirable to him to remain in her Faculty than to accept offers from eastern museums."[26]

The 1892–93 University of Kansas faculty. Standing from left: Professors Canfield, Sayre, Hopkins, Miller, Robinson, Williston, Dunlap, Carruth, Blake, Templin, and Bailey. Seated from left: Professors Hodder, Dyche, Wilcox, Snow, Blackmoor, Penny, and Marvin. Six faculty members were absent when the photo was taken. (University of Kansas Archives)

5 The University Man

Lawrence, Kansas, in 1889 was a town of about ten thousand. Annie Hathaway Williston observed, "This is a one-horse town & the University is the horse."[1] Dyche and his wife and son lived at 1228 Ohio Street, below the hill on which the university perched, on the opposite side of the ridge where Dyche and his Auburn friend had camped in their covered wagon a dozen years earlier. As was often the convention, Dyche and his family took in student boarders. One of these was William Edgar Borah, who later became U.S. senator from Idaho and chairman of the Senate Foreign Relations Committee.

Dyche spent leisure days at the Lake View Shooting and Fishing Club. He loved to fish, and he loved to tell fish stories. Once, when several Topeka members were present at the Lake View Club, Dyche reputedly caught a six-pound bass using his white lawn string-necktie as a lure. He claimed that the "Topeka dudes" then exhausted the supply of lawn neckties in Topeka haberdasheries in their effort to catch bass.[2] As in earlier years working for Professor Snow, Dyche collected specimens in the area around Lawrence. In 1884 his collie, Joe, had flushed and caught a yellow rail, which Dyche believed to be the first collected in the state. In 1885 he had collected a pair of Mexican crossbills and sent them to the Topeka ornithologist Colonel Nathaniel S. Goss, who pronounced them the first of that species found in Kansas.

Early in 1889 Dyche traveled to the ranch of Lee Howard in the Optima Neutral Strip (now in the Oklahoma panhandle) to secure additional bison skins and skeletons for the university bison group. Those specimens, including some live calves, were the last remnants of the great southern herd of bison. A representative of the American Museum of Natural History was attempting to negotiate purchase of the specimens by wire, but Dyche, arriving in person, bettered his offer. Dyche also bought the skins of gray wolves, prairie foxes, lynx, antelopes, coyotes, and prairie dogs, paying Lee Howard seven hundred dollars. The specimens of greatest value, however, were the eleven bison skins, some of which Dyche intended to trade or sell, perhaps to the American Museum of Natural History. Competition for such specimens was heated. Dyche learned that the taxidermist for the American Museum was so angry at having been thwarted in his bid to buy the specimens that he swore that neither he nor the American Museum would have anything to do with Dyche or the skins.

The Museum of Natural History on the upper floor of Snow Hall. Dyche's early efforts in taxidermy were displayed individually on stands, as was the convention at the time. (University of Kansas Archives)

Soon after Dyche's return to Lawrence, the state legislative committees on education and educational institutions visited the university. Professor Snow guided them through the cabinets of geology, fossils, and insects in Snow Hall. Snow took his guests to the zoological museum last, where they were greeted at the threshold of the mammals exhibit room by Dyche, who showed them his mounted bison cow and bull. The state legislators, many of whom had seen and hunted buffalo in the wild, were impressed with the quality of Dyche's taxidermy, although one legislator found the head-hair of the bison too clean, asserting, "I never saw a buffalo whose foretop was not filled with clay and cockleburs." Dyche quickly retorted that he had, in accordance with contemporary fashion, "banged" the bison's hair.[3]

That droll remark notwithstanding, Dyche had taken great pains to see that the bison specimens were true to life. To that end he had begun a correspondence with James R. Mead, an authority on Kansas natural history. An early plainsman, Indian trader, and a founder of the city of Wichita, Mead had hunted bison as early as 1859, killing scores for the tongue ("Cured buffalo tongues had a market value of $1.00 each in 1858," Mead wrote).[4] Dyche relied on the recollections of men who had observed bison in the wild. To Dyche's queries regarding the head of the American bison, Mead responded, *"I never saw a Buffalo Bull or other Buffalo, with sand, and or any other foreign material matted in its forehead."*[5]

Dyche teaching an anatomy class in the 1890s. Note the human skeleton at the head of the table, as well as the cats being dissected. (University of Kansas Archives)

In addition to pointing out the university's state-of-the-art taxidermy to the legislators, it was Professor Snow's intention to exhibit Dyche himself: a home-grown Kansan, educated at both the state normal school and the state university, who was bringing favorable public attention to the university. The legislators ended their tour with luncheon in a Snow Hall classroom: buffalo calf steaks that Dyche had brought from Howard's Ranch.

On March 17, 1889, on a motion by Charles Sumner Gleed, the Board of Regents appointed Dyche to the position of Professor of Anatomy and Physiology, Taxidermist, and Curator of Mammals and Birds, effective July 1. As a full member of the faculty Dyche would come to be known to students and to local citizens as "Prof Dyche," or simply "Prof." The nickname reflected Dyche's pride in his educational achievements, but it was also adopted partly because the title "Professor Dyche" did not quite fit. He had not shed all of his farmboy manner-isms, and Dyche as professor struck some as whimsical. Some considered him to be a rural version of a Horatio Alger protagonist. The 1889 yearbook noted that "Dyche has been held up by the faculty as a brilliant example of what a man can do if he tries. He took two degrees and had grades so high that you had to get out the telescope to look at them. So when some poor devil would hand in a poor exami-nation paper and would return in a day or so for his grade the prof. would fumble around searching for the book and then bring out a paper and say, 'I ran across one of Mr. Dyche's old examination papers the other day. Just look at it; there is not an error in it.' And it is to be hoped that now that Dyche is a professor the other professors will discontinue the practice."[6]

Dyche's role at the university was well established: collector of mammals, taxidermist, teacher. Of the three identities, classroom teaching was the least important to him. He educated in a different way, procuring and preparing specimens for scientific study, thus contributing to the systematic knowledge of mammals. Since he had mounted the two bison, however, he had become increasingly aware that many of the large mammals he wished to collect and preserve were being expunged from North America. He resolved to assemble a representative collection of North American mammals while it was still possible.

In an appeal for funding for this project, Dyche would outline his plan to the Board of Regents the following year: "Allow me to urge upon you the importance of securing at the earliest possible date a good series of representations of other large mammals, such as moose, woodland and barren ground caribou, elk, musk oxen, and polar bears. Each year of delay will make it necessary to put forth a much greater effort as well as demand a much greater outlay of money. It is hardly necessary to remind you that the building of rail-roads connecting with various water courses during the past few years, has practically placed every part of the North American Continent under the foot of civilized man. The exhilarating sport of the chase, added to the hope of being supplied with food, or rewarded by a valuable hide, or set of horns, offer inviting temptations which induce the explorer, the pleasure seeker, the frontiersman as well as the professional sportsman and hunter to wage a war upon the large mammals which continually reduces ranks and will soon result in their utter extermination as wild species.

"The buffalo is already gone and it is evident to those who have given the subject thought, as can easily be verified by an examination of governmental and other reports that other large mammals will soon disappear. Laws are being enacted in most of the states and territories for the protection of large game animals. This action will result, it is to be hoped, in prolonging the existence of certain species at least in favored localities, but from the very nature of the environing circumstances it will be for a limited period only.

"In view of these considerations . . . let me urge upon you again, gentlemen, the importance of continuing the work of securing as complete a collection of our birds and mammals as possible, and particularly that part of the work which has for its immediate object the securing of a good series of specimens of our large mammals.

"Holding in mind this one important fact, namely, that if it is not done now (within the next few years), we may never be able to secure these characteristic species of the American fauna."[7]

Ascertaining that only four Rocky Mountain goats had ever been mounted at any college or museum,[8] Dyche made preparations to travel to British Columbia to collect the elusive mammal. The Board of Regents, convinced by Professor Snow of the urgency of Dyche's mission, granted Dyche a leave of absence. Dyche practiced marksmanship daily, firing some thirty pounds of ammunition from his 1886 Winchester carbine and his 40-75 Remington.[9] He took target practice in a draw near the pond on the north side of Mount Oread (now Potter Lake). A student assistant would roll a wagon wheel down the hill, and Dyche would shoot at the bouncing target.

Dyche left Lawrence on July 3. In Denver he was joined by Frederick A. Williams, a district judge, and J. Wylie Anderson, a dentist. The latter, who weighed an imposing two hundred pounds, was an excellent camp cook and was fond of telling jokes. Williams spent his free time composing heroic poems. Dyche found the two men to be "two broad gauged & most jolly souls for companions."[10] A Denver taxidermist, W. R. McFadden, accompanied the group as its guide. During the days spent in Denver preparing for the trip, Dyche formed a negative opinion of McFadden due to his habit of "communing with spirits," mainly corn whisky.[11] Like Francis Huntington Snow and William T. Hornaday, Dyche staunchly opposed hard liquor.[12]

After a long, hot train journey to Spokane, Washington, the men visited the local bath houses and barbershops, purchased two wagons and about nine horses, and set out north on a wagon trail. The summer was dry, and until they reached the mountains it was difficult to find water for the horses. At Palmer Lake, a few miles south of British Columbia, Anderson and Williams fished for trout. Dyche noted in his fieldbook, "I have no interest in the fishing business. Want specimens."[13]

"Evening in camp was the most pleasant part of the twenty-four hours, for it was spent in profitable conversation, exchanging ideas and constantly developing new thoughts" (Camp-Fires of a Naturalist, p. 142). *Posed photograph originally taken for* Camp-Fires of a Naturalist *but not published. (University of Kansas Archives)*

Further north, in British Columbia near Big White Mountain, the party came across the camp of two skin hunters. The hunters offered advice on where they might find Rocky Mountain sheep (not goats), although they were doubtful that amateurs would have success. Dyche learned that the skin hunters killed over two hundred deer that summer, selling the skins for seventy-five cents each and leaving the carcasses where they had fallen. "O ye mortal Gods what hearts some people have," he wrote.[14] Such slaughter served to strengthen Dyche's resolve to assemble immediately a collection of mammals while there was still time. Heeding the skin hunters' directions, Dyche and his companions spent the next week in the heart of the Cascades. Each man killed at least one mountain sheep, and Anderson and Williams returned to Denver on August 4.

Dyche and McFadden remained to collect additional mountain sheep. When provisions ran low, they began the return trip. The horses were loaded, and travel through the mountainous terrain was difficult. "Have tough—very tough time getting along," Dyche noted. "Packs heavy and stuff hard to arrange. Skeletons very mean stuff to pack."[15] They reached the Loomis Trading Post (now the town of Loomis, Washington) on the afternoon of August 22, and after their extended hunt during which they had eaten little besides meat, Dyche exalted that "melons never tasted so good before. Tomatoes never so luscious. . . . Hurrah for a good nights sleep."[16]

The respite did not last long: Dyche rose at five the next morning and made arrangements to store the specimens and begin another collecting foray. They left the next day, and within a week Dyche and McFadden had followed the Kettle River over a hundred miles. In the Cascades they traveled ten miles a day, looking for caribou but killing nothing but grouse and an occasional deer for food. By September 18 they had returned to the trading post.

After a few days' rest, they undertook another trip to the mountains to the northwest. McFadden was certain they would find mountain goats there, and he referred to the range as "Ibex Mountains" (so unfamiliar were North American goats to the hunters that they used the European genus name *ibex* to describe them). Smoke filled the air throughout the region. Indian hunters were using immense grassfires to drive deer to them. Game was plentiful. On Sundays, however, Dyche refrained from hunting, keeping the Sabbath by suspending "the hunting business," shooting only at game that "got in his way."[17]

Hiking along a high mountain ledge at mid-morning, Dyche heard a noise below him and saw something that looked "like an immense polar bear." He fired carefully with his Winchester, climbed down, and found that he had hit a large mountain goat, the first he had ever seen. The goat had rolled between two fallen trees and could not get up. Dyche examined the animal and took several photographs before killing it with another shot and taking measurements.

After pausing for lunch, Dyche skinned the specimen and disassembled the skeleton. Finished by four that afternoon, he packed his camera, the carcass and bones, the skin, his rifle, and a shot-sack full of tallow, slung them all over his back, and started a slow descent down the mountain. At dusk he killed another goat. Having failed to bring a canteen, Dyche was so thirsty that he resolved to drink blood from the freshly killed goat, but decided against it after smelling the animal. Finding himself with more than he could carry and night upon him, he hung the two goats from a tree limb and made his way down the mountain in a fast, sliding descent. Smoke from the Indian fires sharpened his thirst, and all he could think of was reaching the river. "Was wet with perspiration and hot with Excitement, and dry, O! how dry," Dyche wrote. "Had not had a drop of water since breakfast and had been working and sweating all day. . . . Such rock—such trees, such gulches, such brush and briars, such darkness I do not believe mortal man ever made his way through before."[18]

He reached the river and refreshed himself, and then he set out in the darkness to search for the camp. He became wound up in logs, stones, and brush, fell down thirty or so times, and asked himself in frustration, "What is man made for anyway?" He heard gunshots in the distance, presumably a signal from McFadden. Dyche responded with a shot from his rifle, and headed in the direction of McFadden's shots. After a while shots were exchanged again, and Dyche judged that he was five miles from camp.

The distant forest fires produced a "weird rushing sound." Dyche made his way through the rocks and patches of forest, hoping to reach camp in time for a few hours' sleep before dawn. At the edge of a clearing he stopped when he heard "some great beast" crashing in the brush before him. Thinking that it was a bear, he stood motionless for five minutes, waiting for it either to leave or come into the open where he might shoot it. Finally he called out, "Mac, is that you?" There was no answer. He started to walk again, and immediately the animal stirred in the brush. This time, however, Dyche recognized the sound of iron horseshoes on rock. He entered the brush and found his horse, Charlie. Dyche was standing on the edge of camp. McFadden, he later learned, was several miles on the other side of camp, firing his rifle in the hope of finding camp himself.

Bruised, scratched, and exhausted, Dyche spent most of the following day searching for the spot where he had left the goats. During the next five days he carried down the skins, skeletons, and carcasses, and he dressed the skins. McFadden assured him that each goat was worth a hundred dollars.

"Hurrah for good luck; for Ophelia and Walter; for old K.S.U.; for Prof. Snow and for the regents too!!"[19] Dyche's fieldbook entry on October 1 was jubilant: He had killed four mountain goats. And on the following day: "Hurrah for good luck, Old K.S.U., wife and baby too, if it is a true Black tail Buck. Hurrah! anyway for he is a splendid specimen."[20] The next two weeks were filled with fruitful hunting before Dyche and McFadden returned south.

But Dyche was not ready to leave British Columbia. He had not found caribou. He arranged to hunt with two local trappers and hunters, Maurice Farrell and George McLaughlin. For six weeks they combed the mountains, following reports of caribou sightings. The weather turned cold, and Dyche began to pine for his wife and son and the comfort of his home. "Where and how is wife and boy tonight[?]" he ended one diary entry. "All's well that ends well! Only the brave deserve the fair."[21] Ophelia Dyche in turn signed off a letter to her husband, "Yours with oceans of love from your little son and wife . . . . The winter season is hastening upon us and will drive you homeward, I expect, before a great while."[22] By November 21 Dyche was ready to give up. He wrote, "Have just about as many specimens of deer as I came for. I have lost all hopes of getting caribou on this trip, although we have made a grand effort. There are no caribou in the country, and, of course, we cannot get them where they are not."[23] On December 3 he began a roundabout journey home.

From Spokane he traveled to San Francisco, and at the San Francisco Rifle Club he demonstrated his marksmanship, honed by five months of hunting. He placed a fifty-cent piece on edge a hundred yards down the beach. No one would accept his challenge to shoot at the target because they could not even see it. According to his own account, Dyche put the Winchester to his shoulder, fired, and the coin disappeared. He responded to the onlookers' exclamations by remarking that it was not necessary to see the coin; one only needed to know where it was.

The Union Pacific Railroad provided free transportation for Dyche and his specimens. Dyche stopped briefly in Denver, dining with Judge Williams and sleeping in Dr. Anderson's office. On December 23 he arrived in Lawrence. He had been away six months. He paid Miss Gertrude Crotty, an advanced biology student, $130.00 to assume his teaching duties while he was in the Cascades. The cost of the entire expedition amounted to $451.80, for which the Board of Regents reimbursed him. Through his hunting, buying, and trading he had secured over a hundred specimens: eight Rocky Mountain bighorn sheep, twelve Rocky Mountain goats, two mountain lion skins, and numerous other mammals.

Soon after his return, Dyche delivered lectures about his collecting exploits in local schools and churches. The lectures were popular, with newspaper accounts indicating that he often filled the halls where he spoke. The Reverend R. D. Parker noted wryly that "his account of some of the shots he made at mountain goats rather tested our faith, but Professor Dyche is a member of Plymouth church in good and regular standing and that ends all questioning."[24]

But one hyperbolic newspaper article too many reached the eyes of William T. Hornaday, who wrote to Dyche: "My dear fellow, I assure you that we are, so far as I am concerned, just as good friends as ever, and if you were here again you would soon realize it. I value a good friend too highly to cry quits the moment some little thing comes up that is not altogether to my notion. To be perfectly frank, I will admit that your local newspapers have done much to chill the ardent enthusiasm I once felt toward you and all your undertakings, but they never affected me at all seriously or permanently. In several instances in speaking of you and your work they used expressions that seemed to be aimed particularly at me; but in this I may have been entirely mistaken. The only one of these which I preserved is the last that came to hand, and its spirit is unmistakable. Here it is:—

Prof. Dyche, instructor in Anatomy and Physiology at the University of Kansas, also Curator of Birds and Mammals, called on us recently between trains, on his way home from one of his usual weekly lectures. The Professor has recently returned from a six months hunting expedition in British America, well supplied with skins of the larger mammals found in that country, all of which were killed by himself. He is a Taxidermist of national reputation, rivaled by no one, not even excepting Hornaday, and as he gave particular attention to the anatomy of the specimens obtained, the University will shortly possess the finest group of Mountain Sheep, Mountain goat, American Lions, etc. in the U. S. as it now possesses the finest group of stuffed American Bison in the world. The Professor is a very pleasant gentleman and we trust it will be convenient for him to call often."[25]

Evidently Dyche wrote Hornaday a conciliatory letter. Their friendship weathered the episode.

Since Dyche had apprenticed with him at the Smithsonian, Hornaday had worked to establish a Department of Living Animals at the National Museum. That undertaking quickly expanded into the groundwork for a zoological garden in Washington, D.C. In 1889 Congress passed a bill founding the National Zoological Park, appropriating two hundred thousand dollars. Hornaday selected the land, and he designed many of the buildings and grounds. When control of the park was transferred to the Secretary of the Smithsonian Institution, however, Hornaday learned that his position in the zoo hierarchy would be subordinate. The Secretary of the Smithsonian, Professor S. P. Langley, took charge of the new zoological garden and began to refashion Hornaday's plans for it. Hornaday was thoroughly demoralized, believing that he would "be expected to do all the work, take all the kicks, and see the credit go entirely to two or three others." He wrote Dyche: "I am disgusted with Mr. Langley & am now going to quit natural history and make money." Hornaday moved his family to Buffalo and began working in real estate. Although his comprehensive manual on taxidermy, *Taxidermy and Zoological Collecting*, would be published the following year, the nation's leading taxidermist was, as he told Dyche, "out of taxidermy finally and forever."[26]

Joshua Allen Lippincott had resigned as chancellor of the University of Kansas in 1889, and for a nearly a year the Board of Regents contemplated his replacement. Their choice was Francis Huntington Snow, who was inaugurated as the university's fifth chancellor on June 11, 1890. With Dyche's champion now chancellor, Hornaday prophesied that Dyche's career was sure to "rise and shine."

That year the university was granted charters from Phi Beta Kappa, the oldest honorary fraternity in America, and from Sigma Xi, the honor society of research scientists. Both were the first chapters established west of the Mississippi, and the chapter of Sigma Xi was the fourth established in the country. Snow served as Sigma Xi's vice president during its initial year, and Dyche as its treasurer. The university's Sigma Xi chapter would eventually replace the Science Club, which had been started in the mid-1880s. The Science Club yell ("Rah, rah—Jay Hawk, K.S.U.") eventually became the university yell ("Rock Chalk—Jayhawk, K.U."). At Science Club meetings papers were read on various scientific topics, and the gatherings were concluded with the Science Club yell. At the Science Club banquet, known as the "It," however, proceedings were not so sober.

THE HELIANTHUS.

Science, Psychology & Rock Chalk.

The old professor in his room,
Hears youthful yells which filter through

ROCK !

The book-lined walls & gas-lit gloom,
And ring: "Rock-chalk-Jay-hawk-
K.U.—"

As school-day mem'ries
in him bloom, CHALK !
He tries the yell a time or two.

At first his voice is weak & low,
In whispering uncertainty.
But soon in power the accents JAY !
grow;
Till with his mouth uncurtained he
Gives forth a howl which well might flow
From Injuns wearing shirt only.

HAWK !

And as he sings he bares his soul,
And his digestive fixtures too,

KAY !

Which make upon e in the hole,
U-U-U A very interesting view.
And that's why scientists extol
oo-oo-OO-! Our yell: Rock-chalk-Jay-hawk-K.U.

The Science Club yell ("Rah, rah, Jay Hawk, K.S.U.") eventually became the university yell ("Rock Chalk, Jayhawk, K.U.!"). From the 1893 Helianthus *(KU yearbook). (University of Kansas Archives)*

The 1889 student annual, *The Helianthus,* reported that the yearly "jamboree" consisted of "a banquet prepared by the members . . . and a burlesque program liberally interspersed with songs and comic 'business.' The 'It' begins early and lasts late, and is one of the features of university life."[27]

At "It" banquets, dining tables were decorated with scientific apparatus and various specimens from the university collections. Sometimes a skeleton was placed at one end of the table with a knife and fork in its hands. One student, Eugene W. Caldwell, remarked that it was not the refreshments, "but the feast of dethroned reason, and the flow of soul that made the 'It' the 'It.'"[28] Club members parodied papers that had been read during the year. Professor Edgar H. S. Bailey, credited with originating the Club yell, might give a yearly weather summary that imitated the style of Professor Snow. Clyde Kenneth Hyder wrote that one year "some-body devised a strange 'polar animal,' alleged to have been tamed by Dyche; it was compounded of feather-duster tail, burlap neck, and nail-keg head and, when praised, wagged its tail joyfully."[29] One "It" banquet featured the latest innovation in photography: A pair of students devised a "camera," made from a dry goods box with a piece of stove pipe sticking out of one end. The "camera" produced pictures that showed the future or the past. Caldwell described it: "In the demonstration portraits were made of various members of the faculty. The button was depressed with a blow from a bung starter and this was followed instantly by the report of a pistol inside the box, then smoke came out of the stove pipe, then there was much rattling, grinding and pounding of the machinery inside the camera, and finally from out a little trap door was thrust a well-timed portrait of Professor Dyche showing him in the act of buying from an Indian guide the skins of the big bears he told us he had shot."[30]

Dyche decided that moose and elk should next be added to the university's mammals collection. James R. Mead informed Dyche that he could provide him with one dozen each of all ages of moose and elk, but Dyche had discovered that most specimens sent to him by hunters or other taxidermists were inadequately prepared. He declined Mead's offer and left Lawrence in July 1889 to undertake an expedition to northern Minnesota.

Dyche met his guide, E. L. Brown, a hunter and Indian trader, in Warren, Minnesota. The two men bought ponies, outfitted a light wagon, and headed northeast toward Thief Lake. The land was marshy. The ponies suffered so much from mosquito and fly bites that they were difficult to control. Dyche and Brown had to light smudge fires whenever they stopped, and the horses would not leave the smoke to feed or drink. At one point Dyche could not make out the color of Brown's clothing for the insects swarming around him. Each night the men closed themselves in the tent, plugging every hole and seam, and piling dirt along the edges, and then spent the next half hour killing all the insects inside. Dyche sewed a muslin "mosquito" lining into sleeping bag. "Mosquitoes come by the 10000000000," he wrote in his fieldbook.[31]

As soon as the two men reached Moose River in the second week of August, they began to notice signs of moose. Brown killed a cow and calf on August 12, and Dyche spent the next morning drawing them, making anatomical notes and measurements, and then the afternoon skinning them. On subsequent days he dressed the heads and feet, salted the hides, and grilled moose steaks.

Early one rainy morning Dyche went to look for dry wood while Brown started breakfast. When he returned to camp he found Brown unconscious, face down in the mud. Dyche revived Brown and discovered that he had cut his foot deeply with an axe. "This is embarrassing out here in the woods," Dyche wrote in his fieldbook, "but we will do [the] best we know how for the foot."[32]

Within a few days Brown's foot had improved enough that he could ride, and he resumed hunting. He had shot a moose cow several days earlier, but the wounded animal had escaped in the brush. He now reported to Dyche that he had found the cow—swollen and rotten. Dyche thought the skeleton at least could be salvaged, but Brown assured him that it was "swollen up ready to burst and that bugs and worms are swarming in her." After dinner they rode to the carcass. It was badly decomposed, but Dyche thought that the skeleton of such a noble animal should be saved. As they fell to cutting off the rotting flesh, the stench was horrible, but in three hours they had the skeleton out. The next day they dragged it to a creek to soak.

An experienced moose hunter, Brown had killed all of the moose thus far. On September 19, however, Dyche shot a bull moose. As with the cow Brown had shot, the wounded animal evaded him. "I give up the trail in disgust," he recorded. "A most miserable Experience. Never had worse luck in all my hunting. Am sorry that I hit the animal at all. If I had not hit him he would be living to be hunted another day, but now he will go off and die and do no body any good."[33]

In early October, as Dyche and Brown poled a flatboat down Moose River, they came upon a group of moose standing near the shoreline. Dyche shot a calf and fired at a cow, but it disappeared. He jumped from the boat, waded to shore, and climbed the bank. He ran fifty yards after the cow but could not find her. Then he spotted a large bull moose a hundred yards away. He wrote, "A glance at the old monarch sends a thrill of electrical excitement through my being. My gun goes to my shoulder, the old bull turns his head to look at me. I perceive that I am a little nervous (excited) and hence take unusual pains with my first shot. Pull trigger and let her go—The old bull starts and turns half way round—By this time—The rifle cracks again—Bull makes a few jumps in the brush and I send the 3d shot—and the fourth follows in quick succession—at this moment I see the cow moving through the brush and give her two more shots in quick succession—I make a few quick steps to the south so as to get a better view—when the calf jumps up and starts through the brush—another shot brings him down. The smoke clears away—I take the boat—cross the river and rush over and proceed through the thicket to where I saw the cow last. Saw her lying dead and I rush around the point of brush and see an immense pair of horns[34] sticking up. They belong to the old bull who has settled down in the brush to die. I rush up to him and take observations on his eye and nose. He lingers a while but soon passes away without a groan or sigh—only a few vigorous kicks. O—what a monstrous animal—a giant—a perfect giant of the kind in every sense of the word. What massive horns—what a noble appearance—what grand proportions of body and limb, what a magnificent head—what a phenomenal nose—Large—massive and wonderful in its anatomical combinations. What a neck—it looks as large as a barrel. But the immense horns take my eye and command most of my eager & enthusiastic attention."[35]

Brown meanwhile struggled with the wounded calf as it attempted to wade away. The strength of both men was required to pull it to shore. The bull was an exceptional specimen.[36] Together with the cow and calf Dyche had collected a superior family group.

Winter was closing in. The swamp had begun to freeze over. By mid-November Dyche decided to transport his specimens to Warren, where they could be shipped by train to Lawrence. He was assisted by two men from Warren. On the trail, as Dyche climbed onto the buckboard to relieve the driver, the horses started and the wagon ran into a rut. One wheel hit a rock and Dyche was thrown forward onto the double-trees and then to the ground. A front wheel of the laden wagon rolled over his abdomen, then the back wheel struck his shoulder, but he rolled out of its path before it, too, ran over him. He was taken to a nearby ranch house, but when his condition did not improve the wagon was emptied of its load and he was taken to Pembina Farm where a surgeon could examine him.

After two weeks of recuperation at Pembina Farm Dyche felt well enough to arrange for the shipment of his specimens back to Lawrence. He then made plans for another hunting trip before returning home, even though prior to the accident he had intended to depart immediately. Brown took Dyche to a village of Chippewa Indians near Brown's cabin to hire a party of guides. Two days were required to convince the Indians that Dyche wished to accompany them on the hunt and to pay them for whatever game was killed. Dyche had a difficult time assuring the Indians that he would pay them for game he shot himself. A bargain was struck, however, and Dyche and a small group of Indians set out.

They had little luck. Game was scarce, and the temperature was cold—eight degrees below zero almost the entire two weeks they hunted. Dyche's mustache and eyebrows froze as he huffed along at a trot with the Indians, his side still aching from the wagon accident. At night the men rested around a fire, eating moose meat a previous hunting party had stored in the lake. Thawed by the fire, the meat still tasted good. The Indians smoked pipes and ate bits of browning moose meat, which they cooked on twigs stuck in the ground around the fire. With the help of an interpreter, they traded hunting stories with Dyche. Dyche questioned them about the moose's habits and about their techniques for stalking the animal.

Gone for nearly six months, Dyche returned to Lawrence on December 22. As in the previous year, he was barely in time for Christmas. He had collected nineteen moose.

As its contribution to the Kansas exhibits in the 1893 World's Columbian Exposition in Chicago, the University of Kansas proposed to display Dyche's mounted collection of mammals. Consequently Dyche maintained a harried pace of collecting, buying, trading, and mounting specimens. He had a free hand when trading extra specimens for ones that he lacked because often the specimens belonged to him personally. Although the mammals that he mounted ultimately became the university's property, many of the animals he collected or bought were not. In purchasing, trading, or selling specimens, he might at any given time be representing himself, the university, or both; but he found that it was more convenient and expedient to manage specimens that belonged to him, as the transactions therefore required no approval or justification from above.

Maurice Farrell, George Mclaughlin, E. L. Brown, and other hunting companions served as Dyche's field collectors, shipping him animal skins and skeletons. Dyche had taught them how he wanted the skins prepared and transported, although he preferred to use specimens he had prepared in the field himself because some of the most vital work necessarily took place immediately after the animal's death. Dyche also preferred to accompany his own specimens to ensure their timely arrival. One large shipment of skins from Maurice Farrell, for example, was lost en route and remained on board a boxcar for four months before finally reaching Lawrence, spoiled and useless. Specimens Dyche did not mount were used by the Natural History Department for instructional purposes, or they were traded or sold to other institutions. For example, J. A. Allen of the American Museum of Natural History bought several mountain sheep and mountain goat skins Dyche had collected in the Cascades. Dyche also conducted an extensive correspondence with Frederic W. True, Curator of Mammals at the National

Museum, and sold and traded specimens with him.

In his annual report to the Board of Regents, Chancellor Snow reported that "the most conspicuous enlargement of the natural history equipment has been made in the collection of mounted mammals. The tireless energy of Prof. L. L. Dyche has led to the capture by his own prowess of most of the large animals of western America, and his unexampled artistic skill has enabled him to represent these animals in life-like forms and expressive attitudes. By a rearrangement of class-work in his department, it has been possible for him to devote himself to the task of preparing a large number of these animals for the University exhibit at the Columbian Exposition. This collection will contain upwards of 100 individuals, and will be arranged in natural groupings and with natural surroundings in the Kansas building at Chicago. This exhibit of mammals is not approximated in artistic excellence by any other taxidermic collection in American institutions of learning. But I respectfully call your attention to the fact that, in securing this magnificent collection for the University of Kansas, Professor Dyche has expended $2,500 of his private means. For this expenditure he should be reimbursed at the earliest possible date." In an appeal for a building to house the natural history museum, Snow continued, "I also invite your consideration of the fact that, when this collection of animals is returned from Chicago, the capacity of the natural history building will be taxed to its utmost extent to give it shelter."[37] However, funding for such an enterprise was not forthcoming.

Ellen P. Allerton, "Poetess," wrote in the *St. Joseph Herald,* "If you are introduced to Professor Dyche your first impression will be one of surprise that he should be still so young a man, having accomplished so much. . . . This [taxidermy] room is the place of transition—or progressive resurrection. In the air is a lingering odor of mortality—protest against art. Professor Dyche has himself hunted and shot most of the specimens, tramping through tangled woods, over wild prairies, following lonely rivers, but that another might have done. Many a man can shoot and kill, but few indeed are they who can so bring the dead to life."[38]

Endeavoring to complete the mammals collection in time for the world's fair, Dyche met Dr. Anderson, Judge Williams, and Jim Kennicott in Denver to conduct a month-long hunt in the Rocky Mountains. Williams had written Dyche that he was eager to participate in an expedition that had secured a "World's Fair king."[39] On October 12 that wish was realized when Dyche killed a bull elk that would crown his world's fair collection. Although the elk was not especially large, it was a magnificent representative of its species, its hair being especially rich in color.

Back in Lawrence, on November 7 Dyche received a telegram from the Seventh Cavalry Regiment telling him that the venerable horse, Comanche, had died. Comanche had been a veteran of the Battle of the Little Bighorn and was popularly known as "the only U.S. Army survivor of Custer's Last Stand."

The fresh specimens (including the "world's fair elk") that Dyche had secured on the Colorado trip awaited preparation, but the opportunity to preserve the famous war horse took precedence. He gathered his tools and materials and left for Fort Riley on the next train. Arriving after midnight, he began measuring, skinning, skeletonizing, and soaking the hide. He also consulted photographs of Comanche. He brought Comanche's bones, hoofs, and hide back to Lawrence to complete the taxidermy in Snow Hall's laboratories.

The history of Comanche has been widely recorded, but Comanche's significance to Dyche's career necessitates the following synopsis: On April 3, 1868, an Army quartermaster in St. Louis purchased a number of horses that had been caught wild in Texas and Oklahoma. Among those horses was this six-year-old.[40] He weighed 950 pounds and stood fifteen hands tall. He was purchased for ninety dollars and shipped by rail from St. Louis to Fort Leavenworth, Kansas. On May 16 he and forty others under the care of Lieutenant Thomas W. Custer (brother of General George A. Custer) then were shipped from Fort Leavenworth to the Seventh Cavalry Regiment at Camp Alfred Gibbs, Kansas. En route to their destination, the horses were delayed for three hours in Lawrence. It is noteworthy that Comanche saw, albeit from a crowded livestock car, the city where ultimately he has stood in a lifelike pose since 1893.

After his delivery to the Seventh Cavalry, Comanche was purchased for ninety dollars by a distinguished cavalryman, Captain Myles Keough. On September 13, 1868, Captain Keough rode into a skirmish at Bluff Creek, Kansas, and his mount was wounded by a Comanche arrow. Because of the horse's steadfastness in action, according to one account, Captain Keough named him "Comanche." On the afternoon of June 25, 1876, Captain Keough, General Custer, and all men under Custer's direct command were killed in fierce fighting with a combined force of Indians at the Little Bighorn River.

On June 27th U.S. Army forces commanded by General Alfred Terry arrived at what would come to be known as Custer Hill to find a grotesque mass of dead soldiers and dead horses. The soldiers had been stripped of their uniforms, and many of their bodies had been mutilated. Dead bodies and the stink of corruption dominated Custer Hill, so it is understandable that General Terry's soldiers felt a surge of joy when they saw Comanche alive. Accounts of how the horse was found differ. The following is representative: "He was found with one of the cheek straps of the bridle broken, which permitted him to slip the bit out of his mouth, but the throat latch kept the bridle on him. The saddle had turned under his belly, and the blanket and pad were missing."[41] Comanche was severely wounded, and the men who found him speculated that the departing Indians had left him because he was too weak to be of use. His serious wounds included a bullet through the neck, one behind the front shoulder that had passed clear through, and one in the hind quarters, which had passed through between the hind legs.

Comanche was led fifteen miles to the junction of the Little Horn and the Big Horn Rivers, put with wounded soldiers aboard the steamboat *Far West*, and evacuated to Fort Abraham Lincoln, North Dakota. The wounded soldiers, members of Captain Benteen's and Major Reno's battalions, had fought Indians on June 25th also, but they had not been at Custer Hill.

At Fort Abraham Lincoln, Comanche was suspended from a bellyband sling and treated by Veterinarian Stein and Blacksmith Korn. After Comanche's recovery, an order was issued stating "he will not be ridden by any person whatever under any circumstances, nor will he be put to any kind of work."[42] On ceremonial occasions the old horse, saddled and bridled, under a black mourning net and with trooper's boots reversed in the stirrups, paraded with the regiment.

General E. A. Garlington described him: "Comanche was a substantial and hardy animal well suited to the cavalry service of that day; a good walker and feeder; could live on what the plains afforded when grain was no longer available. In color he was a yellowish bay—or what we called a claybank—with a black stripe down his back."[43] During the ensuing years of his life Comanche became the mascot and "Second Commander" of the regiment. He wandered wherever he pleased on the army post, sometimes responding to bugle calls for mounted drills, sometimes relaxing in mud wallows or tipping over garbage cans searching for snacks. He acquired a taste for beer, and the troopers treated him often.

By early January 1892, Dyche was well along on the preparation of Comanche. J. C. "Charlie" Saunders, who served as an assistant in the Natural History Department for fourteen years, worked on the wooden ribs of Comanche's manikin in his workshop at home, soaking and bending the wood to Dyche's specifications. Dyche's pocket calendar noted that on January 7 he commenced winding excelsior around Comanche's manikin. Work on other mammals progressed as well: By late summer the *University Courier* reported that sixty-five mammals were ready for the world's fair. Dyche hoped to complete at least thirty-five more before the collection was transported to Chicago in December.

Comanche was completed by fall and was also to be displayed at the fair. The Board of Regents recorded the following on November 20, 1891: "The University of Kansas will mount the horse Comanche for a museum specimen. The University is to have possession of the horse until after the World's Fair at Chicago. The University is to have the privilege of exhibiting the horse with its collections at the Fair. After the exhibit has closed the government can have possession of the horse by paying the University five hundred dollars."[44]

To dress Comanche properly, Adjutant J. T. Bell of the Seventh Cavalry Regiment donated the saddle and bridle that Comanche still wears. These pieces, of the style used in 1891, are not the battle-scarred tack that Comanche was wearing when he was found on the Custer battlefield.

Over the years, William T. Hornaday had urged Dyche to seek a position in an eastern institution. When Snow was appointed chancellor, however, Hornaday recognized that Dyche was unlikely to leave the university. Snow had permitted Dyche to carry out his work without interference, taught Dyche's classes to give him time to work on the university's mammal collection, and championed him to the Board of Regents. But Dyche did consider an offer in 1892. James H. Canfield had been associated with the University of Kansas for twelve years before becoming chancellor at the University of Nebraska. One of Canfield's first actions as chancellor was to offer Dyche a five-year contract. The proposal included five thousand dollars per annum with workrooms furnished (Dyche would provide materials, assistants, and pay his own expenses for field and on-campus work). Nebraska wanted a zoological collection, and Dyche wanted a museum. Dyche wrote Canfield that he would be occupied with the world's fair exhibit for two more years, and consequently "a five year contract would have no place in my plans. I am only 35 years old and the next twenty years will bring out my best work. I . . . expect to make 'Rome howl' in my line of business after the big show is over." He confidently informed Canfield that he believed he could obtain appropriations for a museum from any state in the Union if he was given the opportunity to carry out his work and show it to the public. The city of Denver apparently also had offered Dyche a museum building, but leaving the University

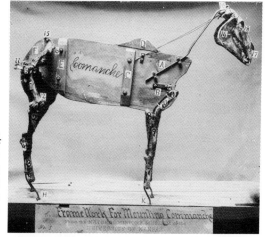

The stages of mounting Comanche, "the only U.S. Army survivor of the Battle of the Little big Horn." A body board is constructed generally representing the height and length of the body. (University of Kansas Archives)

Perpendicular side strips and lathing are fastened to the body board. (University of Kansas Archives)

Excelsior is wound and sewn onto the manikin. (University of Kansas Archives)

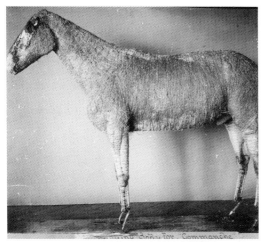

The manikin is finished in clay. (University of Kansas Archives)

Stretching the skin around the manikin. (Thomas Swearingen, Director of Exhibits at the Museum of Natural History, has noted that in photographs such as these, Dyche is invariably posed at the head of the animal while his assistants are relegated to less flattering positions.) (University of Kansas Archives)

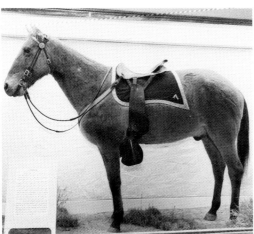

The finished Comanche, complete with the saddle and bridle donated by the Seventh Cavalry. The Seventh Cavalry was to have paid Dyche $400 for his work on Comanche, but since it was a marching regiment and "could not carry a dead horse around with it," it instead struck a deal with Dyche whereby the University of Kansas could keep the animal if Dyche's fee was waived. The U.S. Army later regretted the agreement. (University of Kansas Archives)

of Kansas would mean that he would have to begin his work again, and Dyche insisted that he would not consider leaving the university unless his specimens were left "in the best of shape." He wrote Canfield that his ambition was "to leave in some institution the best collection of North Am. mammals in the world."[45] For the time being, the University of Kansas appeared to be a satisfactory setting.

Concurrent with these other endeavours, Dyche had been writing a book of his hunting experiences. He had drafted over six hundred pages in his hurried scrawl, resulting in a manuscript that read more like field notes than a coherent narrative. With his mammals exhibit nearly ready for a world audience in Chicago, the time was propitious for the book to appear. In the midst of hectic preparations for the world's fair, Dyche decided to hire someone to rewrite and edit the manuscript. He collaborated with Clarence E. Edwords, a reporter for the *Kansas City Journal* who frequently had written on natural history topics. Edwords had spotlighted Dyche's taxidermic work in a series of articles for his newspaper— peppy accounts, unabashed in their admiration of Dyche and his work. Edwords had written that "were the professor to give a detailed account of his trips to the world it would make one of the most interesting books of travel and adventure that is published. Nor would this be all, for it would be so full of scientific interest that it would at once be accepted as a text book on the animated nature of North America."[46]

Dyche and Edwords met intermittently, Edwords sometimes taking dinner with the Dyches in Lawrence. What agreement the two reached is uncertain, but it seems that initially Dyche wished his own name to appear on the book's cover. Perhaps he viewed Edwords merely as an editor, or maybe he intended for Edwords to ghostwrite the book. Hornaday was under the impression that Dyche was writing the book by himself, and he spurred him on: "*let me have that book!* I can do you no greater service than to give you a vigorous prod every now and then, when your work on the MS. lags a little. Believe me, my boy, there is no other joy in this world like the joy of handing that first copy of a nice book over which one has toiled and moiled for weary nights and days and Sun-days,—stolen from other work. After you pour out your soul's best treasures and put them between the covers of a book, with your name swiped across its back to stare your enemies out of countenance, you hold your brain child in your hand and say over and over to yourself, 'Thank heaven! That job is *done.*' . . . Now my boy, you hustle with that 'ere book. Make her *popular,* lively and breezy, so that reading it will seem to a tired office man like a breeze from a mountain . . . ."[47] *The Kansas City Scientist* recorded that Dyche was working on a book, "a book for 'boys' both old and young, a book for all lovers of nature, . . . worked up in a readable and popular style."[48] Dyche hired an artist, George F. Little, to sketch illustrations, and he posed for studio photographs depicting scenes from the book.

Whether or not Dyche intended to represent himself as the book's author, the manuscript became Edwords's brainchild. Instead of utilizing Dyche's descriptive first-person accounts, Edwords wrote his version in third person, with Dyche as the principal character. Although Dyche's original manuscript had meandered, Edwords's version was no improvement. To incorporate scenes of "scientific interest," for example, Edwords invented absurd campfire dialogue in which Dyche's hunting companions became stick figures whose only apparent function was to ask an all-knowing Dyche questions about wildlife.

Evidently Dyche panicked when he read Edwords's typed draft (with Edwords's name hand-stamped at the top of every page). Dyche informed Hornaday of the true state of affairs, and Hornaday advised, "you are about to be victimized. Now *don't* let any fool scribbler 'give you away' by writing a book *about* you in reportorial style, and with a result that you are not satisfied with. *Don't do it,* or you will regret it when it is too late. Don't let anybody spoil forever the good materials in the line of adventure & observation that you have accumulated thus far. Don't let anybody give you away! Write the book *yourself* when you get ready & it will be a world of satisfaction to you when done . . . . Were I in your place I would say to him, 'What will you take to drop it?' & buy him off if necessary. You will soon regret it if you do not."[49]

By the time Hornaday's letter arrived, however, Dyche had sought the counsel of Charles Sumner Gleed. Gleed was one of the most active of the university Regents, a lawyer, and, as William Allen White put it, "the receiver, or something like that, of the *Kansas City Journal,* representing the Santa Fe Railroad of which he was a director, and which had in some way taken over the ownership and managership of that paper."[50] A few years later, in 1896, Gleed would buy the *Kansas City Journal* outright. In any event, when Dyche contacted him, Gleed was Clarence Edwords's boss.

Gleed had the reputation of being a political power broker, and he often wielded his considerable powers to assist would-be authors. Undoubtedly that was why Dyche approached him. But Gleed's assessment was hardly encourag-

Lewis Lindsay Dyche defending himself against a rattlesnake. This posed studio photograph was one of several intended for publication in Clarence Edwords's Camp-Fires of a Naturalist *that was not used. (University of Kansas Archives)*

ing: "I have read the manuscript 'all over in spots.' I have dipped into it at random all through, and am prepared to say that it is a breezy and interesting narrative, amusing and instructing and very decidedly readable. It will not, however, bear critical examination from a literary standpoint, and I do not believe any publisher will accept it as it is,—that is any publisher who has to take the risk himself. Furthermore, it is not now in a condition where you can 'father' it as proposed. I should not like on your account, and on the university's account, to have it appear with a preface by you just as it now stands. I do not think it needs an absolute new construction, but I do think it needs a great deal of pruning and polishing. I do not know that I am at liberty to touch it with my pencil, and of course I do not want to touch it until I know I am at liberty. The task is a big one and I do not desire particularly to undertake it. I would only do so as a favor to you. I do not wish to read it all straight through if I am to correct it, until I get authority to correct it, because I do not wish to read it twice. . . . You must be the judge about how much interference Edwords will tolerate. Please instruct me to return the manuscript as it is, or correct it as I please. I will comply with your instructions."[51]

Camp-Fires
of a Naturalist

The Story of Fourteen Expeditions after North American Mammals. From the Field Notes of Lewis Lindsay Dyche, A.M., M.S., Professor of Zoology and Curator of Birds and Mammals in the Kansas State University

By CLARENCE E. EDWORDS

12mo, cloth, illustrated. Price, $1.50

For sale by A. C. McCLURG & CO., 117 Wabash Ave., Chicago

Poster advertising Clarence Edwords'
Camp-Fires of a Naturalist. *"My story is taken from the note-books and diaries of the professor, and not one word has been added to the facts which he has noted to make the book more interesting or exciting." (University of Kansas Archives)*

Gleed revised the manuscript considerably, and his version was leaner and more readable. Wishing to distance the "popularly written" book from the university, Gleed deleted most references to Dyche's association with the university, including a description of Dyche's work on the mammals exhibit. *Camp-Fires of a Naturalist* was essentially Edwords's book, however, and few seemed pleased with the result. In the preface, Edwords noted without irony that "My story is taken from the note-books and diaries of the professor, and not one word has been added to the facts which he has noted to make the book more interesting or exciting. I offer simply a description of the life of a naturalist-hunter and of the pleasures of camp life . . . ."[52] A noteworthy passage in the book is its beginning:

"One raw March evening, in the early days of Kansas, a covered wagon drawn by oxen stopped on the banks of the Waukarussa River. In the wagon lay a babe close to the side of its mother, whose illness was so severe that but little attention could be paid to the child. The sturdy pioneer, who had left his Eastern home to make a new one in the West, cheered his wife with a word and placed the child on a bed of grass before a bright fire. Near the spot selected for the camp was the winter village of a band of Indians, and the fire had been hardly started when a number of the red men gathered around the wagon. The condition of the sick mother appealed to the womanly instincts of the squaws, and tender hands ministered to her wants. The infant was taken from its improvised bed, and soon was drawing a new life from a red breast. For weeks the mother hovered between life and death, and all the while the babe was cared for in the village of the Indians. He thrived, and when the mother was restored to health the baby boy was strong and lusty. This babe was Lewis Lindsay Dyche and his life almost began at a camp-fire . . . ."[53]

Camp-Fires of a Naturalist was published by D. Appleton and Company in the summer of 1893, probably due to Gleed's influence (Edwords dedicated the book to Gleed, calling him a "true friend, a careful critic, and a wise counsellor . . . who, by word and deed, has helped the writer over the rough places and made smooth his pathway in placing this book before the public"). Heeding Gleed's advice, Dyche did not allow the foreword he had written to appear, nor was his name printed on the book's cover. *Camp-Fires of a Naturalist* sold for $1.50.

Understandably, the *Kansas City Journal* gave the book a favorable review: "The reader is carried into the midst of the very scene of which the author tells, not by elaborateness of description, but by the directness and vividness of every sentence. He is given no opportunity to abandon the companions with which the book has provided him, for incident is made to follow incident with no intervening literary padding. In fact, the book is all action. . . . It may be that it is the very absence of conventional bookishness that makes this volume which deals so seriously yet so trippingly with science and adventure, so unlike any other work in the domains with which it has to do."[54]

Camp-Fires of a Naturalist received scattered reviews across the country. Most of them were favorable, with many reviewers depicting it as "a boy's book." "The fact that it belongs to neither science, history nor fiction will attract many readers," reported the *Columbus Ohio Dispatch*.[55] A magazine for schoolchildren, *School Education,* published an excerpt, complete with illustrations of several of Dyche's mounted animals, and noted that those animals were part of the magnificent collection currently on exhibition at the "White City": The World's Columbian Exposition.

"Viewing the Animal Exhibit in the Kansas Building." From the Chicago Inter-Ocean, *September 18, 1893. (University of Kansas Archives)*

6 "The Stuffed Animal State": Kansas in the White City

The United States first hosted a world's fair in 1876 to celebrate the centennial of the Declaration of Independence. Attracting thirty-two participating countries and over eight million visitors, the Philadelphia fair was a huge success. But plans for another American fair, larger and grander than the first, had begun even before the Philadelphia fair closed. Its theme was to be the 400th anniversary of Columbus's discovery of the New World. Anticipation for the "World's Columbian Exposition" grew as the Third Paris Internationale took place in 1889. The Paris Internationale flourished such spectacles as the Palais de Machines (the largest enclosed building constructed to that time) and the Eiffel Tower. To host a fair so soon after the Paris fair, the United States would have to produce a truly great exposition or suffer by comparison.

Numerous cities vied to host the fair, but Congress ultimately selected Chicago. Although not as accessible to foreign visitors as East Coast cities, Chicago was strategically located on Lake Michigan and Chicago River waterways. More importantly, Chicago had come to represent to many Americans exactly that pioneer spirit and "can do" attitude they wished to project to the rest of the world. Chicago's rapidly growing industries had attracted thousands of immigrants from the rural Midwest and from Europe, and the city's rapid recovery from the Great Fire of 1871 signified its inner strength and ambition.

Ground was broken in the lakefront Jackson Park on July 2, 1891. The fair's planners utilized new techniques of iron and steel manufacture to construct enormous structures quickly and economically. The buildings' skeletons were covered over with white staff, a plaster and fiber material resembling stucco. Because most of the buildings were left unpainted, the exposition grounds came to be known as "The White City."

Western and midwestern states acted quickly to appropriate funds to enter "state buildings" and exhibits in the fair. Kansas was among the first, with the Kansas State Board of Agriculture calling for a special delegation to meet in April 1891. The delegation determined that one hundred thousand dollars would be necessary to fund a Kansas building and exhibits, which would be assessed from each county and from the railroads operating in the state. In the fall of 1891, a newly created Kansas Board of World's Fair Managers sent a committee to Chicago to apply for space in national buildings and to select a site for the Kansas Building. A Topeka architect, Seymour Davis, won the competition for designing the Kansas Building. A Topeka company was awarded the construction contract with a bid of $19,995. On October 22, 1892, the Kansas Building was dedicated, the first state building to be erected at Jackson Park.

Seventy-six "Columbian Associations" had been formed across the state to collect funds and organize exhibits for the Kansas Building and for Kansas exhibits in national buildings, including a large pavilion for the Agricultural Building. The major educational institutions in the state undertook to prepare exhibits. The State Agricultural College in Manhattan assembled a display of trees for the Forestry Building, as well as an exhibit depicting work at the college. Likewise, the State Normal School provided an educational exhibit representing various of its departments. The Kansas School for the Deaf planned a display of its artistic, industrial, and regular classroom work. At the University of Kansas, Professors Samuel Williston and Erasmus Haworth prepared a Kansas mining exhibit for the Mines and Mining Building. But the university's principal contribution to the fair was to be Lewis Dyche's collection of North American mammals.

From the outset, Dyche and Professor Snow recognized the opportunity the World's Columbian Exposition would provide to display Dyche's work. Even before plans for the Kansas Building were submitted, Dyche and Snow arranged, with the help of regents Charles Gleed and Cyrus K. Holliday, to provide space for the mammals exhibit. Consequently, the plans submitted by architect Davis included a chamber designed especially for Dyche's mammals: a sixty-by-eighty-eight foot annex, which constituted the north wing of the building. A Board of Regents biennial report expressed confidence that the collection of North American mammals would be recognized as "one of the most remarkable exhibits at the Exposition," and that the university exhibits would "impress all strangers with the fact that Kansas is a State of magnificent capabilities throughout the whole range of civilized pursuits."[1] The Kansas Board of Managers appropriated only $750 for Dyche's exhibit to cover "all expense of placing his display in position, scenery, painting, labor, and superintendence."[2] It is likely that one reason the mammals group was to be the principal Kansas exhibit was the fact that virtually all costs of the exhibit already had been assumed by the university.

Dyche's taxidermy laboratory on the third floor of Snow Hall was a flurry of activity. Five assistants helped Dyche prepare the exhibit: Charlie Saunders,

W. W. Wyland, Charles E. Hite, Joe Shaffer, and W. S. Smith. The *University Courier* reported that at one point fifty separate specimens were in the process of being mounted, and that the workroom resembled a combination "blacksmith's shop, tanner's establishment, artist's studio, drug store, and carpenter shop."[3] Due partly to his extra work preparing the Kansas exhibit, in April 1892 Dyche's salary was increased to $1966.67 per annum by the Board of Regents, and on June 7 "Professor of Zoology" was added to his title, thus extending his official position to Professor of Anatomy, Physiology, and Zoology, Taxidermist, and Curator of Mammals and Birds.

In June the *University Courier* reported that two-thirds of the preparations for the mammals exhibit was completed. The remainder was "coming fast; with head up; and tail arising."[4] By November the animals were ready. Dyche ordered eight railroad cars to transport the collection to Chicago, including a flatcar for the larger animals and one car for Dyche and his assistants to live in while the exhibit was being set up and the groundwork constructed. The university's zoological museum closed temporarily as the third-floor workroom became a carpenter's shop, with crates built for each specimen. Before sunrise on Friday, December 9, the train departed. Each furniture car was decorated with a canvas banner reading "Kansas University World's Fair Exhibit" (these were painted by Adam Rohe, who a few months earlier had painted the backdrop for the university's production of *Twelfth Night*). As the train paused at stations along the way, small crowds gathered around the open flatcar on which the big bull elk stood. Although the body was covered by its crate and canvas, the antlers poked out into the open air, and in a telegram to Lawrence the following day, Dyche reported that "urgent requests" compelled him to open the doors of the large furniture cars several times to allow people to see the animals on the inside. The train arrived in Chicago the evening of the same day. "We were greeted with cheers and the waving of hats and handkerchiefs," Dyche wrote. "As the cheers went up for Kansas and the world's fair we responded with 'Stand up for Kansas' and our old Kansas University yell, which set the crowds to howling and the dogs to barking and running."[5]

The day the train arrived in Chicago, an editorial appeared in the *Topeka Daily Capital* criticizing the fact that so much space in the Kansas Building had been apportioned for the university's natural history exhibit. "The best and most advantageous site in the whole building is to be devoted to an exhibit which does not even in the slightest particular represent the state," the *Capital* complained. "Agriculture, horticulture, manufacturing, mining, education and charities, on all of which Kansas particularly prides herself, and which it is supposed to be the special province of our proposed exhibit at the World's fair to foster, must give way to a huge display of dead beasts."[6] Newspapers throughout the state soon echoed the *Capital*'s complaint. "What we need at the great fair is to show the world how all men can make a living in Kansas, not simply how Prof. Dyche makes a living," asserted the *Newton Republican*. "Very few Kansas people want Kansas to be known to the world as the stuffed animal state."[7] Some newspapers characterized the mounted mammals as "mummies." The *Salina Republican* posed the question, "What is the use for Kansas to exhibit a lot of stuffed animals at the World's Fair when the parks will be full of the same animals living and in good health?"[8]

Several newspapers rallied around the university exhibit, however, arguing that the mammals would attract many more visitors to the Kansas Building than might otherwise come. The *Kansas City Star* stated, "Editors fail to recognize that the collection is valuable not as an assortment of 'dead animals stuffed,' but as an exhibition of scientific taxidermy; as such it will be the wonder of the world; for nothing in its line in Europe or America excels it. The display will show that Kansas has made progress in natural history beyond Agassiz; it will be an indication of Kansas culture and Kansas progress that all the corn, and wheat, and cattle, and editors and hogs in the state in one pen cannot equal."[9]

The editorials continued with such profusion that the *Emporia Gazette* wryly noted that "Prof. Dyche and his natural history collection are getting an immense amount of free advertising."[10] Newspapers from other states began previewing the Kansas University exhibit, and the *Chicago Inter Ocean* hired *Camp-Fires of a Naturalist* author Clarence E. Edwords to write a piece titled "Mounting a Moose." Although few persons had as yet viewed it, Dyche's exhibit was well known. The *Lawrence Journal* mused that perhaps Dyche himself had initiated the "kicks" about his exhibit as a publicity scheme.

Another controversy emerged following the publication of a letter in the *Denver Times:* W. R. McFadden, the Denver taxidermist who had served as Dyche's guide on the 1889 British Columbia expedition, claimed that he, McFadden, had killed and mounted several of the mountain goats and mountain sheep in the Kansas exhibit, and that Dyche was taking credit for his work. To students writing for the *Students' Journal,* the charge that that Dyche had not performed the taxidermy on those animals was absurd, since hundreds of persons had witnessed Dyche and his assistants preparing the specimens in the Snow Hall workshop. Whether Dyche had killed the animals personally was a another question, but the student reporters were willing to take Dyche at his word.[11] Dyche rebutted McFadden's accusation in a letter to the *Denver Times,* insisting that none of the specimens in the exhibit had been "furnished or mounted" by anyone but himself. Dyche contended that hides he had bought from McFadden had been improperly prepared and were therefore worthless.[12]

The winter of 1892–93 was severe, with snow covering the exposition grounds from December through March. Temperatures fell to twenty below zero. The heavy accumulation of snow on the roofs caused leaks in buildings throughout the fair and slowed final preparations as many items could not be uncrated nor paint applied under such conditions.

To guard his "big animals" in the Kansas Building, Dyche set up living quarters within the panorama's artificial mountain. A hinged papier-maché rock behind the group of mountain lions served as the doorway to his bedroom. (University of Kansas Archives)

But thanks to the newly invented electric light bulb, twelve thousand men and women worked around the clock preparing for the May 1 opening day.

The Kansas Building was unheated, making work on the mammals exhibit unpleasant. Dyche and three assistants, E. D. Eames, W. W. Wyland, and Charlie Saunders, constructed a wooden framework to support a twenty-foot-high papier-maché mountain for the mountain goats and mountain sheep. Since it was necessary to safeguard the exhibit, Dyche set up living quarters within the artificial mountain. A hinged papier-maché rock, directly behind a group of mountain lions, served as its door. Alone with his collection during the Christmas holidays, Dyche wrote a letter to William T. Hornaday from his den under the artificial rocks expressing "wonderful relief to see all the big animals here in the Kansas building and all in good shape . . . . The great problem I have on hand now is the ground work. If I make a success of it, I think I will have a show that will attract some attention. People like to look at a collection of animals." Remembering that it was Christmas Eve, he added, "What a nice time I would have if I was at home. How I would like to prepare a number of things for my little son Walter to find in the morning."[13] Surrounded by his "big animals," a tired and homesick Dyche signed off to his teacher and friend.

"You will surely have a stunning exhibit at the Fair," Hornaday advised Dyche. "The success of my landscape-&-animal frieze & ceiling in my library leads me to believe that it would help you out amazingly and make a great hit if you were to call in Miss Palmer or somebody equally good & have the dead wall back of your groups painted in a continuous landscape representing, as I have done, the habitat of each species. The effect would be *very* stunning. I assume that you will be obliged to arrange your groups around the wall, close up, to leave the central space for them asses—I mean *the masses,* of course. A proper amount of paint on your dead wall, properly distributed, will give your exhibit an out-door and Wild West effect that will make it simply stunning. Were I in your place I would do it at all hazards."[14]

Hornaday had made use of scenic backdrops in wall-case displays. In *Taxidermy and Zoological Collecting,* Hornaday noted that "the beauty of . . . any group in a flat case is greatly enhanced by the addition of a painted background of the proper character to represent the home surroundings of the living creatures in front of it. Of course the back must seem to be a harmonious continuation of the bottom, where the real objects are. The tints of the picture should be very quiet, and by no means gaudy or striking, and should not attract attention away from the zoological specimens. The objects to be gained in a painted background are distance, airiness, and, above all, a knowledge of the country inhabited by the bird or mammal."[15] Hornaday had introduced this technique a decade earlier in his group "Coming to a Point," which depicted a white setter dog discovering six partridges in a bush. The case holding the specimens was only ten inches deep, but the painted backdrop provided a fully three-dimensional effect.

Hornaday had left the field of taxidermy before the technique of the painted backdrop had become common practice, especially in museum display. The animal and landscape frieze he mentioned in his letter to Dyche, for instance, was in his home in Buffalo. Few persons had witnessed the effect of a well-prepared specimen set in surroundings resembling the animal's natural habitat. "As yet the museums will have no painted backgrounds," Hornaday asserted in *Taxidermy and Zoological Collecting.* "If I am ever at the head of a museum, it shall have groups with painted backgrounds galore . . . . There is in this direction a vast field which has hardly been touched, and when it is once developed the world will be the gainer. Museum managers the world over are too conservative by half."[16] Dyche's display in Chicago would be among the first to exploit Hornaday's taxidermic techniques and his concepts of display. And the scale of Dyche's panorama would be among the largest attempted.

Dyche and his assistants used wheat straw pulp, glue, and plaster of paris to create the papier-maché groundwork for the exhibit. Trees, rocks, logs, and mountains were composed of the same material. A nail keg was converted into a burnt-out stump. When possible, Dyche combined real plants and rocks with his artificial props. A large walnut log taken from the Kansas River bottom was shipped to Chicago and used in the exhibit.[17] The pillars supporting a balcony above were covered with bark, and real limbs were placed on them. The setting was panoramic, with rocky crags for the mountain animals, moss-covered and swampy ground with water holes for the moose, grassy plains for the antelope, wolves, and bison. Although different portions of the panorama represented different geographical regions, the time of year was the same for the entire exhibit: early fall. Leaves had begun to scatter on the ground, and the trees were acquiring rich colors. The grasses were turning brown, but green spears were still apparent.

The University of Kansas exhibit in the process of being installed on the world's fair grounds in Chicago. The interior of the Kansas Building can be glimpsed through the open canvas flap at far right. (University of Kansas Archives)

The animals were in full flesh and high spirits, their hair thick and glossy. Dyche hired a Chicago artist to paint the walls behind the exhibit, with the effect that the landscape seemed to extend as far as the eye could see.

The Columbian Exposition opened on May 1, 1893. An international naval review also took place on the Hudson River. In Chicago, President Grover Cleveland pressed a gilded telegraph key, an electric circuit closed, and the White City came to life: lights glowed, machinery rumbled, flags were raised, statues were undraped, cannons and whistles sounded from the harbor, two hundred white doves were released, and an orchestra played "America."

Chicago's White City included over two hundred twenty buildings, housing over sixty-five thousand exhibits. The Manufacturers and Liberal Arts Building covered thirty acres. Replicas of Columbus's three ships floated in the harbor with a mock-up of the battleship *Illinois,* fully equipped and manned by U.S. sailors. The Krupp Iron Works of Essen, Germany, exhibited the largest military cannon ever cast. Technical innovations included the Linotype, Pullman railway cars, an elevated electric railway, and the electric light bulb. Assembled on the Midway Plaisance, north of Jackson Park, were the "popular" exhibits intended not so much to edify as to entertain: ethnological exhibits, such as mock African and Eskimo villages, bazaars, jugglers, and, in the Algerian and Egyptian theaters, dancing girls. There was an ostrich farm, a balloon ride, a model of a Hawaiian volcano, and a scale version of Blarney Castle. Sitting Bull's cabin from Fort Yates (in front of which he had been killed in 1890) had been dismantled and reassembled on the Midway. Rain-in-the-Face, the Sioux warrior who by some unlikely accounts killed Custer (and according to Henry Wadsworth Longfellow cut out his heart as "a ghastly trophy") was another sideshow attraction. Dominating the Midway was George Washington Gale Ferris, Jr.'s immense wheel, 264 feet high, with thirty-six cars each as large as a railway coach.

Bands paraded through the streets, including John Philip Sousa's marching band and the Royal Scottish Pipers. Within the White City Carl Hagenbeck presented his Zoological Circus, and Florenz Ziegfeld, Jr. produced his first musical comedy revue. Buffalo Bill's Wild West Show was set up just outside of Jackson Park. Ignace Jan Paderewski, whose long hair caused ladies to swoon, played Chopin on his Steinway piano in the Court of Honor's Music Hall, while Scott Joplin played ragtime on the Midway Plaisance.

Virtually every nation on earth was represented at the fair. As many as 716,881 persons visited on one day; over twenty-one million paid admissions were recorded. To many Americans the Columbian Exposition symbolized the emergence of the United States as a world power and marked the end of the country's frontier era. The White City was an illusory world, a world of promise and optimism.

The third largest of the state buildings, the Kansas Building was advantageously located near the northern edge of Jackson Park, not far from the 57th Street entrance. The Texas and North Dakota state buildings stood on either side of it, and an Eskimo village directly behind. The building was two stories high, with a rectangular observatory on the southwest corner. Flanking the two side entrances were large pyramids of coal taken from the state mines at Lansing. Near the main entrance lay a five-thousand-pound piece of rock salt from Lyons and a fountain contributed by a Hutchinson women's group featuring an ear of corn carved from limestone.

Inside the Kansas Building, the walls were adorned with sheaves of wheat, corn, flowers, and other state products that had been shipped to Chicago literally by

The Kansas State Building at the 1893 World's Columbian Exposition. This photograph originally was published in Kansas at the World's Fair, *1894. (University of Kansas Archives)*

the boxcarful. Latticeworks were interwoven with cornstalks, and scrollworks were made up of wheat. Under the entrance arch hung a Liberty Bell made of grasses, golden grain, and bronzed cane seeds and lined with tufts of milkweed, with a golden ear of corn serving as the clapper. In the main floor exhibit room stood a twenty-foot high pyramid of receding shelves covered with glass jars of grains and seeds and samples of Kansas soil from each county. Other pyramids included upright ears of corn, sheaves of wheat, grasses, millet, flax, and alfalfa. The main exhibit room contained a twenty-foot-high "Pagoda of Grain," made from cylindrical glass columns filled with wheat and oats, with sixteen-foot cornstalks in the center. Overlooking the main floor exhibits were second-floor galleries, composed principally of "women's exhibits."

The Kansas Building contained a silk exhibit, the State Normal School exhibit, the State Agricultural College exhibit, a historical and reading room, and ladies' and gentlemen's parlors. Railroads operating within the state also presented exhibits. A miniature electric train displayed by the Atchison, Topeka, & Santa Fe Railroad was especially popular. There were eight water basins in the building; next to each were statues of prairie dogs and jack rabbits inviting visitors to "Come and drink with the boys and girls of Kansas."

Roughly a third of the building's space was devoted to the natural history exhibit in the semicircular north wing: 121 mammals,[18] arranged in separate groups, usually families, with young and old of the various species and both genders displayed. The exhibit included white-tailed deer, mule deer, moose, woodland caribou, wapiti (North American elk), pronghorn, mountain goats, mountain sheep, grizzly bear, mountain lions, coyotes, lynx, black-tailed jack rabbits, wolverines, black-tailed prairie dogs, gray wolves, cross foxes, red foxes, a silver fox, ocelots, and bison.

Natural light, admitted by skylights and directed by curtains, illuminated the exhibit. The specimens were protected from overzealous onlookers by a pole fence, but Dyche had constructed a path through the groundwork on which he conducted tours for special groups. Comanche, looking solemn in his fresh saddle and bridle, stood apart from the main exhibit. Fearful of a band of organized thieves that had plagued the Exposition and to protect his exhibit from the public, Dyche remained with his mammals at all times. Short of funds, he had discharged Wyland and Eames, both of whom had been sick a good part of the winter, leaving Charlie Saunders as his only assistant.

Fighting bull moose. Note the cyclorama. The exhibit was "rendered more beautiful and realistic by a scenic painting which extended the woodlands and prairies as far as the eye cared to look. The deception was so good that many people asked every day whether or not this, that or the other animal was real or painted." (University of Kansas Archives)

The success of the university's natural history exhibit exceeded all expectations. As the 1851 London world's fair had revealed the products of new taxidermic methods, thus marking the beginning of a new era in the craft, so did Dyche's exhibit, based on Hornaday's methods, present a new paradigm in taxidermy. Taxidermists and museum administrators who visited the exposition were unanimous in their praise for the exhibit. *Scientific American* wrote: "In the north wing of the Kansas building is one of the most remarkable exhibits to be seen at the great Fair. . . . the work of a man who is recognized by naturalists as the best taxidermist in the country, if not in the world . . . . Artists and professional men from all over the world who have seen it say this is the finest group of mounted animals they have seen, and that there is nothing like it in the world."[19] *The Book of the Fair,* a three-volume commemorative guide to the Columbian Exposition, directed considerable attention to the exhibit. In describing taxidermy exhibits in the Anthropology and Ethnology Department displayed by such institutions as Ward's Natural Science Establishment of Rochester and the Agassiz Association of St. Louis, the guide pointed out that not those, but the Kansas exhibit contained "the best specimens of taxidermy displayed in the Exposition and one of the best in the world."[20] In an exposition rife with taxidermy, this was no slight praise.

Dyche's secret entrance to his bedroom beneath the papier-maché rocks figured prominently in several newspaper stories. Ophelia Dyche visited her husband once during the fair, and years later she recalled that she had stayed with him under the papier-maché mountain. She was pregnant with their only daughter (Ruth Ophelia was born in Lawrence on August 8, 1893).

Due to the natural history exhibit, the Kansas Building was immensely popular, especially for a state building. Even before the fair had officially opened, as many as ten thousand persons a day passed through the building. After opening day, an average of ten to twelve thousand visitors per day was recorded, and during the last two months of the fair, eighteen to twenty thousand. Dyche reported that several attempts were made to purchase the panorama or individual specimens. The Field Columbian Museum reportedly offered fifty thousand dollars for the collection just as it stood in the Kansas Building. A "gentleman from London" offered to pay five thousand dollars for the two fighting moose. And a Chicago cement company proposed to move the entire exhibit to another location in the city where a separate admission price could be charged and the profits divided with the university.

As the exhibit's creator as well as its custodian, Dyche enjoyed the plaudits resulting from its popularity. Although his request to sell *Camp-Fires of a Naturalist* at the fair was denied by the Board of Managers, souvenir handouts distributed in the Kansas Building advertised the fact that Dyche was responsible for the exhibit. And displayed beside Comanche were photographs depicting the successive stages of taxidermic work on the horse, some of which featured Dyche standing next to the animal. Those photographs also were used in an article Dyche published in *Scientific American* describing his method for mounting large mammals.

The Book of the Fair noted that the mammals in Dyche's panoramic exhibit reflected the art of sculpture more than traditional taxidermy. In fact, Dyche took lessons from sculptors working at the exposition. Conversely, he gave sculptor Preston Powers lessons on animal anatomy. Mammals in the Kansas exhibit reportedly served as models for many of the animal statues that lined the fair's lagoons.

Planners of the Columbian Exposition had determined that this world's fair would exhibit not only material objects, but also, as Charles C. Bonney proposed in the *Statesman Magazine,* the *nonmaterial* aspects of culture. To this end a series of worldwide congresses were held on topics such as government, law, finance, labor, religion, and education. Dyche participated in the Congress on Zoology, delivering a paper on "Mammalogy and Mammalian Taxidermy at the World's Columbian Exposition."

As one means of popularizing the fair, special days were held in honor of various cities, states, and nations. The Committee on Ceremonies had designated September 15 and 16, 1893, as "Kansas Days," but the Kansas Board of World's

The Panorama of North American Mammals at the World's Columbian Exposition. This photograph was one of several sent to William Temple Hornaday in a souvenir album. "The pictures are without exception magnificent," *Hornaday wrote Dyche. "They represent work that every honest taxidermist in the United States must feel proud of, proud to know it is all the production of the brain and hands of an all-wool-yard-wide* American, *without a foreign drop of blood in him." (University of Kansas Archives)*

Fair Managers deemed two days to be insufficient and unofficially voted to extend the Kansas celebrations from September 11 to September 16. The governor and his staff, judges of the state supreme court, state senators and congressmen, state legislators, the National Guard, and the press were invited to participate. A large platform was built at the rear of the building. Seats were provided for two thousand. The six "Kansas Days" were filled with speeches by Populist governor Lorenzo D. Lewelling, former governor Charles Robinson, and other state politicians, with music by Marshall's Military Band, the Modoc Club, and the Alhambra Mandolin Club, and with banquets and fireworks. One notable participant in the festivities was the elderly Captain John Brown, Jr., son of the famous abolitionist. The World's Columbian Exposition lasted six months, closing on October 31, 1893. The night before the fair ended, an unknown man came to the door of Chicago mayor Carter Harrison, and when Harrison answered, the man shot and killed him. The closing of the exposition was to have been as gala as its opening; instead, flags were lowered to half mast and the great fair ended quietly.

Salvage rights to the Kansas Building were sold to a Chicago company for two hundred dollars. The building was dismantled for materials, and the grounds cleaned. It was the intention of the Kansas Board of World's Fair Managers that the grains and grasses on exhibit in the Kansas Building be transported to Topeka for display, but an entomologist of the U.S. Department of Agriculture advised them that grains, grasses, and cereals at the fair were infested with weevils and other insects. The agricultural exhibits therefore were destroyed.

E. D. Eames and W. W. Wyland returned to Chicago to help Dyche and Saunders prepare the Kansas exhibit for transportation. When the crating was completed, Dyche quietly returned to Lawrence alone, leaving his assistants to accompany the collection. He had gained weight during the inactive months of superintending the exhibit, and on a morning walk down Massachusetts Street he went unrecognized by persons who knew him well. Dyche encountered a reporter on his walk, and revealed to him a piece of news: Comanche would return to Lawrence with the exhibit. The *Lawrence Evening Gazette* recorded: "[Comanche] was to have gone to the National Museum at Washington. The government officials failed to go about it in the right way to take Comanche, and Gen. Forsyth, who presented the animal to Prof. Dyche, is anxious that the mounted horse should remain here."[21] Army historian Barron Brown described the situation differently: "Captain Nowlan called a meeting at Ft. Riley of the officers of the regiment to determine what disposition should be made of the remains; at which it was set forth that the Seventh Cavalry was a marching regiment; here today and gone tomorrow; subject to field service on telegraphic orders; that it had no home, and no facilities for taking care of the horse and could not carry a dead horse around with it."[22] And the recollections (in 1931) of General William H. Sears provide yet another account of the horse's ownership: "Prof. Lewis Lindsay Dyche told me that after he completed the work of mounting Comanche, he sent a bill to the officers of the 7th Cavalry for $400 for his services; but told them if they would leave Comanche at the Dyche Museum at the University there would be no charge for the mounting. By a sort of tacit consent the old war horse was permitted to remain at the University, and surely the statute of limitations has run against any right of removal, many long years ago, and property rights are now vested in the University, through the generosity of Lewis Lindsay Dyche."[23]

Over the years there have been numerous attempts to remove Comanche from the University. A museum was constructed on the Custer Battlefield in 1939, and promoters of the museum petitioned to have Comanche for exhibition, but their request was denied by the Kansas legislature. General Jonathan M. Wainwright requested in 1946 that the horse be returned to Fort Riley, but the university chancellor refused. In 1951 South Dakota Senator Francis Case tried to borrow Comanche to mark the state's seventy-fifth anniversary, but the chancellor refused. The Kiwanis Club of Lewiston, Montana, asked for Comanche, as did the World Publishing Company. All requests for Comanche have been refused.[24]

William Temple Hornaday, who had viewed the natural history exhibit in Chicago, wrote Dyche, "The farther away the Fair gets, the more we cherish its memory. . . . They [Dyche's mammals] represent work that every honest taxidermist in the United States must feel proud of, proud to know it is all the production of the brain and hands of an all-wool-yard-wide *American,* without a foreign drop of blood in him." Once again, Hornaday urged Dyche to consider a position in the East, possibly at the Carnegie Museum, and offered to work in his behalf toward that end. "You are known all right in the West, but there are an everlasting lot of people in the East, and you are not known here *half* as you ought to be. Now I believe in *advertising,* and in advertising my friends when I advertise anybody.— so there you are!"[25]

To many persons, including some journalists, it seemed a foregone conclusion that Dyche would leave the University of Kansas for greener pastures. Dyche declined to answer one Lawrence reporter's question as to whether he had been offered a position at an Eastern museum, but he did admit that he would prefer to stop teaching in order to devote more time to laboratory work and his collection. With his now-famous natural history exhibit as leverage, Dyche was inclined to remain at the University of Kansas, under his own terms. The Board of Regents and Chancellor Snow were inclined to do whatever necessary to see that he did. In its 1893–94 annual report, the Board of Regents recorded: "The ambition of Prof. L. L. Dyche is to make the largest and most complete collection of mammals than has been, is, or ever can be, made in the world. It is estimated by naturalists that, in 25 years, all the larger mammals, such as deer, elk, moose, lions, tigers, etc., will be practically extinct, no living specimens remaining except the few that may be held in captivity. In these 25 years, with the splendid beginning already made, Professor Dyche can bring together a collection that can never be duplicated. This collection may belong to the University of Kansas, if provision is made to take care of it. Considering that the cash value of such a collection would be many times the cost of its collection, and would be continually appreciating, is it not good business sense to secure it? Professor Dyche is recognized as the foremost taxidermist of the world. He has been offered a much larger salary than he is now receiving to go elsewhere, but he is loyal to Kansas and desires to stay here. The only thing he asks is an opportunity to make this grand collection, and a place to put it. The state certainly owes it to herself to retain the invaluable services of Professor Dyche, and to seize the opportunity that is now offered to build up a natural history collection that can never be equalled in the world."[26]

Dyche's first order of business was to house the world's fair collection. The seven railway cars of exhibits returning from Chicago were more than could be displayed in Snow Hall. A new building on campus designed solely to house the collection was the next logical step, although Dyche also suggested the possibility of building a university museum in downtown Lawrence. But with the new Spooner Library, Blake Hall, and chancellor's residence already on the construction program, a museum building was, for the time being, out of the question. The exhibit returned to Snow Hall.

Late in 1893 Dyche collected small Kansas mammals to study their diets relative to agriculture. Dyche corresponded with C. Hart Merriam, head of the Ornithology and Mammalogy Division of the U.S. Department of Agriculture, and sent him nearly forty harvest mice he had collected in the vicinity of Lawrence. Merriam added those specimens to his national collection, which was in turn given to J. A. Allen, the most prestigious mammalogist in the country. In 1895, based on the mice Dyche had contributed, Allen described a new species of *Reithrodontomys dychei,* and a new subspecies, *Reithrodontomys dychei nebrascensis.* Subsequent taxonomic analysis disallows Dyche's species and subspecies, combining them as a single subspecies, *Reithrodontomys megalotis dychei.*

Dyche wrote Frederic True at the National Museum: "I am still collecting and am getting a pretty good series of skins on hand of large mammals. I have just commenced to do something with small mammals. Put up 300 skins last month and will about reach 200 this month. Most of the collection I have here belongs to me individually. I do not know anything about small mammals. Have some small stuff on hand that I am unable to name for a certainty. My library is not complete and I cannot do much. I expected to see you at the World's Fair but did not. I had a few large mammals on exhibition there; they were specimens mounted for show and I had them arranged on an artificial ground work in a way which I thought would please the mass of the people."[27]

At Chicago, Dyche's exhibit had pleased thousands of spectators as well as taxidermists and museum preparators. During the summer of the fair, Dyche, acting independently of the Kansas Board of World's Fair Managers, entered the exhibit in a special competition administered by the World's Columbian Commission Executive Committee on Awards. It won a first prize, one of the few state exhibits to do so. By the time the award arrived in Lawrence, however, Dyche was on board a ship bound for Greenland.

"On June 12, the question of having exhibits in the state buildings examined for awards came up...No examination of exhibits was made in our building, except in the case of Prof. L. L. Dyche, who acted independently of the Board and secured an examination of his famous exhibit of American mammals and obtained the first medal..." (University of Kansas Archives)

Go North!

GREENLAND'S ICY
MOUNTAINS AS A
SUMMER RESORT.

A Trip to the Arctic Regions for
Recreation under the Direction of

DR. F. A. COOK,

Ethnologist of the Peary Expedition, Originator
and Commander of the coming

AMERICAN ANTARCTIC EXPEDITION.

*Flier promoting Dr. Frederick
Cook's expedition to north
Greenland. (University of Kansas
Archives)*

7 The Last Voyage of the *Miranda*

For some time the world had been enthralled by the adventures and the tragedies being played in the arctic regions, and inevitably "polar fever" reached Kansas. A former student of Dyche's, Charles E. Hite, served as zoological preparator for the Peary Relief Expedition and helped retrieve Lieutenant Robert E. Peary and his party from Whale Sound, north Greenland, in the late summer of 1892. In 1894 Dyche, together with Hite (then a professor at the University of Pennsylvania), responded to a flyer promoting "a trip to the arctic regions for pleasure and recreation." The expedition was headed by a twenty-nine-year-old physician, Frederick A. Cook.

After a Dickensian childhood spent helping to support his siblings and widowed mother by toiling in a glass factory and then a food market, Frederick A. Cook put himself through New York University medical school by working nights as a door-to-door milkman. Six months after his graduation he had accumulated only three patients. Then he read an

*Dr. Frederick Cook at about
age 29. This photograph was
given to Dyche by Cook.
(University of Kansas
Archives)*

announcement in the *New York Herald* that Lieutenant Peary, on leave from the Navy, was seeking a surgeon to accompany his independent expedition to north Greenland. Although the position offered no wages, Cook responded at once and thereafter spent a year with Peary on Whale Sound.

After their return to New York, however, Cook parted ways with Peary because the latter refused him permission to publish his ethnological studies of the Polar Eskimos. Peary insisted that no member of the expedition other than himself or his wife be allowed to publish accounts of their experiences, lecture before the public, or give interviews to the newspapers. Members of Peary's party had been required to sign a contract to that effect, and they were obliged to turn over to Peary all diaries and journals they had kept during the expedition. So Cook decided to organize his own expeditions.

Initially he planned an expedition to Antarctica, but failing to arrange the necessary financing, began organizing "tourist cruises" to Greenland. In the summer of 1893 Cook attempted to direct a chartered yacht, the *Zeta,* on an excursion to northern Greenland, but upon encountering substantial ice floes, the ship's captain refused to sail even as far as Cape York. Cook wished to take some of the yacht's small longboats farther north, but the captain would not allow it. Cook's "expedition" was forced to content itself by touring fjords in south Greenland and studying the Eskimos.

In advertising his cruise of 1894, Cook tried to appeal to a broad range of people. Scientists could study "RICH FOSSIL BEDS" and the "AURORA BOREALIS." Artists would be afforded the opportunity to paint "ICEBERGS AND GLACIERS" ("he who first paints them will become immortal"). A few staterooms would be "especially prepared for LADIES."[1] And for collectors there was the chance to hunt "REINDEER, CARIBOU, POLAR BEARS, SEAL, WALRUS . . . ."[2] Dyche apparently paid the five-hundred-dollar fare and was named "Official Naturalist" of the expedition.

Dr. Cook made a significant compromise when organizing the cruise: He had hoped to charter the S.S. *Newfoundland,* a wooden steam-whaler suited to breaking through arctic trash-ice, but settled for the *Miranda,* an iron steamer with a history of bad luck.

Named for Prospero's virginal daughter in Shakespeare's *The Tempest,* the *Miranda* was built for the Red Cross Line in Liverpool, England, in 1884. The ship first saw service running between New York, Halifax, and St. John's, New-foundland, but soon ran aground off Point Judith. Later she struck rocks at Hell Gate in New York's East River and sank. She was raised and resumed service, subsequently colliding with a steamer and then a schooner. After those calamities the *Miranda* was withdrawn from passenger service and began ferrying freight between New York, Jamaica, and Central America.

Dr. Cook's Arctic Expedition sailed on the *Miranda* after sundown on July 7, 1894, and she barely made it out of New York harbor. Signal wires to the engine room were crossed, transforming the "full reverse" signal into "full ahead," and as she got under way the steamer nearly ran down a smaller vessel. "This caused great excitement and much shouting on the part of the Captain," Dyche noted in his diary, "much running and crowding together of the people on the pier who also did much yelling and pointing in the way of giving advice. It was necessary to drop the anchor twice before we could get started in the right direction."[3]

The *Miranda* steamed under the Brooklyn Bridge at 9 1/2 knots as the first table was seated for dinner. The second table, including Dyche, was served a little

after nine. Dyche savored the meal and joined passengers on deck taking in the
"small moon and its light and the lights from various points on shore."

Some of the Miranda's *passengers. William H. Brewer of Yale, noted for his participation
in the California Geological Surveys of the 1860s, holds the fishing pole. To the right sits
Henry Collins Walsh, founder of The Explorers Club. Dyche stands at far right. (University
of Kansas Archives)*

After a sleepless night, Dyche was up at six walking the decks for two hours
until breakfast. He ate the large breakfast of beefsteak and eggs and then, an hour
later, became the first seasick passenger. Advice was plentiful. He was told to
drink a quart of sea water; eat a cracker and take a small glass of wine; drink a cup
of hot salt water; go on deck and keep walking; lie flat on his back for thirty-six
hours; drink red-hot lemonade; take a good physic; lie down and be quiet; tie a
piece of fat meat to a string and pull it up and down his throat; keep his mind
occupied with things other than those pertaining to his condition. "I did none of the
above things," Dyche noted. By evening about half of the fifty passengers, most of
them university professors, had joined him at the rail—"a sorry looking lot of
ducks indeed," Dyche noted, "but . . . in as good humor as circumstances would
permit."

On the second morning the passengers learned that a ship's fireman was
missing. He had fought with the engineer the night before, which led to wholesale
conjecture throughout the ship. The captain, William J. Farrell, passed judgment
that the man had jumped overboard and, hopefully, had reached shore safely.
Several days later the missing man was discovered hiding in the hold.

Dyche overcame his seasickness and spent most of his time on deck observing oceanic wildlife. He saw schools of whales and porpoises, "an immense green
turtle," jellyfish, and a Portuguese man-of-war. Whenever a creature came within
range the hunters on the excursion (including a former mayor of Cleveland) fired
their rifles. Henry Collins Walsh, a passenger who wrote about the voyage,
remarked that the deck, "bristling with polished gun-barrels, resembled that of a

pirate ship."[4] While the small-caliber ammunition had no noticeable effect on whales that were hit, Dyche wrote in his diary that "the boys" also shot and crippled birds that they knew they could not eat.

The *Miranda* arrived at Sydney, Nova Scotia, at dusk on July 11. After docking at the coal pier, "the boys" roamed North Sydney, a small community of about five thousand persons. Dyche looked at the town, taking notes, and then returned to unpack his sleeping bag and spend a clear night on deck. The next morning he and F. A. Travis of the American Museum of Natural History walked a mile outside of town and spent the day collecting birds and red squirrels. After his bout with seasickness the excursion was, for Dyche, literally a breath of fresh air.

As the *Miranda* sailed eastward from Sydney, conversation among both passengers and crew turned increasingly toward the ability of their craft to cope with the ice floes off Greenland. Although most passengers were unaware of the *Miranda*'s history, even before she left New York Harbor there had been speculation that she was not a sound ship. One Philadelphia newspaper had reported that the steamer was unseaworthy and might never return from this voyage. Dr. Cook had refuted those reports. "The *Miranda*," he contended in the *New York Times,* "has often encountered more ice off the coast of Nova Scotia in April and May than she is likely to meet on her present trip. . . . During the time we shall be in the arctic regions we shall probably see no ice that is nearly so dangerous."[5] But some of the crew maintained that iron ships were no good in arctic waters because the seams tended to leak when they hit ice. And they recalled that rats had abandoned the *Miranda* in New York harbor.[6] Dyche was content not to speculate: "Having been raised on land—and rather dry land at that—I know nothing about this business and trust to the better judgement of the others. I hope that our ship will be good for the journey."

The doubters' fears intensified the next day when Captain Farrell announced that the ship would make an unscheduled stop at St. John's, Newfoundland, to have the compass repaired. An iron spike had been driven into the compass box when it was being serviced in New York, and the magnetic needle would not function properly. In addition to that bad news, Dyche discovered that superstitious sailors had thrown overboard the fish crow specimens he had collected at Sydney.

The *Miranda* spent most of a Sunday in St. John's, where some of the passengers took small boats a half mile out of the harbor to visit an iceberg, cutting off samples and taking photographs. Dyche took a tour of the *Kite,* the small wooden steam-whaler that had borne Robert E. Peary and his party, including Dr. Cook, to Melville Bay in the summer of 1891 and served as their relief ship in 1892. While in St. John's, Dr. Cook hired Patrick Dumphy, an ice-pilot who had served as second mate on the *Kite* during the 1892 relief voyage. Dumphy's appearance on board eased the fears of the passengers, who, according to Dyche, were beginning to express a lack of confidence in the youthful Dr. Cook. Late in the evening of July 16, the *Miranda* sailed for Greenland.

Hunters continued to amuse themselves by shooting at passing gulls. A gun discharged accidentally and the bullet passed through the crowd on deck, hit iron, and sent three fragments into a man's leg, bringing blood but not cutting him deeply. Dyche was annoyed at the conduct of his fellow "sportsmen" throughout the voyage.

Dyche's wildlife panoramas

Details from the panorama at the Museum of Natural History at the University of Kansas in Lawrence attest to Dyche's taxidermy skills. The majority of the figures, preserved in the 1890s, retain accurate color and form with periodic curatorial maintenance.

The Panorama of North American Plants and Animals in Dyche Hall (above) is divided into principal life-zones. Here, mountain goats, moose, beaver, and white-tailed deer occupy a forest of deciduous trees in the Canadian Life-Zone. The moose were collected by Lewis L. Dyche on Moose River, Minnesota, in 1890. Bison, black-tailed jack rabbit, black-tailed prairie dog, coyote, and badger in the Upper Austral Life-Zone (left). The bison bull was collected in Montana in 1886 by a Smithsonian Institution expedition headed by William Temple Hornaday.

Mule deer and ocelot in the Austral Life-Zone (above). Assisted by university students, George P. Young created the foreground. Sam T. Dickenson painted the background. The desert and tropical rainforest portions of the panorama were added after Dyche's death to complete the representation of North American biomes. Woodland caribou, snowshoe rabbit, and lynx in the Hudsonian Life-Zone (below). Displayed in "lifelike occupations," the animals' hooves and feet are adapted to frozen tundra and the soft, damp forest floor.

Greenland caribou (above) in the tundra of the Arctic Life-Zone. Dall sheep in the Hudsonian Life-Zone (below). Collected in the Talkeetna Mountains at the head of the Knik River in 1896, the white Alaskan sheep gaze down on lowland-dwelling caribou.

Color photography by Wally Emerson

Polar bears in the Arctic Life-Zone (above). Camouflaged the color of polar ice and snow, these large carnivores leave the ice floes only to breed, sometimes migrating long distances inland. Initially criticized as resembling a "boxing stance," Dyche's portrayal of the polar bears has subsequently been vindicated as an accurate depiction. Walrus group in the Arctic Life-Zone (below) collected by Dyche (assisted by Robert E. Peary) off the coast of northern Greenland in 1895. Dyche recorded in his expedition diary: "This walrus collecting is not only dangerous, but the handling of the skins the hardest of hard work."

In the mid-morning of July 17, after she had passed Belle Isle, the *Miranda* encountered a fog bank and soon thereafter hit an iceberg jutting fifty feet above the water. Many passengers were knocked off their feet. Chunks of ice showered the foredeck. Captain Farrell backed the ship away so that Dr. Cook and the officers could inspect the damage. It was not serious, they reported: three bowplates, fifteen feet above the waterline, were stove in.

Dr. Cook held a meeting of the passengers at which it was decided not to steam back to St. John's, but to put in at a fishing village on Cape St. Charles and make the repairs themselves. There they remained several days, with the passengers indulging in, according to Dyche, "a vast amount speculation" as to what would happen next.

Dyche traversed the rocky, moss-covered hills collecting about fifty small birds and talking with the villagers. During the day he strolled through the children and numerous dogs and spoke to the women. In the evenings he watched the men and women clean and pack the day's haul of codfish. They toiled hard, lived in rough board shanties, but struck Dyche as being content. As one woman told him, having enough to eat and drink and fire to keep warm was "enough for anybody."

One evening the *Miranda*'s passengers and crew and the villagers held a dance in a fishing house. The women and girls were too shy to participate, but the Americans sang, and some of the sailors danced in clogs. Among the *Miranda*'s passengers were six Eskimos who had participated in the Columbian Exposition and had arranged for passage back to Labrador with Dr. Cook. Two Eskimo girls were the only female participants in the dancing, and they proceeded to teach everyone a dance in which partners shook fingers at one another in a scolding manner. Their father accompanied on an "Eskimo-style" fiddle.

The next day Dyche and twenty others rowed two longboats across the bay to Battle Harbour. They lost their way on the return trip, however, and it was 2:30 a.m. before they finally found their way back to the ship—and the playful taunts of their fellow passengers.

But the mood was not so merry the following morning. Dr. Cook called a meeting of the passengers in the dining room and Captain Farrell read a formal written statement. Farrell reported that some of the ship's bowplates were cracked and strained and, because a hawse pipe was broken, only one anchor was usable. He was therefore duty-bound to bring the *Miranda* to the nearest harbor for repairs: St. John's again, some three hundred miles to the south. "Ten days has been set as the time required," Dyche wrote, "But judging from our past Experience it will take a month."

Charles Hite had intended to have the *Miranda* drop him and a few other men off farther north so that they could hunt and explore on their own. Given the present situation, he and his party decided to take a mail steamer from Battle Harbor. Five sportsmen decided to leave the *Miranda* and travel inland to hunt and fish. Three others chose to keep one of the ship's longboats and try their luck hunting right there. The Eskimos elected to find other means of transportation back to their home villages. At dawn on Sunday, July 22, the *Miranda* departed. Two church services (one Episcopal, one Presbyterian) were held in the dining room that day, presumably petitioning for better luck. The passengers, their ranks depleted, took turns in the bow watching for icebergs.

By Tuesday they had reached St. John's. Dyche spent his days setting traps outside of town, but had limited success. One day's catch was "nothing except one sparrow and a few large slugs." He added to his collection of small birds, mice, and rats, but held out his hope for large mammals if he could only reach Greenland. A few of the passengers discussed leaving for New York, but Dyche resolved to stay with the ship, "if she goes anywhere." Crews were working day and night on the bowplates, and the constant hammering reassured Dyche that something useful was being done.

On Sunday, July 29, slightly ahead of the original estimate of ten days, the *Miranda* again sailed for Greenland. The sea was free of bergs for the first few days, and spirits on board kissed the clouds. In the evenings the professors presented lectures to one another, and during the day they played leapfrog on deck. Dyche donned gloves and boxed with Frederick Gay of Harvard. Below decks, a fight broke out between two of the firemen, and the loser came topside to have Dr. Cook bandage his cut head. The days of boredom and waiting had passed.

A man on the wharf at St. John's told Dyche, "A man who would go to Greenland for pleasure would go to hell for recreation." But Dyche was anxious to reach that island. He discussed with Dr. Cook the possibility of having the *Miranda* drop him off with supplies so that he could collect on his own. He attempted to complete preparation of the skins he had already collected so as to have time to devote to his anticipated specimens. One afternoon he became so absorbed in working on two rats that he forgot to go to dinner.

At six in the morning on August 3, Dyche was the first to sight Greenland. Other passengers joined him on deck, and they studied the mountains and bergs through their binoculars. The *Miranda* soon reached large bergs and the ice floating off shore, with Captain Farrell steering the ship along the edge of the main mass, avoiding any contact. So careful was he, in fact, that at one point the *Miranda* was heading southwest, provoking remarks from the passengers on deck: "He is afraid of his shadow." "He is no good." "He has no heat." "I wish he would get sick so that Dumphy could run the ship." "He never goes except when the ship is headed towards St. John's."

Nevertheless, the mood remained frisky. Dyche reported, distinctly in the third person, that "the boys amused themselves by pulling a few tons of ice on deck with ropes." As the ship gradually poked its way northward the men stayed close to their rifles, ever ready for the captain to blow his whistle when seals were sighted. The "seal whistle" was sounded many times, but no seals were hit. At one point half a dozen Winchesters blazed at a seal on a piece of ice two hundred yards away, but "he only bobbed his head up and down as if recognizing a salute."

Thick fog forced the *Miranda* to stop several hours at a time, evoking more assertions that Captain Farrell was "chicken." During one stretch of riding at anchor, Dyche gave his moose hunting lecture in the dining room.

On the morning of August 7 the *Miranda* put in at the village of Sukkertoppen, piloted into the harbor by a flotilla of kayaks. "The boys" spent two days taking pictures of the Eskimos, hunting, and trading, strolling through the village with "buckets distended with knives, fish hooks, old ties and stockings, bunches of ribbon" to exchange for "sealskin pocket books, Kayacks, spear heads and eider down pillows, duck skins and such goods." An open-air dance was held in the evening, and when Dyche gave two women each a packet of needles, taking nothing in return, they told him twenty times that he was "very good" and escorted him to the dance.

At three the next morning Dyche and H. D. Cleveland of Harvard hired two Eskimo guides and took a boat to some small islands eight miles off shore, to collect birds. That evening Dyche and Edward Avery McIlhenny (from the Avery Island, Louisiana, Tabasco plantation) collected a few young black-backed gulls on a higher mountainous island. An accomplished ornithologist, McIlhenny had established a large private bird refuge in 1892 on Avery Island.

The *Miranda* left Sukkertoppen on August 9, her decks adorned with sixteen kayaks, eiderdown boots and blankets, several stuffed seals, an assortment of skins, and Dyche's bird specimens hung out to dry. Dr. Cook's program called for the ship to steam northward along the coast of Greenland toward Melville Bay where she would pause to allow passengers to hunt seal and polar bear, and then sail to Robert E. Peary's headquarters near Whale Sound. The *Miranda* was not the relief vessel for Peary's expedition—another ship, the *Falcon,* had already embarked on that mission. The *Miranda*'s visit was to be merely a social call.

Seven miles out of Sukkertoppen, with the wind blowing hard, the sea rough, and Dyche working below decks dressing his birds, the *Miranda* struck a submerged reef. Swells knocked the ship twice more against the rocks before she could be steered clear. The foghorn began to blow, distress flags were raised, and pandemonium reigned on deck, with passengers and crew retrieving clothes and money from their cabins and heading for the lifeboats. Since there were no women and only one child on board, no time was lost in deciding who should get in first, and two boats quickly were lowered. Passengers rushed about the deck with small bundles of belongings and life jackets. The ship's signal cannon fired at rapid intervals. Rudolf Kersting, a German photographer, was seen stuffing tobacco into the pockets of his hunting jacket. He cried out, "The boat is sinking, save your tobacco, boys!"[7] Dyche clutched his Winchester rifle and three hundred cartridges, which a ship's officer said he could not take with him. Dyche "thought otherwise."

Although water was leaking into the boiler room and a few other compartments, the pumps appeared to be keeping up. Captain Farrell declared that the ship was not in imminent danger of sinking. He was afraid to sail back to Sukkertoppen unaided, however, so six men were selected to take one of the lowered longboats to shore for an Eskimo pilot to guide them back. Dyche, in order to relieve his mind and "to allow things to settle," returned to the hold and resumed skinning his birds.

Once safely ashore in Sukkertoppen, passengers learned that the *Miranda*'s aft water-ballast tank, previously empty, was now full of water. With the pumps unable to clear it, the top of the thoroughly holed ballast tank now served as a false bottom to the ship. Captain Farrell had no confidence that the thin, rusted metal would hold at sea. The *Miranda* was, for the time being, stranded in Sukkertoppen.

Lieutenant Peary's relief ship, the *Falcon,* would pass Sukkertoppen on her way to north Greenland, but it was decided that even if they could signal her, the schooner was too small to accommodate them. Therefore Dr. Cook and a few men elected to take one of the ship's boats and a Sukkertoppen longboat and row to Holsteinborg (140 miles north) to intercept a fishing vessel. Volunteers for the open-boat journey included a surveyor from Boston, two Yale students (one a member of the crew team), and two newspapers correspondents—four men living the action, and two reporting it. Six Sukkertoppen Eskimos accompanied them.

Once again the excursionists indulged in "oceans of speculations" regarding what would happen next. Most tried to make the best of the situation, realizing that this was all of Greenland they were likely to see. Professor G. Frederick Wright of Oberlin College organized a trip to examine a nearby glacier, and another group mounted a hunt for reindeer. Dyche hired Eskimo guides to help him collect whatever he could find, which amounted to gulls, guillimots, and ravens. He prepared and stored the skins on deck, under wagon sheets, to keep them away from the rats.

"The Esquimo are swarming all over the deck and coming and going in their smooth running Kayaks," Dyche wrote. "How interesting they are. I hope to be able to study their habits and know something of their life history before we get away from here as this will be the only point in Greenland that we will visit." Dyche spent a considerable amount of time with the Eskimos, compiling a vocabulary list, taking photographs, making notes. Although he bought a few things from them with Danish crowns, he had not come prepared to barter as had many of his fellow passengers. "Our fellows are continually trying to drive bargains with them," he noted. "It is quite easy to cheat them as they have little idea of the real value of the articles offered them. They want to trade more than is good for them."

The Danish governor of the town and his wife took pity on the stranded excursionists, who were running short of provisions, and invited them on several occasions for dinner, wine, coffee, and tea. Dyche requested permission to remain in Sukkertoppen over the winter so that he could collect mammals, but the governor informed him that he could not remain in Greenland for such a period of time without a permit from the Danish government. This policy had been adopted to protect the Eskimo population from prolonged contact with outsiders. With the governor's assistance, Dyche applied for a permit for the following year.

Faculty and students from Oberlin College vandalizing a glacier. This photograph originally was published in Henry Collins Walsh's The Last Cruise of the Miranda, *1896.*

A few days after Dr. Cook and his small party had left, the stranded *Miranda* passengers held a meeting. Dyche described the scene: "We have a mutiny after dinner at the suggestion of Dr. Brewer[8] who with others recommend that the captain be put in complete charge of our stores of provisions. All seem to favor the idea. I suggested that such an arrangement be made temporary and to last until Dr. Cook returns when other arrangements could be made. For this I was jumped upon. I still contended for it as I thought the stuff belonged to Dr. Cook and he should at least be represented. I was told that the stuff was purchased with our money, that the arctic Expedition was over, that Cook had shown his inefficiency to manage the business, that he was not our commander, that the Cook Arctic Expedition never existed except upon paper; that this was a case of self preservation, that Cook was nothing more than one of us, that he evidently knew now if he never did before that he had no ability for managing such an expedition. I thought different and made a fight for the Dr.'s rights, stating that he is surely the commander of our party, that he provided and arranged all details of the Expedition, and the simple fact that we consented to it and allowed it was evidence that he had charge of our party and the captain had charge of the ship. After much discussion the matter was allowed to go over until 9:30 p.m. I did not wish to attend this meeting as I had had so much to say at the dinner meeting. I went ashore with Cleveland."

Dr. Cook returned to Sukkertoppen on August 20 with an American fishing schooner, the *Rigel*. The *Rigel*'s captain, George W. Dixon, agreed to carry the excursionists "to civilization or Gloucester" for four thousand dollars.[9] Such a fee was not unreasonable since the *Rigel* would be foregoing her fishing voyage, and the captain and crew normally were paid with a percentage of the catch. In fact, Captain Dixon offered to ferry the Cook expedition for free if they would wait a few weeks until the fishing was completed. A shortage of provisions on the *Miranda* and the necessity that some of the passengers return to their homes and jobs ruled out that possibility, however. In any event, the excursionists believed that the responsibility for paying Captain Dixon and his crew lay with the *Miranda*'s owners. Hence the four-thousand-dollar fee seemed imminently reasonable.

The fishing schooner Rigel *comes to the rescue of the stranded* Miranda *passengers and crew. This photograph originally was published in Henry Collins Walsh's* The Last Cruise of the Miranda, *1896.*

Dr. Cook's plan called for the *Miranda* to steam back to St. John's with the small schooner in tow, as a sort of oversized lifeboat. All passengers would travel on board the *Rigel*. As space would be extremely cramped, each was allowed to bring only one small bag of belongings on board. Boats would travel back and forth from the *Miranda,* bringing supplemental food and supplies during the voyage. Dyche spent the last night in Sukkertoppen preparing his birds ("Work myself out of my wits almost to get my birds and things in shape—a dreadful rush."). On the morning of August 21 the *Miranda* set out with the *Rigel* close behind her. The excursionists crowded together on the afterdeck cheering and hurrahing to the Eskimos on shore, who formed a line and fired their rifles in salute. Exhilarated by the U.S. flag above them (the *Miranda* flew the Union Jack), the men sang the "Star Spangled Banner" and "My Country, 'Tis of Thee" as they departed Sukkertoppen harbor in a drizzling rain.

Inside the tiny *Rigel*'s hold, dubbed the "Sucker Hole," passengers were packed "as thick as sardines." Indeed, the hold reeked of fish. On the open sea most of them, including Dyche, were sicker than they had been on board the *Miranda.*

At two in the morning on August 23 Dyche heard the three-whistle warning signal from the *Miranda.* He woke Dr. Cook and then went out on deck, but he was too nauseous to stay long and returned to his sleeping bag. The *Miranda* was in distress. The ballast tank had finally given way. Captain Dixon drew the *Rigel* alongside the failing steamer and hailed Captain Farrell to cut the tow cable and drop off in the lifeboats. Farrell replied that he wished to stand by his ship until daylight. The *Miranda*'s firemen, who had come on deck and were preparing to abandon ship, were sent back to plug the holes with pillows and mattresses. The leaks slowed, but the ship was sinking.

In the bow of the *Rigel,* Captain Dixon stood with an ax ready to cut the hawser lest the *Miranda* founder and take his vessel down with her. The *Miranda*'s lifeboats were lowered, but proved clumsy in the heavy waves; one in fact was smashed against the *Miranda*'s hull. Thus it befell the crew of the *Rigel* to effect the rescue. The skillful fishermen maneuvered their small dories back and forth in the turbulent water, transferring all those left on board the steamship (save a few live pigs). The *Miranda* was last seen at 61°15' N latitude, 58°40' W longitude, midway between Greenland and the Labrador Coast, her lights burning, her rudder lashed to one side, the propeller still turning. Sluggishly she steamed out of sight into the thick fog.

Dyche, lying sick in the hold through most of the excitement, managed only a few words in his diary to record the events of that early morning: "At 4:15 all the *Miranda*'s crew have reached the schooner in safety. The toe [sic] rope has been taken in and the *Miranda* is seen for the last time floating in the fog with all our baggage except a few clothes and a little stuff in our hand bags. A gloomy and sad looking crowd in the schooner and most of us sea sick and not able to express our views of the situation. I am one of such." Dyche had collected and purchased over four hundred and fifty bird skins, sixty-five mammal skins, and a barrel of bones and skulls. All went down with the *Miranda.*

The *Rigel,* already crowded, was now forced to accommodate the thirty-five crewmen of the *Miranda:* Ninety-one persons were aboard the ninety-nine-foot sailing vessel. Dyche was one of thirty men assigned to the twenty-foot-square hold. He wrote, "The sight of the surroundings and the odors are nauceating and would make any well trained stomach shudder. This proceeding on a schooner is slow business, however we all feel much safer than we did in the old *Miranda*."

But Captain William Farrell would not blame his ship for their misfortunes. Instead, he blamed two of her passengers—the clergymen: "Always have devil's own time when we have those people on board. Have storms and all kinds of accidents. Took five days to make trip from New York to Halifax when it should have been made in two. Always have trouble when they are along. I knew we were going to have trouble. I told the cook so when he asked me to come down to services. Had two of these people on board and we were shipwrecked twice. I knew we were going to have trouble. The rats left us. Never saw it fail in all my life."

After the *Rigel* crossed the Davis Strait her progress was inhibited by head winds. As she worked her way south toward Sydney she put in at small harbors, giving Dyche and the others an opportunity to get over their seasickness and to buy food from fishing households (most of their foodstores had gone down with the *Miranda*). Dyche collected several birds during these brief stops and hung the skins from the ceiling in the hold. As the *Rigel* passed other schooners sailing in the opposite direction, their crews stood on deck and gaped at the men overflowing the small vessel, shouting, "Where did you get them? Where did you get all the people? Three cheers for the American fishermen—Hip Hip Hoorah!"

The *Rigel* arrived in Sydney, Nova Scotia, on September 5. Dyche immediately checked into a hotel, had a bath, a "fine breakfast," and bought new, clean clothes. He sent Mrs. Dyche a jolting telegram: "Ship lost. Saved by schooner. Send letter to New York." That evening the excursionists organized a banquet at a South Sydney hotel to honor the captains of the *Miranda* and the *Rigel*. The banquet lasted until the early morning hours, and the men who had been through so much together "had a very good time with toasts and wine and a general exchange of opinions." A collection was taken to purchase a testimonial gift for Captain Dixon, and a sum of two hundred fifty dollars was secured. A month later the *Rigel*'s captain was presented with an inscribed, ornamental clock. The clock was all that Captain Dixon and his crew would receive for their rescue of the passengers and crew of the *Miranda,* however. The *Miranda*'s owners did not find themselves bound by the arrangement Dr. Cook had made with Dixon, declaring that the law did not hold a company responsible for a contract made under such circumstances. If Dixon had managed to bring the *Miranda* into port, he could have claimed salvage rights to the ship, but as it was, he had gained nothing but the gratitude of many men.

The next day the passengers bid farewell to the crews of the *Miranda* and the *Rigel* and boarded the *St. Pierre,* bound for Halifax. Dr. Cook, unfazed by the disasters of his expedition, was so impressed by the wooden steamer that he contrived to form a stock company in order to buy her.

Remarkably, the voyage had not discouraged the excursionists either. They changed steamers again in Halifax and, according to Dyche, were having "a delightful journey" to New York on board the *Portia,* reading accounts of their shipwreck in the New York newspapers, enjoying "well served and moderately clean" meals ("Only found one meal worm in my biscuit this morning," Dyche noted), and, in the smoking room, organizing "The Arctic Club of America," which would "meet once a year and have a dinner and do such other business as may be of interest to the members."[10]

The *Portia,* Shakespearean sister ship of the *Miranda* on the same Red Cross Line, was steaming through a heavy fog on Vineyard Sound, intermittently sounding her horn, when she struck a three-masted schooner. The schooner was cut cleanly in two. Dyche looked on as the coal-laden *Dora M. French* quickly sank: "A wild rush follows and then the din of the rushing feet, mingled with the screams of the women and the cries of the children. I push through the crowd and get on deck .... The bow end of the schooner was going down. The great broken masts standing in every direction. The tangled sails and ropes were in a worse fix than if a Kansas cyclone had passed through them. The stern end of the schooner was standing at an angle of 45 degrees. Three men were clinging to the wreck. As it sank out of sight they were left in the water. Two of them soon disappeared but the third kept swimming from one piece of the wreck to another until he reached a broken piece of mast that held him up. After a course of time a life boat was let down. One of the drowning men floated for some time and his hand could be seen going under the water. It was an awful sight." Only one man on board, the mate, survived the collision. Four others, caught in the wreckage, drowned.

The next day the *Portia* arrived in Brooklyn.[11] "Warm but same old New York," Dyche wrote. "Shake hands all around and bid good bye to friends— shipwrecked friends, who I may never see again. Such is life. After such a long trip upon uncertain waters, it seems good to get back to the United States . . . ."

Dyche would spend the next few days calling on acquaintances in New York, including the noted taxidermist John Rowley, and then stop in Buffalo for three days to visit William Temple Hornaday before beginning the long train ride back to Lawrence. On September 11 he stayed with Dr. Cook at his home in Brooklyn. Cook was visited on that same day by several newspaper reporters, who questioned him about his Arctic expedition.

"A delightful trip," Cook told them, "replete with adventures, abounding in situations, not free from danger, and, taken all in all, I have not heard one member of the party that had a complaint to make."[12]

Dyche and Eskimo woman at Cape York, Greenland. (University of Kansas Archives)

8 Greenland, Peary, and the *Kite*

Lieutenant Robert E. Peary was stranded in north Greenland. On leave of absence from the U.S. Navy Corps of Engineers, Peary had established a base camp on Inglefield Gulf in 1894 from which he had launched an expedition to explore the northern coast of the island. His first attempt failed miserably. As soon as Peary and his men had constructed their headquarters, "Anniversary Lodge," a giant iceberg had broken loose from a glacier, smashed the party's steam launch and two other boats and carried away the fuel oil drums. In response to the disaster, Peary exclaimed, "The fates and all Hell are against me, but I'll conquer yet!"[1]

Following the first aborted attempt to cross Greenland's ice cap, all but two of Peary's men decided to return to the States aboard the *Falcon,* the relief ship scheduled to pick them up. Remaining with Peary were Hugh Lee, a youthful newspaper reporter, and Matthew Henson, who the newspapers referred to as Peary's "colored servant." Peary called Henson and Lee his "small but experienced, effective, homogeneous and loyal party." With them he successfully crossed Greenland's "Great Ice."

But Peary had made no arrangements to be picked up from his base camp after the second trek. His wife, Josephine, tried desperately to raise money to charter a ship by delivering public lectures, showing magic lantern slides of Greenland, and exhibiting a north Greenland Eskimo girl. But she failed to raise the necessary funds.

Morris K. Jesup, director of the American Museum of Natural History, came to her rescue. He agreed to complete financing of an expedition to retrieve Peary with the understanding that the American Museum would send a geologist to examine three large meteorites Peary had discovered and a collector to bring back arctic mammals. Jesup left the selection of men for these two positions to the museum president, William Wallace.

To inspect the meteorites, Wallace secured the services of Rollin Salisbury, professor of geology at the University of Chicago. To collect mammals for the museum, he called on Lewis Lindsay Dyche. Wallace knew that Dyche, after his failure to obtain specimens during the previous year's dismal *Miranda* cruise, had made plans to return to southern Greenland early that summer. Wallace arranged for the relief ship to rendezvous with Dyche as she sailed north to Anniversary Lodge. Whatever specimens Dyche could secure in north Greenland—walrus, polar bear, or musk oxen—would be divided equally between Dyche and the American Museum. The relief vessel was to be the *Kite,* the small steam sealer-whaler that Dyche had surveyed the previous July in St. John's.

Dyche left Gloucester, Massachusetts, on May 16, 1895, bound for Greenland on board the American fishing schooner *Golden Hope,* "a flyer," according to Dyche. She passed every ship in sight on a smooth, uneventful voyage northward along the Labrador coast and across the Davis Strait. Dyche suffered mild bouts of seasickness, and he ate little for several days at a time. "I am no sea dog and do not want to be one," he wrote. "A land lubbers life is good enough for me." But all in all he found the voyage pleasant, "a great contrast" with his experience on the *Miranda* the previous year.[2]

In the early morning hours of June 9 the *Golden Hope* came within sight of Greenland. Dyche rose from his bunk at six and took his field glasses on deck: "Icy in every sense of the word this morning. Clouds were overhead but the sun was lighting up the mountain peaks which were covered with snow and ice. There were bunches of white and grey clouds floating between and about the peaks. The water at the base of the mountains was covered by a low cloud of white mist. At one moment the entire cyclorama would appear as a cloud mass, then all appeared as a land mass. In reality it was a great picture of such fine grey and soft blue tints, mingled with an infinite amount of pure white and dark shadow, that it could not be painted or described with any justice to nature. Such a scene is seldom witnessed and such an hour I have seldom spent."

Late that afternoon the *Golden Hope* arrived at Holsteinborg, 140 miles north of Sukkertoppen. No Eskimo kayaks greeted the schooner. "The reason was no fault of the huskies however," Dyche noted, employing the American sailors' jargon. "They would have surrounded us, but for the order of the governor keeping them ashore. The Governor does not like to have the fisherman in the harbor as they come ashore and more or less interfere with the natural order of things in Eskimo life."

Holsteinborg, like all Danish colonies in Greenland, was established to maintain a trading district (four trading outposts lay in the Holsteinborg district). The Danish government maintained a trade monopoly with the Greenland Eskimos not only for financial reasons, but in order to protect them from the influences of outside civilizations. Not until after World War II were outsiders admitted to Greenland without special permission from the Greenland Board in Copenhagen.

Dyche met the governor of the district, R. Müller, and presented him with a letter of introduction from the Danish delegation in Washington and his permit to collect in Greenland. Müller greeted Dyche warmly and invited him to his house. "The natural form of introduction among these people with a drop for the health of the king and all present was gone through with, and that natural uneasiness of how I should fare when I reached Holsteinborg began to wear off," Dyche recorded. Dinner soon followed. "This as well as a thousand other things on hand was all new to me. Wines and old country ales in abundance. Rye and other bread stuff and for meat, something entirely new, Greenland hare for one course, and the skin of the white whale, prepared somewhat as my German grandmother used to prepare pigs feet for 'sons.' This dish as well as the Greenland hare more than pleased my palate after the diet of three weeks on the schooner."

Dyche secured a room in one of the Danish houses and arranged with the governor's wife for board. At eleven he was alone in his new room, writing that "a little fire is burning bright and the room is as cozy as one could wish in any country. I hardly know how to get into my bed, two thick of Eider down. I finally crawl in between them."

The next morning Dyche tramped through snow that had fallen during the night. The village consisted of three or four Danish houses, surrounded by about twenty-five large Eskimo huts, built of turf and stone and entered by means of a short tunnel. About five hundred Eskimos inhabited them. "I am the wonder of the town," Dyche wrote. "A few follow me at what they think to be a safe distance. The children scamper and run when I come near them. Dogs everywhere—they surround me but do not bark or offer to bite." Rubbing a small boy on the head brought screams and sobs from the surrounding children, who believed that Dyche had somehow harmed him.

But after setting up a workshop in a storehouse attic, Dyche soon had two Eskimos—a man, Gustav, and a boy, Elias—to help him work on skins as they were brought into the shop. They were able to adapt quickly to Dyche's requirements for skinning birds, as Dyche complacently noted in his diary after the first day of work. Villagers continuously brought Dyche varieties of birds and eggs or told him where he could find them, and his "bird business," as he called it, was established.

Dyche made collecting trips almost daily, although heavy rains kept him from venturing out as long as he would have liked. Governor Müller was a companion on those trips, and frequently they hired Eskimos to row them out into the bay. In his field notebook Dyche carefully logged where he had found each specimen, its condition, and its environment. When possible, he took photographs. He soon discovered that the clothes he had brought with him were not warm enough, so he hired a woman to make him a heavy dogskin coat for 17 Danish kroner (about $4.60).

Dyche described how seals were brought to him: "A whole seal is drug from the shore up to the store house where I am at work. Soon two more huskies appear each with a seal skin. I get my camera and take pictures both of the seals and huskies. Measure the whole seal and take some notes. The animal is drug up to the village and two women proceed to skin it—after my directions. . . . The animal is all taken and I finally leave the skin in charge of one of the huskies. He takes it—

to the sea and returns it to me well washed. The skins are balls of fat and all over grease and like indian rubber. I finally make arrangements to get two women to shave the fat off. They come to my bird establishment and are soon at work with their half moon knives which they use with great skill—after the feet were dressed they began pushing the fat off with the knife by placing the skin on a sloping board about the shape of a wooden snow shovel turned upside down. In half a day one woman had dressed one skin and did it remarkably well." All the while Eskimo children stood by waiting to be given pieces of blubber to chew. Dyche paid his assistants well by Holsteinborg standards: 10 ore, or 2 1/2 cents, an hour.

Dyche was up most mornings between five and six. His days were filled with collecting, making measurements, taking photographs, skinning birds and seals, blowing eggs, packing specimens, writing field notes, cleaning his guns. Due to the damp weather he had to clean and oil the guns immediately after use. The humidity also hampered bird preparation: Blood on the birds would not dry, and Dyche could not skin them without blood smearing the feathers. He used cornmeal to soak out most of the blood, and then wiped it off with a small sponge. After one month he had skinned 361 birds: eider duck, fulmar, jaeger, dovekie, mallard duck, guillimot, gyrfalcon, razor-billed auk, thick-billed murre, and kittiwake; glaucous, Iceland, and great black-backed gulls; common and Arctic terns; and red and northern phalarope. He had collected or purchased over two thousand eggs, sixteen seals, and numerous bird and seal skulls.

Dyche frequently accompanied Governor Müller as he made his rounds of the village. As far as Dyche could tell, the governor's main preoccupation was dogs, "training his young dogs to swim . . . . Feeding dogs, attending dog concerts, superintending dogs fights, tieing and running after dogs, repairing damage dogs do the yard, etc." When Dyche first arrived in Holsteinborg, he proposed to set up his tent as a workshop, but the governor assured him that the dogs would eat it. Dyche could not even crack the door of his room for air because dogs would nose their way in. And after-dinner entertainment with the Müllers often consisted of going outside to watch dogfights.

Dyche ate his meals with the Müllers. They had homemade beer instead of coffee for breakfast, rye and white breads, cold meats, and white whale sauce. The evening meal sometimes lasted hours. A Dutch man-of-war visited the Holsteinborg harbor, and the Müllers and Dyche were invited on board for a three-hour meal, "a Danish dinner served in several courses with a half dozen kinds of wine." The Müllers invited the ship's officers to dine with them the following evening. Dyche wore his Scotch tweed, as he did not have a dress suit with him "in Greenland or anywhere in the world." The meal overwhelmed him—native oysters cooked in soup and raw on the shell, Greenland ptarmigan, brown potatoes, green beans imported from Europe, cold caribou tongue, boiled ham, cakes, wine, cognac, and coffee. "We finally reach the end of the bill of fare and the Evening," Dyche wrote in his diary. "I go to the little stream which comes down from the mountains near the village and get a good old fashioned drink of water which pleased my stomach more than all the combinations I had tasted of."

Dyche described another social occasion late in his stay: "At supper the subject of the Eskimoes dancing came up and it was suggested by Mrs. Müller that as it was Sunday and they had their good clothes on that perhaps I could get them to dance by offering a pound of coffee and a pound of sugar. Louisa, the Eskimo girl who works in the Governor's house was made the agent and the proposition was soon heralded through the village. A party of dancers soon gathered in front of the Governor's house, the fiddler came and the dance was soon headway. . . . It is hard to get them to dance this time of the year. Most of them are away fishing and hunting, especially the younger part of the population, those who organize and start the dance agoing. However they are all passionately fond of dancing and dance with much ease and grace. They have dances of their own, but have learned European dances and waltz with much good grace. The violin music is of the old Missouri river bottom catfish kind. By the time I had finished making photographs, the whole village had collected about the dancing grounds. However all soon departed after the dance was over to make the coffee. . . . This was intensely more interesting to me than the dancing business. They were not Exactly in the humor of dancing but they were surely in the humor of coffee. This coffee drinking held the mob together for nearly an hour or until bed time, 10 p.m. They made the coffee very strong as they always do when possible and are very fond of it. Some one now produced a rope and some Experts began showing what they could do. Jumped on one foot, then on the other, then on the hands and feet, then sat down and jumped the rope."

Dyche accumulated a sparse vocabulary with which he could communicate with the Eskimos. He found himself alternately impressed and repulsed by them. He held a high opinion of Elias, his young assistant, believing that "if he had the same opportunity as some of our American boys he would make a good man." On the other hand Dyche found Gustav, although skillful at his work, exceptionally lazy, full of excuses, and always begging. "He wants Every thing I have," Dyche complained in his diary. "He wants every new thing he sees me have and all the old things." Dyche also suspected Gustav of coaching other villagers on how to trade with him, telling them what prices to demand for their skins and eggs. Dyche admitted, "They are sharp and shrewd and usually get the best of me in a bargain— as compared with the prices the governor pays them." Dyche found abhorrent the villagers' method of killing dogs—strangling them with a rope. Perhaps more than anything else, Dyche was put off by the uncleanliness of the Eskimos. "So few people ever take a bath in this country that it was quite a surprise to the water," he noted after bathing.

Dyche was most impressed by Eskimo women. "A family camped just across from my work shop has many things to 'truckum' or trade," he recorded. "The woman is very clever about making things out of seal skins. Says she has a smart man, meaning that he is a good seal hunter. The men bring the seals to the shore, then their work is done. The women do the rest of the work. Take the women away from the village for one year, and I much doubt if many of the men would live the year out. Women seem to do everything."

Dyche took numerous photographs while in Holsteinborg, although he found it difficult to photograph the Eskimos spontaneously because the dim light required a slow shutter speed (therefore relatively immobile subjects), and also because the Eskimos were unwilling to pose in what they felt were unflattering attitudes. On one occasion he hid his camera under a black cloth in order to photograph women carrying loads of fish. When discovered, one woman cursed him "in good vigorous Eskimo language" as he covertly took another snapshot of her.

The *Kite* was due to rendezvous with Dyche between July 8 and July 16, and Dyche began preparing his specimens for shipping, drying bird skins, packing them into crates and kerosene barrels, painting his name in red on each one. He did not venture far from the village for fear that the *Kite* would come while he was away, and he did not collect anything that he could not prepare immediately.

Dyche packed away the souvenirs he had acquired, and they were numerous. He had arranged a colossal trade with the Müllers: Dyche's dory, two rifles, and three hundred dollars for Müller's collection of fourteen hundred eggs, numerous skulls and bird skins, Mrs. Müller's collection of over two hundred eggs, and two eiderdown robes. Dyche did not have three hundred dollars, but the Müllers trusted him to send it later. Mrs. Müller also gave him a cap and muffler for his daughter, Ruth. Dyche traded a shotgun, a Winchester rifle, and 150 cartridges to the assistant governor for 132 kroner, a walrus skull, thirty bird skins, an eiderdown robe, and a pair of sealskin pants. With the Danish minister he traded a shotgun for some skulls and a kayak. And he bought two pairs of sealskin pants and boots, two pairs of purple-topped sealskin boots for Walter, and two pairs for Mrs. Dyche. (He had only intended to buy one pair for her—he thought he had bargained twice with the same woman to make a pair, but had in fact bargained with two different women, and each brought him a pair.)

July 16 passed, the last date projected for the *Kite*'s arrival, and then July 17, and July 18. Dyche began to worry about what would happen to him and to his specimens. A distant steamship finally was sighted on July 18, but when it continued northward Dyche became frantic. Steam-powered vessels were rare that far north, and Dyche and Governor Müller concluded that the ship that had passed must have been either the *Kite* or a ship on its way to search for Fridjof Nansen's polar expedition. Dyche became quite upset, writing, "If it was the Kite & something has happened by which the New York arrangement has been broken up, I think that I should have been notified at least, so as not to keep me here on such suspense—not knowing whether to wait for the vessel or not, not Knowing for a certainty whether to wait for the vessel or not, not Knowing for a certainty whether she has gone north or not. . . ."

The passing ship, the *Kite,* found Holsteinborg harbor the following day. After meeting his fellow passengers (Professor Salisbury and Emil Diebitsch, Peary's brother-in-law), Dyche began to organize the moving of his collections on board. He hired Eskimos, making arrangements "to have four of them well fed so that they would be willing to work at night." Dyche went to bed at two that morning and got up at four. "Hurry about as fast as possible getting small things picked up," he wrote. "It takes time to bid these danish people goodbye. Their customs of hospitality are not like those of Americans. They seem to [be] an easy going people, at least those I have met. Like good beer & grog & are hard smokers—using their large Danish pipe with stems some 3 to to four feet in length. It is eleven a.m. before I am on board the Kite and already to start. The Gov. & the two second Govs. accompany me and they stay on board until the Kite is about a mile away or at the mouth of the harbor, when I bid them a final goodbye. I do not leave Holsteinborg without feelings of regret. I had many pleasant hours notwithstanding the fact that the weather was bad all the time. . . ." That afternoon, bound north on board the *Kite,* Dyche reminisced in his diary, ten pages that day, about the men "coming and going in their Kayaks—this one with a seal, this one with some birds—another with fish, and another with a small whale or porpoise. . . ."

The *Kite* was a barkentine, that is, the front mast was square rigged, and two others were rigged fore to aft. She was a small ship, forty yards long and weighing 208 tons. She carried auxiliary steam power. Specially designed for Arctic sailing, with her propeller sunk deeply to avoid ice and her bow constructed of massive oak timbers bolted and keyed together, the *Kite* was strong enough to plow through floating ice. She had borne Peary to northern Greenland in 1891, and while ramming a passage through the ice of Baffin Bay, a thrashing blow from her iron tiller had broken both bones of Peary's lower right leg. Dr. Frederick Cook set the breaks. And with Dyche's former student assistant, Charles Hite, on board, the *Kite* had served as Peary's relief ship in 1892.

The Kite *in ice floes off north Greenland. Photograph by Dyche. (University of Kansas Archives)*

The *Kite* paused in Disko Bay, where Dyche and two Eskimos shot fifty fulmars. Dyche needed a place to prepare the birds. He offered the cook "a good price . . . in American gold" to allow him to use his bakery as a taxidermy workshop. The cook was willing, but pointed out that "it was impossible to do justice to the people on board in the cooking business if he did." Dyche instead set up his tent over the main hatchway, where, after arranging a few of his crates, he had just enough room to stand and work.

"Thousands of huge ice bergs," Dyche noted as the *Kite* made its way northward, "in places the ocean seems to be a solid mass of ice—great ice masses towering up in the heavens. The sun is up in the east and the ocean in the west—a grand panorama, the white city of the gods . . . ."

On July 29, while he was working in his tent, Dyche heard someone shout, "That looks like a bear!" Dyche rushed to the rail with his field glasses and he saw a polar bear, two or three years old, standing by a carcass. All hands scrambled for their rifles. As the bear took to the water Dyche let off a shot at its head. Then everyone was shooting, the bear was bellowing, Dyche took another shot at its neck, and then it was dead. A boat was lowered and the 600-pound carcass hoisted on board. Four bullets had hit the animal, a male, and on skinning it Dyche determined, with satisfaction, that his shot to the back of the neck "did the business."

The *Kite* passed Herbert Island, twenty-five miles from Peary's headquarters, but it jammed in the thick ice of Inglefield Gulf. Dyche went ashore to hunt auks. He had never seen so many birds at once, and he returned to the ship with a hundred. While he was away hunting, two Eskimos had brought the news to the *Kite* that Peary was at Anniversary Lodge. They offered to guide a party to Peary, and Dyche and Emil Diebitsch elected to go. Two sleds with teams of six dogs each were prepared, Dyche donned his Eskimo garb. By eight that night they were off.

Dyche skinning a polar bear on the deck of the Kite. *(University of Kansas Archives)*

Each sled was rigged with two large air-filled skins for bouyancy. Diebitsch and his sled immediately spilled into the water. Channels and leads, some difficult to see, slowed travel. At times the men detoured as much as a mile to find a favorable crossing. If a lead was narrow, they used the sleds as frail bridges. If a suitable piece of ice could be found, they ferried the sleds across. If the water was shallow, they simply waded, letting the dogs pull the floating sleds. Diebitsch was dumped into the water again. Then Dyche spilled twice "so as to make up for lost time." His sealskin costume kept him dry.

At 2:30 a.m. they spotted a seal, and Dyche watched their Eskimo guide stalk it: "He gets quite near it by a creeping wriggling motion, keeping his side to the animal & by imitating the motions of the seal, especially those made by the seal's head, he imitated with his head which was covered with [the] hood of his seal skin coat. . . . The motions of the seal's tail he imitated with his foot. It is said that they make the noise of the seal with their mouths & scratch on the ice so as to imitate the scratching of the seal & cause them to come out of the breathing or air holes. The seal Killed we are all soon on the spot. . . . The seal is skinned by one of the Eskimos after my directions for a specimen. The dogs are then allowed to have the carcass and make very quick work of it. Eating & fighting & grabbing meat from each other. All the seal is food for them. When they were through nothing remained not even blood or bones."

As the men worked their way along Redcliffe Peninsula toward Anniversary Lodge, they encountered a channel so wide that schools of narwhal were swimming in it. Unable to cross, they followed it five miles. A little after eight o'clock, within sight of Anniversary Lodge, they realized that they would be unable to get across. They headed back to the *Kite*.

The return trip was difficult. Some of the channels they had crossed had widened, and new ones had opened. By noon they found that wide channels in all directions cut them off from Peary's lodge, from the Redcliffe shore, and from the *Kite*. Dyche and Diebitsch "debated seriously" about their situation. But Dyche noticed that the Eskimos did not seem concerned: "In fact they did not seem to be alarmed at anything. When the sled broke or got out of repair, or when we could not get over the rough ice or across the channels—they acted as though it was a huge joke."

Dyche and Diebitsch followed a channel, watching narwhals and seals in the water. In frustration, Dyche shot a seal, but his shot was too good, breaking its neck and killing it instantly. The seal sunk before Dyche could spear it. When Dyche and Diebitsch returned to the sleds, they found the Eskimos prying loose a large piece of ice on the edge of the channel. Soon dogs, sleds, and men were all packed on one cake of ice and under way. They reached the *Kite* at 4:40 p.m. after twenty-one hours of continuous travel, "which despite its hardships," Dyche noted, "I enjoyed very much."

While Dyche slept, Captain John Bartlett was able to maneuver the *Kite* into

Robert E. Peary in north Greenland, photographed by Dyche. (University of Kansas Archives)

McCormick Bay. From there it was an easy journey overland to Anniversary Lodge, where Peary, Mathew Henson, and Hugh Lee were discovered safe and well. The *Kite* was too far from the lodge to load Peary's equipment and belongings, however, and as it appeared that ice in Inglefield Gulf and Bowdoin Bay would prevent the *Kite* from getting closer for another week, Bartlett, Peary and Dyche decided to collect walrus. The *Kite* steamed to Karnah, an Eskimo village on the southern coast of Redcliffe Peninsula, where they hired Eskimos to harpoon the seals they shot and to assist Dyche in preparing the skins.

The men spent several days hunting walrus, which Dyche later described in an article for *The Cosmopolitan:* "At this juncture I noticed a walrus some distance off. He was swimming away from the herd. 'There he is!' said Lieutenant Peary. 'I believe, professor, you got a good sight in on him.' 'No,' said another, 'that is not the animal; that one is not large enough.' The command was given to put the boat after him, and the boat shot forward.

"I did not know much about throwing an Eskimo harpoon, but I had practised a little at Holsteinborg, and was anxious to test my skill. The boat was now between the wounded animal and the main herd. While it was moving along, the walrus dived and unexpectedly came up quite near us, making his way back to the herd. His neck was bleeding, and as he went down with a deep groan, throwing the water in the air, I threw the harpoon, holding my breath, gritting my teeth, and using every ounce of strength in my body. The harpoon handle flew off to one side

Hoisting a walrus aboard the Kite.
Dyche took this photograph.
(University of Kansas Archives)

and splashed in the water, the animal pulling on the line. I had him! Lieutenant Peary called out: 'Professor, did you fasten him?' I was so overcome for a moment that I could not answer; but the surging line told the story for me. In a moment the line was paid out, and the old bull was speeding away, rushing the boat through the water, until finally, worn out, we dispatched him with a bullet. It was the particular bull for which I had longed. His tusks were the largest of any I secured in the Arctic regions."[3]

The deck of the *Kite* became a taxidermist's shop, strewn with bones, blubber, blood, and walrus skins. "Worked all night with my six Eskimos butchering the walrus,"
Dyche wrote. "A hard nights work. The animals were very heavy and hard to move. Yet my Eskimos stuck to in fine shape. I was surprised to see them work so hard & to see how quick they could remove the skin from one of the large brutes. At one a.m. we had coffee & crackers. This seemed to put new life into the men & we had a long hard pull until 8 a.m. when breakfast was ready. We all sleep until noon & then work until past midnight skinning out heads. The heads were cut off & not skinned. This was another heavy job as the large skins had to be pulled out flippers & all and dragged to a place where we could get at them. A great mess of meat & blood. Every body in blood to the Knees. Ships men good to help. Grease & fat—Piles of skins, animals piled up on each other. Blood & tusks. Pull animal by small hole in skin. Tough skins." "This walrus collecting is not only danger-

ous," he added, "but the handling of the skins the hardest of hard work."

On Sunday, August 11, the *Kite* finally reached Anniversary Lodge, a large, rectangular wooden building covered in tar paper. Dyche took the outside doorknobs as souvenirs. He photo-graphed the small band of Eskimos who had assisted Peary in hunting, as guides, in maintaining the

North Greenland Eskimos skinning walrus heads on the deck of the Kite. (University of Kansas Archives)

lodge, and, in the case of the women—Peary made little attempt to hide it—in providing sexual comforts. In fact, in his two-volume account of the expeditions, *Northward Across the "Great Ice,"* Peary published nude photographs of his Eskimo assistants, including his fourteen-year-old mistress Allakasingwah, calling

Another of Dyche's photographs, this is of the Kite *anchored near Anniversary Lodge, Robert E. Peary's headquarters on Ingelfield Gulf, north Greenland. (University of Kansas Archives)*

them "ethnological flash-light studies." During the two days his equipment and supplies were being loaded onto the *Kite* and later at Cape York, Peary utilized the sunny weather to take additional photographs. Evidently Dyche stood behind him during a few of those sessions because his collection of photographs also included a few such "ethnological" shots.[4]

Anniversary Lodge was so abundantly supplied with food that after Peary's supplies were transferred to the ship the passengers' meals actually improved. The *Kite* sailed to Olrik's Bay to give Dyche an opportunity to collect caribou. Dyche was able to shoot a few, but he was convinced that he could have secured more if men from the ship had not accompanied him. "Too much foolish Excitement, much as is often shown by inexperienced hunters," he wrote. "Of course such a crowd did not see the deer."

They made another walrus hunt near Saunders Island, more successful than the first. "My blood is hot with excitement," Dyche wrote. "Six big bull. All Killed by my own rifle. What a grand lot of specimens, what a fine experience & what supreme excitement. A day among days. Whoop, Hurrah, Rock Chalk Jayhawk K. U. Now I am full of business. I cut holes in the skins. Have the mate & sailors to help me and get all six animals on board."

With the mammal-collecting phase of the Peary Relief Expedition complete, the *Kite* steamed toward Cape York and the three meteorites. Eskimos had named them "The Tent," "The Dog," and "The Woman," but after centuries, as pieces of iron were chipped away to make knives and cutting tools, the meteorites bore little resemblance to their namesakes. Peary, a skilled engineer, was able to coax "The

Dog" and "The Woman" on board the *Kite*. Dyche helped drag "The Woman" (fifty-five hundred pounds) across the ice. "It looked once as though it was going down in the ice," he wrote, "but the chains & ropes held it after the ice began to give away." "The Tent," weighing ninety tons, could not be blasted loose or split and was left to be retrieved another time.

One afternoon while Peary and "his forces," as Dyche called them, prepared the meteorites for removal, an Eskimo off shore harpooned a narwhal.[5] Dyche quickly organized an Eskimo crew for the *Kite*'s whaleboat. They pulled alongside

the animal and Dyche fired as it surfaced, striking the brain and killing it. They towed the body to a nearby ice pan, where Eskimos from shore joined them in removing the skin and blubber. The boat crew received the largest shares of meat, with the harpooner taking the most. Dyche kept the skeleton and tooth.

North Greenland Eskimos as photographed by Dyche.
(University of Kansas Archives)

Dyche described how Peary made a grand show of paying the Cape York Eskimos: "They all collect in a group near the shore where he is dealing out the articles. . . . Mr. Peary finally gets settled with them & as a final finish gives them a box of tools, iron, old duffels, files etc. etc. He pours those things out on the rock. What a time they have gathering them up and dividing them. The whale boat is traded to them for 5 Kayaks. Guns given & traded to them. Every one is happy and all are boiling over with jabbering. We finally at 12:30 get aboard the *Kite*. The natives are all placed in the whale boat with good bye, the anchor is raised and we are soon on our way to the coast."

As she crossed Baffin Bay and journeyed south toward Baffin Island, the *Kite* paused to trade with passing whalers. Dyche took advantage of these opportunities to gather additional skins, buying five adult polar bear hides from a ship's captain for twenty-five dollars each and two cub skins for seventeen dollars each. But after the *Kite* had zigzagged back to Greenland's west coast and encountered a Scottish whaler, the *Eclipse,* a quarrel developed. Annoyed that Dyche had been buying all available specimens, Diebitsch and Peary boarded the *Eclipse* without Dyche. "They simply kept him out of the market," Matthew Henson later told reporters. "Prof. Dyche . . . has been mad ever since."[6]

This was not the first confrontation between Dyche and Diebitsch. When the relief expedition was first organized, Diebitsch had asked Dyche to sign an agreement stating that Diebitsch was commander of the expedition and that Dyche was not to publish any accounts of the expedition. Dyche refused Diebitsch's proposal, stating that he would "talk and write for publication when and wherever he pleased." To the Kansas City papers he later stated, "the Peary party tried to muzzle me. But you can't muzzle a Kansas man. It is one of his state rights to talk and write pieces for the paper."[7]

Dyche also refused to concede command of the expedition to Diebitsch. As a representative of the American Museum of Natural History (which was principally responsible for financing the expedition), Dyche felt he should at least share command. But William Wallace had been unwilling to mediate, writing Dyche that as he had been assured Diebitsch would offer Dyche "every facility" and would cooperate with him in every way, it was therefore unnecessary to place someone in charge.[8] Outnumbered by Diebitsch and the Peary party, Dyche now found it difficult even to find out where the ship was heading.

As the *Kite* worked her way south through the Davis Strait, Matthew Henson told Dyche "the inside history" of their expedition across the Greenland ice cap. He described incredible hardships—how Lee had begged to be left to die, and how the meat of a single rabbit had saved their lives. "When Matt saw the rabbit it was sitting on its haunches," Dyche wrote in his diary. "However it soon settled down.

Matt wanted the Lieutenant to shoot & the Lieutenant wanted Matt. Lieutenant said he wanted it too bad & was afraid that he could not hit it. Matt responded that he was snow blind, said his eyes had been sore for some time, & he did not think he could see well enough to shoot. Lieutenant said that he would not hit the hare, & insisted on Matt shooting. Matt said that he laid flat down on the

Matthew Henson and a north Greenland Eskimo near Ingelfield Gulf. Photograph by Dyche. (University of Kansas Archives)

ground and took a dead rest & missed the rabbit. The rabbit sat up on his haunches & looked in great surprise & wondered what was happening. Matt said he put in another cartridge & the second shot was fired & the rabbit fell over dead." Peary decided to give the dogs the last of the walrus meat they had saved while Henson cooked the rabbit. They decided they would eat only half of it for the time being. But Peary was too tired to feed the dogs. He told Henson he would feed them later.

"The rabbit was put on the oil stove but before the water got hot Lieutenant cut off one hind leg & began eating. Matt said he could not stand it to see eating going on without eating himself. Said he was hungry and took the other leg. The whole rabbit was soon finished without waiting for it to cook and not saving a morsel for another meal."

The story Dyche heard was one the public back in the States would be eager to hear.

In St. John's, Newfoundland, Dyche transferred his collections to the steamship *Sylvia*. Henson accompanied Dyche on the *Sylvia* to New York. Peary and Lee elected to take a train from Halifax—Peary to his mother's home in

" 'About This Time Expect Peary Relief Expedition.' — Almanac." By 1899 *"Peary relief expeditions"* had become a biennial event, prompting this cartoon in the New York Journal. *Note Peary's well-stocked winter headquarters and his well-fed men and dogs. From the* New York Journal, *July 10, 1899. (University of Kansas Archives)*

Portland, Maine, and Lee to his home in Connecticut. That Peary avoided meeting New York reporters reflected his low spirits after the arduous expedition.

In New York, Dyche and Henson were greeted by reporters eager to hear details of the expedition. Henson, bound by the gag contract, said little, but Dyche, who had learned all the details from Henson, felt no inhibition. "I do not think that Peary will try another Arctic expedition," he told the *New York Times*. "His last expedition was a dismal failure. Although I cannot speak officially for Lieutenant Peary in this matter, I understand that he attributes his want of success to the inability to find the rations which he had hidden at advantageous points during his former trip. . . ."[9] Dyche proceeded to tell the newspapers his own story, writing for the *New York Herald* a full-page account of his experiences in Holsteinborg, his collecting successes, and his part in the relief of Lieutenant Peary. The last item was coined by many newspapers as Peary's "rescue" despite the fact that he had been in no danger. Thus Dyche became "the man who rescued Peary."

Other details of the expedition were grossly misreported, usually in Dyche's favor. One headline in the *New York Evening Telegram* read "Peary's Trip a Failure; Such is the Opinion of Professor Dyche, Who Accompanied the Expedition; The Latter's Meteorite Quest a Success."[10] The *New York Mail and Express* reported, "Prof. Dyche secured two meteorites, one weighing 3,000 pounds and the other 800 pounds. He says he left behind him one weighing forty tons."[11] Several newspapers, in fact, reported that it was Dyche and not Peary who had brought back the Cape York meteorites.

Diebitsch did not arrive in New York until after Dyche had given interviews.

When Diebitsch boarded the *Sylvia*, where Dyche and Peary's collections were being unloaded, he would not speak to Dyche or even look at him.

New Yorkers were charmed by Dyche's energetic midwestern manner. He had not cut his hair since he left Kansas, and his long locks were striking. Dyche dined with Paul du Chaillu, the African explorer, and John Brisbane Walker, editor of *The Cosmopolitan*. The Arctic Club, formed by his shipwreck fellows of the previous year, gave a dinner and reception in his honor.

Little was heard from Peary in Portland, Maine, although he was reported to have said, "I shall never see the north pole, unless someone brings it here. I am done with it. In my judgment, such work requires a far younger man than I. The leader of such a party should be able not only to do as much as any one else, but more than any other man."[12] Meanwhile Dyche, only a year younger than Peary, was hinting to reporters that he might be such a man. For the moment, Dyche had stolen the North Pole show.

"Look at the Man! Look at the Man! Look at the Kansas Man!" Cartoon *from the* Kansas City Star, *December 22, 1895. (University of Kansas Archives)*

9 An Arctic Paderewski

I am glad to see you have shied your castor into the lecture ring. Your poster and circular are fine,—and your hair reveals an Arctic Paderewski! The other artist plays on a piano; you play on icebergs.

William T. Hornaday

Dyche hit the ground running in New York. He was photographed at the Garber Photography Studio wearing his Arctic sealskin costumes and flaunting his long locks. He signed a contract with Henry Collins Walsh (a companion on the *Miranda* voyage who later founded The Explorers Club) to ghostwrite a book about his Greenland expedition, an arrangement similar to his collaboration with Clarence Edwords. The book was to be titled *Beyond the Arctic Circle,* but nothing came of it. As had been arranged, Dyche divided the material he had collected in Greenland with the American Museum of Natural History. The museum's annual report noted that the specimens collected were "a valuable acquisition to the Department of Mammals and Birds."[1]

Dyche, who had never agreed to Peary's gag rule, spoke freely to New York reporters, to the irritation of the Peary faction. While he did not malign Peary, he frankly described him as dejected, and he expressed doubt that Peary would ever make an attempt on the North Pole. Peary's isolated comments to the newspapers corroborated Dyche's assessment, but Peary and his backers were irritated nevertheless, especially when Dyche told reporters that "there was still plenty to be had in Greenland," namely the thirty-six-ton "Tent" that Peary had been unable to bring back. Peary claimed the valuable meteorite was his "by right of discovery," and stated his intention to return to Cape York with a larger ship to recover it. But Dyche argued that the meteorite belonged to whomever could bring it back, and that he had every right to do so. Dyche further maintained that he had laid eyes on the meteorite at the same time as Peary, and therefore Peary's claim to the meteorite "by right of discovery," if there was such a thing, was unfounded. In fact, Dyche did see "The Tent" at the same time as Peary. Eskimos had guided Peary and Hugh Lee to the vicinity of the "great iron stones" the year before Dyche arrived, but in the deep snow the men were able to locate only one of the smaller meteorites. Peary had scratched a large "P" on this meteorite and left a written claim to all three meteorites in a cairn. Hugh Lee supported Peary's claim to "The Tent," contending that they had visited the vicinity and knew that it was there, even if they had not seen it. Lee told his hometown newspaper, "The snow was very deep over it and we did not locate it exactly but we walked all over it. I claim that Peary has first right to it."[2]

Dyche in his Arctic sealskins. This photograph was one of several taken at the Garber Studio in New York. (University of Kansas Archives)

After Dyche returned to Lawrence, Peary wrote him:

"I see according to clippings from western papers sent me by friends that you contemplate an attack upon the North Pole next summer & also propose to bring back the large meteorite which I left in Melville Bay. While I have had sufficient experience to know that implicit confidence cannot always be placed upon what one sees in the papers, I think it best to repeat what I said in my first letter, that there may be no possible chance for any future misunderstanding.

The large meteorite which I left last summer owing to lack of proper appliances for its removal is mine by the right of discovery just as much as those that I did bring back. Further I shall send a ship for the meteorite next summer.

As for the North Pole if it be true that you are going after it, you have my best wishes for your success & safety."[3]

Peary eventually secured "The Tent" (later renamed "Ahnighito"), the largest meteorite recovered to that time, in the summer of 1897. In 1905 Josephine Peary sold all three meteorites to Mrs. Morris K. Jesup, who gave them to the American Museum of Natural History where they still stand.

Dyche's declaration to mount an expedition to the North Pole was in earnest. "Give me ten physically perfect men and equip me with provisions enough to last ten years and I will discover the North Pole," he told reporters.[4] While he did not believe that ten years would be required to reach the Pole, he felt that a ten-year supply of provisions was necessary for a methodical, safe approach. "The sole and fatal obstacle which has stopped Arctic explorers from finding the pole is not cold, but hunger," he stated. "Give me plenty to eat, and I can get to the North pole as easily as I got within 800 miles of it [on the *Kite*]. Good old fashioned 'grub' should be the watchword of the Arctic explorer."[5]

Dyche's plan called for a ship to plow north through the Baffin Bay ice. On Greenland's northwest coast he would stockpile provisions and establish a permanent base. Using whaleboats, Dyche and his men would methodically transport a chain of smaller caches further up the coast, each a day's travel apart. The greatest time and effort in the expedition would be devoted to moving provisions north. Food was cheap, Dyche reasoned; better to spend a great deal of time preparing for the final journey than risk loss of life. "Success lies in going slow and taking good care of your men, feeding them well, and not allowing them to become fatigued," he asserted. "Nor am I going to eat dog or chew walrus hide to keep from starving."

"I have been quoted as saying that finding the North Pole was not a difficult thing," he continued. "I don't think I said that. It is not easy, but I think it is possible, and the secret is—plenty of provisions. The Kansas papers joke me about that. It's a way

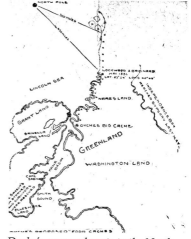

Dyche's proposed route to the North Pole. He hoped that land might be discovered to the north of Greenland, thus making the trip easier. From the Kansas City Star, *December 22, 1895. (University of Kansas Archives)*

we have in Kansas—this joking a man on a serious proposition, but expecting him to accomplish it just the same. One paper called my scheme the 'Plum Pudding Route,' and said that I would walk a mile and eat terrapin and plum pudding, then walk another mile and eat a sponge cake and tutti-frutti, and so go stuffing myself until I reached the North pole the victim of dyspepsia and gout. But no matter, my idea is that failures have been made because of lack of provisions and not from extreme cold."[6]

Dyche proposed to remain in north Greenland for approximately five years, placing caches, securing additional provisions by hunting game, learning hunting and sledge-driving techniques from the Eskimos, and exploring the northern coast of Greenland before making his cautious trek across the polar ice. He hoped to find islands between the northern coast of Greenland and the Pole on which he could place additional caches. To shorten the distance traveled over ice, Dyche set the jumping-off point for the final leg of the journey at Independence Bay, the point Peary, Henson, and Lee had reached on their 1895 journey across Greenland. Dyche intended for his expedition, unlike Peary's, to travel along the shoreline of Greenland instead of crossing the barren ice cap.

For transportation, Dyche rejected such suggestions as a hot air balloon, donkeys, or vehicles propelled by gasoline and coal-dust combustion. "I shall pin my faith to the dogs," he declared. "Without dogs the journey to the pole will never be made." As for the members of his expedition, Dyche insisted, "Not one of them shall use tobacco or spirits. These create thirst, which is often inconvenient and time wasting, and sometimes dangerous . . . . I shall take no heavy men. Lean, healthy men will stand the work better and not be so liable to accident. I shall also have a large force of Esquimaux."[7] Dyche felt that Eskimos were essential to an attempt on the Pole. They were expert sledge drivers and were accustomed to living in the harsh climate and terrain. Dyche proposed that all members of his party adopt "the living, diet, and mode of travel of Eskimos."[8]

It is uncertain how Dyche intended to finance the expedition. He suggested that he had "several wealthy friends in New York" who were willing to back the venture, but he would not reveal their identities.[9] Some newspapers reported that he would receive funding from the University of Chicago and the Chicago Columbian Museum. Dyche also pointed out that recovery of the Cape York meteorite would help finance the expedition.

In retrospect, many elements of Dyche's plan seem self-evident, but at the time they were not so obvious. Dyche's proposal to use Eskimos was discredited by Hugh Lee, who had more experience in Arctic exploration than Dyche. Because Eskimos had abandoned Lee, Peary, and Henson on their trek across the Greenland ice cap, Lee thought it foolhardy to rely on Eskimo participation in an attempt on the Pole. "We lived with the Eskimos for two years and found them a race of home-loving people," Lee stated. "Professor Dyche would find it hard indeed to take a force of them away from their homes." Lee also discredited Dyche's proposal to push a ship so far north, asserting, "There is not one year in ten that a ship may count upon being able to reach Fort Conger."[10] And not all explorers were convinced that dogs were the best mode of transportation for polar travel, as evidenced by Robert F. Scott's use of ponies and motor sledges on his tragic 1912 expedition to the South Pole.

But Dyche's Holsteinborg host, Governor Müller, believed that the plan was sound. "I am *quite of your opinion* that the first condition for getting up there is plenty of provisions and warmth," he wrote Dyche. "When a man has that, he will be able to stand a great deal, and when you take care to make short marches and not to get so much fatigued, I can see no reason why you should not be able to get as far up as there is any land."[11]

Dyche's public pronouncement that he would launch an expedition to the North Pole may have been one of the factors that induced Lieutenant Peary to do likewise. In January 1897 Peary outlined to the American Geographic Society his plan for attaining the Pole. Although Peary had worked in north Greenland for years, he had never expressed the desire or intention to make such an attempt, although the public naturally assumed that this was his ultimate goal. Peary's plan, which he coined "The Peary System," was in many respects similar to Dyche's. Peary proposed to take his party by ship to Whale Sound, hire Eskimos, and then break through the pack-ice to Sherard Osborne Fjord or further. There Peary would establish a base, placing caches in the same manner that Dyche had proposed (although devoting less time to the task) and hunting for fresh game before making the final attempt across the polar ice.

To support Peary in his bid for the Pole, several wealthy New York men, including Morris K. Jesup of the American Museum of Natural History, founded the Peary Arctic Club. In contrast to the Arctic Club formed by passengers of the *Miranda* cruise, the Peary Arctic Club's sole purpose was to ensure that Peary would be the first man to reach the Pole. Membership dues were one thousand dollars per year. Dyche maintained his membership in the less prestigious Arctic Club by paying one dollar a year, which covered mailing expenses.

Dyche began to give lectures describing his experiences in Greenland and his plans for a North Pole expedition. The lectures were so popular that Dyche hired his lawyer, Eldie F. Caldwell, a former state representative, as his manager. Posters were printed flaunting Dyche's profile and long locks. A lecture tour across Kansas was undertaken, with Caldwell its advance man. Dyche brought "polar fever" to Kansas, and the contagion spread.

The Board of Regents, irritated with Dyche's neglect of his teaching duties while on the lecture tour, declared that the length of his hair was inappropriate for a member of the university faculty (Dyche had not

The Dyche family ca. 1895: Ruth, Walter, Ophelia, and the infant, Lewis, Jr. (University of Kansas Archives)

had his hair cut since leaving for Greenland in May 1895) and ordered him to have it cut. It is indicative of his repute that numerous newspapers across the state covered the noteworthy event.

Lucile Baker, who wrote a column for the *Topeka State Journal* under the pen name of "Becky Sharp," interviewed the Dyche family at their home in February 1896. Three-month-old Lewis Lindsay, Jr.[12] lay on a polar bear rug in the center of the sitting room; two-year-old Ruth sat on Miss Sharp's lap; and four-year-old Walter played near his mother. Miss Sharp described Mrs. Dyche as "a dear little home body, with the most domestic tastes imaginable." Mrs. Dyche was reluctant to discuss her husband's proposed North Pole expedition. "I don't like to talk about the North Pole," she told Miss Sharp tearfully. "It makes me a widow and my children fatherless. Why should I?"

But Lewis Dyche was more than willing to discuss it, although he side-stepped Miss Sharp's repeated requests to accompany the expedition. Showing her a handful of letters, Dyche told her, "I get a great many applications from people who want to go. I had one today from a woman who wanted a place for her 14 year old son, and desired that I take him with me when I go again. Here's another from a boy also. He says, 'I am as good as the average boy and I hope you will consider my application.' As good as the average boy!" Dyche laughed. "I expect he is, and if I wanted a boy, I expect I'd take him." "Becky Sharp" left the Dyche home certain that the professor would "discover for himself a real Kansas United States of America North Pole and exhibit it duly stuffed and mounted in the Kansas University Museum . . . ."[13]

William T. Hornaday, too, was convinced that Dyche's proposal to mount a North Pole expedition was fully serious, and he pleaded with Dyche to abandon the scheme, writing, "I have talked about you amongst all sorts and conditions of men,—and assured many good citizens that Professor Dyche, the Intrepid, is far too valuable a man to be spared for the all-devouring, ever-greedy maw of Arctic Exploration. I read your *Herald* article with avidity, your *Cosmopolitan* article with delight, and your intention to try for that d - - d pole—with genuine dismay! . . . I have been praying (as heathens pray) that the rumor of [Nansen's] pole-finding is true, and that you are so completely forestalled that there will be no excuse whatever for you to

> Leave your home & country,
> Blow in a lot of good money,
> Bury yourself in God-forsaken Greenland,
> Rob your Wife of a lover,
> Rob your children of a father,
> Rob yourself of Everything
> and Waste three to five valuable years,
> all for   _____
>   000.00 !

"In my opinion, the North Pole is a delusion and a snare. It is a devil's bait to a horrible man-trap. It is a fraudulent old stick, cross-grained, knotty, and rotten at the heart. Even if found, it is not worth a frozen toe from a first-class man, let alone an American life. Be sensible. Stay within reach of your charming wife and lovely children, and leave the infernal old pole to rot in Arctic darkness."[14]

For several months it appeared that Lewis Dyche intended to conquer the

North Pole or die trying. His expedition never materialized, however, and gradually he ceased to mention it. Dyche's detractors would allege that he never seriously intended to mount such an expedition, that he was merely cashing in on the publicity it brought him. Dyche himself mentioned to Becky Sharp, "Do you know I call this the guying age? Everything is made an opportunity for us to guy each other. . . . I'm constantly asked, 'When are you and Becky Sharp going to start to the North Pole?' I always say, 'Not this week, anyway,' or something like that."[15] It is possible that Dyche was merely "guying" the public about his North Pole plans, or perhaps he was merely getting Peary's goat. But friends and family were convinced of his sincerity. Perhaps, as he pondered the expedition, Dyche came to the realization that he was not an explorer in the traditional sense of the word (his lecture flyers notwithstanding). He was not a discoverer of new lands, but of new facts. His realm of exploration was to add to the systematic knowledge of the animals he collected. Despite being tempted by the "Devil's bait" of the North Pole, Dyche elected to persevere in collecting mammals.

It came as a surprise to the Kansas press when Dyche abruptly abandoned his lecture tour on June 2 to undertake an expedition to Alaska. Some newspapers speculated that his trip was not a collecting expedition but a secret dash for the North Pole. Topeka newspapers called the collecting expedition a ruse, insisting that Dyche's "game" was the large meteorite in Greenland. Such stories not only had Dyche traveling to Greenland via the unlikely route of Alaska, they had him navigating the Northwest Passage to get there. (The Northwest Passage had not yet been traversed and would not until Roald Amundsen accomplished the feat in 1906—and Amundsen's journey required three years!)

Newspapers throughout the country picked up the Topeka story, and a fantastic "race for the meteorite" was on. The farther the story strayed from Kansas, the more outlandish it became. The *Buffalo Commercial* reported that "Lieut. Peary . . . claimed the meteorite by right of discovery, and warned the professor not to attempt to move it. As the meteorite weighs dozens of tons, Peary's warning was of necessity heeded at the time, but Prof. Dyche stated distinctly that he intended within a few years to return to Greenland for the meteorite."[16] Other newspapers, while skeptical of the story, carried it nevertheless: "Dismissing the class and ramming a change of underwear into his bag, the professor ran to the depot and took a ticket for Seattle. From that point he will . . . start for Bering strait and thence take the northwest passage to Greenland."[17] The *Denver Times* conceded that Dyche really had gone to Alaska, but declared that his mission was "to learn something of the truth of the stories which are told of a living mastadon in the upper valley of the Yukon river."[18]

In truth, Dyche sought the white Dall's sheep. After four days of traveling by train (pausing to visit the Custer battlefield), he arrived in Seattle. He collected invertebrates for two weeks in Puget Sound and then booked passage to Sitka on the steamer *City of Topeka*. From Sitka he took the ship *Dora* to a trading outpost near Homer, on Cook's Inlet.

There Dyche met Creasing, an agent for the Alaska Commercial Company who operated a trading post on the Knik River in the Talkeetna Mountains. Creasing told Dyche that white sheep could be found in mountains beyond his trading post, and he offered to ferry Dyche upriver in his sloop. "It was a tough journey," Dyche recorded. "The tides and whirlpools and sand flats all conspire against the sailor. The tides go out and leave boats stuck in the mud. They come in with a roar, a wall of solid green water that bears down upon the boat struck in the mud. When the wave strikes the boat over it goes, and a man would have as much chance for his life in the Niagra rapids. Hundreds of men are drowned in it every year. . . . Creasing knew the tides thoroughly, however, and we got to his camp safely."[19]

With Creasing's help, Dyche outfitted a boat and hired four Indian guides to take him to the head of the river. That stretch of river was covered by great sand and mud flats, and the Indians had to drag the boat much of the way. Mosquitoes were rife. In the Talkeetna Mountains at the head of the river, Dyche set up camp and made several short one- and two-day hunts for sheep. He had luck immedi-

ately in killing ewes and lambs but had to climb higher to find rams. He found the hunting particularly tricky because if he shot an animal where it would fall down the mountain, it would be disfigured, broken, and worthless for his purposes. Dyche collected seventeen sheep in all: *Ovis dalli,* named for their discoverer, William H. Dall of the Smithsonian Institution. They were a well-defined variety, rarely collected and, Dyche claimed, not displayed in any museum.

Dyche took numerous photographs of the Indians and their camps. Like the Greenland Eskimo children, the young Knik Indians were terrified of his camera equipment. Dyche met an elderly woman who had been spurned by her clan, left in a tent to starve. Dyche gave her food, but he believed that she would not live long after he had gone.

Dyche paused in several towns on his return trip. In Kodiak he paid $240 for a collection of twenty-five sheep heads and a collection of moose and caribou

The notorious Tlingit Indian Princess Tom. (Courtesy University of Kansas Archives)

antlers. He thought the price cheap, having learned how costly it was to hire Indian labor to carry the specimens from the mountains. In Sitka he visited Florence Campbell, an Indian woman who had studied at Haskell Indian College in Lawrence. Miss Campbell introduced Dyche to Princess Tom, a wealthy Tlingit Indian. Princess Tom had made her fortune, some fifty thousand dollars, by trading molasses, sugar, flour, and other cheap goods she procured in Sitka to the Indians for valuable artifacts, which she in turn sold for large profits to tourists and other white men passing through the port city. Her grand house and Princess Tom herself were tourist attractions. She sold Dyche two woven baskets that she claimed she had made with her own hands—but she was notoriously unscrupulous in trade. She recently had acquired her fifth husband, whom Dyche called "almost a boy," giving five hundred blankets and a small sum of cash to the boy's father.

Dyche asked permission to photograph Princess Tom. At first she declined, but she relented when he convinced her that no one would want to look at her after she became old and wrinkled (she was in her mid-sixties). When he returned the next day to take the photograph, she had put on a red dress and was sporting nine bracelets made of ten-dollar gold pieces, five bracelets made of twenty-dollar gold pieces, and a necklace made of five- and ten-dollar pieces. After being photographed, Princess Tom took from her finger a silver ring set in turquoise, engraved with a bear's head, and placed it on Dyche's hand. A New York newspaper later reported that Princess Tom intended to buy Dyche as her sixth husband.

DASHING KANSAN!

Prof. L. L. DYCHE,

At the Melvern Opera House, Feb. 8,

AFTERNOON AND NIGHT.

Prof. Dyche is now the most popular Arctic Explorer, and Melvern feels proud that she has secured him for Saturday, February 8.

Beginning in South Greenland, he carries you

TO THE NORTH POLE,

with 400 illustrations, taken from Nature. Don't miss the opportunity.

Tickets on sale at all business houses in the city.

Poster promoting an 1896 lecture. (University of Kansas Archives)

10 "Dashing Kansan!" The Magic Lantern Lectures

In the nineteenth century, writers, preachers, showmen, professors, and explorers (including Frederick Cook and Robert E. Peary) traveled from town to town edifying and entertaining the public for profit. Imitating the Chautauqua Literary and Scientific Circle established at Lake Chautauqua, New York, small communities organized their own "Chautauquas" to meet annually and educate the adult public. The first such Chautauqua in Kansas, organized by Presbyterian minister Duncan C. Milner, was held at Bismarck Grove near Lawrence.

For some time university faculty had delivered lectures in Kansas towns. In the fall of 1891 some of those lectures were organized into regular courses: twelve weeks, one lecture each week, featuring some of the strongest members of the faculty. The Board of Regents urged professors to participate in this "University Extension," a forerunner of Continuing Education, to remind them that they were servants of the state, and to invigorate their minds "by contact with men and women in practical life."[1]

Lewis Dyche took part in the University Extension lecture series, but for many years he had also lectured independently. As early as January 1887 he gave a schoolhouse lecture describing a New Mexico collecting expedition, and the following month he audaciously told hunting stories to Indian students at the Haskell Institute. Following the World's Columbian Exposition, Dyche delivered a lecture at Plymouth Congregational Church in Lawrence entitled "Behind the Curtains at the Fair." And after his return from the 1895 Greenland expedition, he delivered lectures across Kansas describing his experiences in Holsteinborg and with the Peary Relief Expedition, illustrated by "magic lantern slides," glass-plate slides he had taken in Greenland.

On returning from his Alaskan expedition, Dyche undertook a lecture tour more ambitious than the one he had made in the spring: six months of lectures in towns throughout Kansas. Lantern-slide-illustrated lectures were popular in the 1890s, as evidenced by a Sears, Roebuck catalog of the era that offered lantern-slide projectors and ready-made slide shows, complete with a printed lecture script, a thousand advertising posters, and two thousand admission tickets. Small-town people generally expected lectures to be solemn and educational; they filled lecture halls with the aim of self-improvement as much as entertainment. Dyche's programs fulfilled that purpose, although he was careful to heed the rallying cry of

Dyche's stock poster for his 1895–96 lecture tour.

William T. Hornaday: "Make her *Popular.*"

Dyche's lawyer and former classmate, Eldie F. Caldwell, served as his advance man, placing advertisements in newspapers and taking with him from town to town some of Dyche's mementos from Greenland and Alaska—a mannequin clothed in Eskimo sealskins, eiderdown robes, sealskin garments and boots, Eskimo dolls, a cradleboard, a narwhal tusk, and other curios—to exhibit in storefront windows.[2] Stunning posters for Dyche's lectures featured the Garber photographs of him in his Arctic attire. Handbills and flyers usually exaggerated his exploits. One handbill for a lecture to benefit a town's high school library proclaimed him "The Greatest Hunter On The Continent—in Costume." An Effingham flyer touted Dyche's "renowned lecture on Perils of the Explorer in the Arctic regions" for its high school lecture course: "Dr. Dyche has made 16 expeditions into the Arctic Zone and has killed more of the large animals of that region than any man now living. On his last expedition he was shipwrecked and suffered extreme privation for ten days." A Melvern handbill read: "Prof. Dyche is now the most popular Arctic Explorer, and Melvern feels proud that she has secured him for Saturday, February 8." The flyer for a Beloit lecture read: "HE IS COMING! . . . His recent Arctic explorations have made his name a household word throughout the nation, and the fact that he came nearer reaching the North Pole than any of his predecessors, gives him the place at the 'head of the class' of

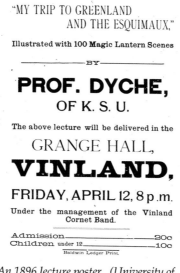

"MY TRIP TO GREENLAND AND THE ESQUIMAUX,"

Illustrated with 100 Magic Lantern Scenes

———— BY ————

PROF. DYCHE,
OF K. S. U.

The above lecture will be delivered in the

GRANGE HALL,

VINLAND,

FRIDAY, APRIL 12, 8 p.m.

Under the management of the Vinland Cornet Band.

Admission_____20c
Children under 12_____10c

Baldwin Ledger Print

An 1896 lecture poster. (University of Kansas Archives)

Arctic explorers."

A gifted promoter, Caldwell was proficient in drawing attention to his client. An Emporia newspaper remarked, "For many years Emporia people have been taught to believe that Dick House, the hardware drummer, is the noisiest man in the world. This is a myth. Eddie [sic] Caldwell, the manager of Dyche, is so noisy that he makes Dick House sound like a piano with the soft pedal on. Caldwell was in town today and the fire department made five runs mistaking his laugh for the alarm."[3] A man who placed advertisements and distributed flyers for Caldwell in Washington, Kansas, boasted that Dyche had been advertised "as extensively as . . . Pears Soap."[4]

Local newspapers did little to dispel the fervor for Dyche's lectures. A headline in the *Kansas City Times* read, "Lecture on the North Pole; Prof. Dyche Has Been There and Knows All About It."[5] The *Emporia Gazette* reported, "Mr. Dyche is today the best advertised man in the west. He gets more money for his lectures than Mr. Ingalls.[6] That is because he has a story to tell and tells it well. His lecture will pack the Whitley for twice. There has been no greater advance sale this winter . . . . Everyone is going. The collection of furs and northern relics is attracting a big crowd. Dyche's lecture will be the biggest thing Emporia has seen this year."[7]

Titles for Dyche's illustrated lectures included "Camp-Fires of a Naturalist in Alaska," "Greenland and the Arctic Regions," "Wild Animals of North America,"

"Scenes from the Land of the Midnight Sun," "The Arctic Highlanders and the Problem of the Pole," "Land of the Earthquake and Volcano, or Life and Conditions in the Interior of Alaska," "Perils of the Explorer in the Arctic Regions," "My Trip to Greenland and the Esquimaux," "A Hundred Pictures and a Hundred Stories," and "Hunting Anecdotes, Wise and Otherwise." One lecture, "Wild Animals and their Haunts," was designed especially for schoolchildren, although Dyche offered a children's version of his lectures at matinee performances. For the

An 1896 lecture poster. (University of Kansas Archives)

latter, Dyche appeared in sealskin costume.

The lectures were illustrated by glass-plate slides Dyche had taken in Greenland and Alaska. Photography had been Dyche's hobby for some time. In 1884, the year he received his bachelor's degrees, he had founded a university photography club, and since the early 1890s he had made a practice of taking a field camera with him on expeditions. Photographs of a freshly killed specimen were imminently useful to a taxidermist, and Dyche also photographed the animal's habitat. The scenic and enthnological photographs and the visions of exotic locales held a fascination for Kansas audiences.

The lantern slides were made by projecting the five-by-seven-inch dry-plate negative onto a 3 1/4-by-4-inch glass plate coated with a dry albumen gelatin emulsion. The emulsion was protected by a glass cover of the same size, its edges bound together with pasted paper tape. That process usually was carried out by Elbert S. Tucker of Lawrence, who frequently performed photographic work for the university.[8] Dyche hand-tinted many of the black-and-white slides himself to produce a colorful effect. The lantern slides were illuminated by calcium light (an intense white flame produced by incandescent lime) and projected onto an eighteen-by-twenty-foot canvas screen. Cylinders of calcium gas were shipped to the town where Dyche was lecturing by the Kollman Brothers Kansas City Calcium Light Company. Eldie Caldwell or Charles Bunker operated the stereopticon projector. The stereopticon directed two lamps at the screen so that light could be cut off from one lamp while light from the other was allowed to fall on the screen, thus producing the effect of one picture dissolving into another. Posters advertised that Dyche had over 500 slides, but he showed no more than 100 to 150 in a single

*An 1896 lecture poster. (University of
Kansas Archives)*

lecture.

Newspapers gave varying accounts of Dyche's style of lecturing. The *Abilene Reflector* called him "one of the stammerers . . . but with a good story to tell. . . ."[9] Some complained that he spoke too quickly, and some that he spoke too long. The secretary of a Wichita mortgage company wrote Caldwell: "The Professor tries to do too much in the limited time he has at his command. He delivers a lecture a good deal as he hunts bears, gathers beetles, or prepares a Latin or Greek lesson. He does it with all the energy that is in him. This suggestion is made, and it strikes me to be a very reasonable one, that if the Professor would speak not longer than one hour and a half, and speak slowly and distinctly so that all the persons in the house could understand and mentally assimilate, the lecture would give much greater satisfaction."[10]

Most accounts flattered Dyche's performances. His vivid narratives, his self-deprecating humor, and the colorful lantern slides attracted large audiences. Dyche consistently filled lecture halls, opera houses, churches, and school auditoriums, and frequently he was invited for return engagements. Speaking as a guest of the Modoc Club of Topeka, he lectured in Hamilton Hall, a facility intended to accommodate fifteen hundred persons but that held eighteen hundred the night he lectured. The aisles were full, the stage was crowded, and many persons were forced to stand. The *Topeka Capital* reported, "The lecturer announced that he would attempt to cram two lectures into one. . . . Naturally he is a rapid talker, but last night he outdid former efforts. He used words at the rate of over 200 a minute. It was a conscientious effort to tell all he could in the allotted time—and tell it

PROFESSOR L. L. DYCHE,

NATURALIST AND EXPLORER

In his famous lectures at THE ROHRBAUGH,

Friday, April 17th, '96.

Students' Matinee, 4 p. m.   Admission 15 and 25 cents.
Evening Lecture, 8 p. m.   Admission 15, 25 and 35 cents.
Reserved Seats for Evening Only.

The program for one of Dyche's lectures.
(University of Kansas Archives)

interestingly."[11] Dyche's presentation that evening lasted two and a half hours.

Dyche did not use notes, although he did compose a stock introduction to his lectures:

"Ladies and gentlemen,

The idea of building up a fine collection of mammals and birds for the state at the University of Kansas has been an ambition with me for many years. Specimens enough have already been collected to fill a large-sized building if they could be put on exhibition and properly arranged.

While visiting different parts of the continent in search of these specimens I have had some experiences which will never be blotted from my memory: The killing of my first deer in New Mexico, my first bear in the Spanish Mountains, big horn sheep in Washington, mountain goat in British Columbia, elk in Colorado, moose in Manitoba, seal in Davis Strait, polar bear in Melville Bay, walrus in Kane Basin, and white sheep in the Alaska mountains, might be mentioned as a few of the exciting events which have attended my expeditions.

The pleasure of the chase spurred on by the scientific interest I have always had in North American animals turned days, weeks, and months of what otherwise would have been considered the hardest kind of labor into intensely interesting work."[12]

Dyche's Greenland lectures began with a brief description of the *Miranda* excursion, then a recounting of his 1895 expedition to Holsteinborg. He illustrated the life-style of West Greenland Eskimos with lantern slides. Then he narrated Lieutenant Peary's crossing of the Greenland ice cap and the voyage of the *Kite* to relieve the Peary party. The walrus hunt with Peary off Herbert Island was described in detail, complete with dialogue, and it figured prominently in newspaper accounts of the lectures. "The description of the walrus hunt was very vivid and thrilling," wrote the *Norton Champion*. "While we were personally gratified that the professor escaped alive, yet we could not but sympathize with the poor walrus whose battle for her babe was as heroic as though her affections were held a sacred matter by the cruelty of scientific exactions."[13] Dyche concluded the lectures by displaying a map and addressing the problems of mounting an expedition to the North Pole, outlining his own "plum pudding" route.

Dyche's lecture tour kept him on the rails. A page from his pocket diary shows, for example, that he lectured in Beloit on April 1, 1897; in Stockton on April 2; Cawker City on April 3; Concordia on April 5; Washington on April 6; Marysville on April 7; Sabetha on April 8; and Wetmore on April 10. Ticket prices were fifteen and twenty-five cents for children and twenty-five and fifty cents for adults. In the smaller towns Dyche took in about fifty-five dollars a day in ticket sales for one matinee and one evening lecture. Daily expenses for his manager, train fares, hotels, meals, advertisements, and calcium gas consumed much of the profit. Additionally, Dyche paid an instructor to teach his classes while he was away from the university.

Not all his lectures were for profit. Dyche gave many to promote worthy causes, such as school libraries and athletic clubs. In Lawrence, although he was an opponent of the newly introduced game of football, he gave a benefit lecture for the Kansas University Athletic Association.

An enraptured young fan carefully printed:

DEAR PROF DYCHE

EVERY SINCE THAT TIME US HAVE BEEN TO THE LECTURE ON GREENLAND US HAVE BEEN PLAYING PROF DYCHE KILLING WALRUSES. BEN ASKED MAMA IF THAT LONG STICK WHAT WAS IN YOU HAND WAS THE NORTH POLE. I DID AJOY YOU LECTURE. I WOULD LIKE TO BE A LITTLE ESKIMO BECAUSE I WANT TO GO TO BED WHEN I WANT TO.

DEAR-LOVE-OF-ESTHER-HASKELL[14]

While on his lecture circuit Dyche suffered a gunshot wound in a Newton hotel. Bending over to untie his shoelaces before retiring, he was struck in the shoulder by a spent bullet shot through the ceiling by a drummer occupying the room above. Dyche was not hurt. The offender had been drinking Kansas whiskey, no doubt reinforcing Dyche's dim view of men who consumed hard liquor.[15]

On the evening of February 22, 1897, the Kansas state legislature met in Representative Hall to hear Dyche lecture on "Camp-Fires of a Naturalist in Alaska." The following day the *Topeka Daily Capital* noted sardonically that Professor Dyche was the one man who need not worry about his salary being cut. With the Populist Party controlling both houses of the legislature, the University of Kansas faced severe cuts in general appropriations, including faculty salaries. Dyche's invitation to lecture had been extended before the issue of faculty salaries had been raised. He did not mention the budget dispute during his appearance, although in previous weeks he had spoken against the proposed cuts. He was especially critical of a bill that would have compelled students to pay ten dollars in yearly tuition. "I am opposed to the plan and I know that it will work a great injustice to the barefooted boys of the state," Dyche charged. "By the barefooted boys I mean boys who are struggling to get through college and depending for the necessities of life upon what they can earn by working between recitation hours; just such fellows, for instance, as I was. . . . Instead of the state passing laws to compel the students to pay a tuition, it had better pass laws and make provision for assisting in every way possible the poor boys of the state in securing an education."[16]

When reporters raised the subject of the proposed salary cuts, Dyche told them, "All I need salary for is to hunt more animals. That is where my salary goes anyway, and if they will give me more money with which to search for additions to the university collection I will be satisfied." Asked if he thought his salary would be reduced, Dyche replied, "I don't know, but I suppose I will go down with the rest."[17] Dyche insisted that he would remain at the university even if his salary was cut in half, but when the appropriations bill passed both houses and became law on March 13, Dyche's was the only salary *not* to be cut. Chancellor Snow's $5,000 salary was reduced to $4,000, and full professors' salaries were reduced from $2,000 to $1,800 or $1,750.

Inevitably Dyche's retention of his whole salary stirred ill feelings among the faculty, especially since he was earning additional revenue from his lectures while neglecting his teaching duties. However, the financial basis for Dyche's collecting and taxidermic work always had been complex, and Chancellor Snow and the Board of Regents tended to be liberal with him. Dyche often financed his expeditions from his own salary or from the profits he made by trading surplus specimens or from his lectures. Although the Board of Regents might reimburse him for specimens or for a portion of his expedition expenses, he never could count on reimbursement, and he planned his expeditions and his finances accordingly. For example, after Dyche's return from the 1895 Greenland trip, the regents appropriated $125 for bear skins and $66 to pay an instructor who had taught Dyche's classes, but they declined to purchase the enormous egg collection Dyche had bought from Governor Müller. The egg collection therefore remained Dyche's, either to donate to the museum, to keep for himself, to sell and pocket the profits, or to sell and apply the profits toward another expedition. Furthermore, when the regents did reimburse Dyche for his expenses, the reimbursement usually came out of funds already earmarked for the Natural History Department, so when he accepted those funds he was depleting the resources necessary to run the depart-

Lewis Lindsay Dyche age 42. "Louis [sic] Lindsay Dyche, college professor, Arctic explorer, big game hunter and author, arrived in the city Friday after a three months' trip undertaken for the purpose of collecting specimens of natural history along the California coast. Professor Dyche will lecture before the Academy of Sciences tomorrow . . . . Still a young man, for he is scarcely 40, Professor Dyche believes that his knowledge of Arctic conditions, his strong constitution and experience in outdoor life in the roughest of regions will enable him to make a successful attempt to reach the North Pole . . ." The San Francisco Chronicle, *May 24, 1899. (University of Kansas Archives)*

ment. Such financial ambiguity permeated Dyche's professional life.

The state legislature left Dyche's salary intact, but the Board of Regents put an end to his lecturing for profit. On April 9, 1897, the regents issued an ultimatum, aimed at Dyche and Professor Lucien Blake (who had been delivering a popular series of lectures on electricity and magnetism), stating that no public lecture be given by a university professor for a profit of more than five dollars. The regents' ultimatum was effective: for the next several years, Dyche and Blake limited themselves to occasional weekend lectures. And they no longer charged admission.

Dyche spent the summer of 1897 at Monterey Bay, California, at the Hopkins Biological Institute of Leland Stanford University. Mrs. Dyche and the children accompanied him. The inevitable rumors were published that Dyche was again heading north, but the rumors were mild compared to those published during his previous expedition—these had him only going as far north as Alaska. Dyche studied morphology, cytology, and embryology at the Institute, and he collected marine invertebrates on Monterey Bay. During low tide he donned hip boots and waded the shoreline while Walter, nine, assisted him by carting the specimens away in a little red wagon. Father and son spent afternoons in a dory, Walter holding the boat steady as Dyche hung over the side with his head in a water glass (a bucket with a glass bottom), peering at the sea life. He used a net and a pole with a claw hook to secure specimens. Before returning to Lawrence in the fall, he had collected or purchased 1,000 starfish, 500 sea urchins, 1,000 squids, 500 sharks, 500 shark heads, 200 skates and rays, 300 hagfish, 25 ratfish, 1,000 crabs, 500 ascidians, 500 mussels, 25 jellyfish, 12 sea pens, 12 sea cucumbers, 100 abalones, 100 sea anemones, and "a great number" of eggs. Over a ton of material was shipped to Lawrence for use as study specimens.

In Lawrence Dyche continued to work on mammal specimens, teach anatomy and natural history classes, and lobby for a museum building. For the first time in his career, years passed unmarked by dramatic expeditions. Many of the articles he published in his lifetime were written during these years. Bound to campus by budgetary constraints, he became *Professor* Dyche. But Dyche was not a man to fade into the crowd. A stirring example of the power of his presence is an anonymous letter he received from a woman who had attended the funeral of a mutual friend: "I have always thought of you as one of the first men of the the Age—not only from hearing you spoken of by Ralph in terms of unqualified praise—but also from what I have read of your great learning and wisdom together with your wonderful researches and discoveries, both on land and sea—all of which will *immortalize your name*—but I never fully realized how *truly great* and *noble* you were, until I stood by the side of poor Ralph's grave, and just dreading to hear that sickening sound of the earth striking on the coffin lid,—when I saw you motion to your men to first throw on the beautiful oak branches before filling in the grave—*then* I knew that you were indeed one of *God's Noblemen!*—I shall never forget it! Never!!"[18]

Dyche spent the 1899 summer in Monterey, where he witnessed the systematic killing of California sea lions. For years fisherman had complained that sea lions ingested salmon and other food fish, and they eventually persuaded the state government to reduce the sea lion population. The killing already had started by the time Dyche arrived. He proceeded to open the stomachs of twenty killed sea lions in which he found squid and octopus, but no scaled fish. Five sea lions that he killed himself, for taxidermy, contained no fish either.

A 1901 study by the United States Fish Commission bore out Dyche's findings that the quantity of fish consumed by the sea lions was inconsiderable. In fact, they were consuming animals considered to be the fishermen's enemies. In *The American Natural History,* William T. Hornaday praised Dyche's observations and summarized the lesson to be learned: "Wild animals never should be destroyed on the strength of general opinions; for a supposed enemy may, on careful investigation, prove to be a friend."[19]

The Museum of Natural History under construction in 1902. (University of Kansas Archives)

11 Museum Builder

The University Charter of 1864 directed the Board of Regents to expend the funds necessary to erect "suitable buildings and . . . [a] cabinet of natural history." When the university first convened in 1866, a room of North College was reserved for the "cabinet of natural history," which contained "a scanty number of geological specimens."[1] But on September 14, 1866, the three-member faculty (Francis Huntington Snow, David H. Robinson, and Elial J. Rice) rode out to investigate "petrified turtles" that had been reported near Cameron's Bluff on the Kansas River. Robinson recalled, "I do not remember whether Professor Snow brought back any of those turtles or not; but I do remember that he and I rode so hard, and acted so much like boys, that we quite shocked our venerable President, who never thereafter could be induced to ride with us."[2]

Through such excursions as well as more serious collecting expeditions, Snow added to the collection until, when it moved to the University Hall (Fraser) in 1873, its birds, plants, minerals, insects, reptiles, and fishes filled a large room in the new building. Soon two rooms were filled. Then parts of both the second and third floors of University Hall were required to display "the cabinet." By 1884 the collection was so large that many specimens had to be stored. Snow Hall was dedicated in 1886, and "the cabinet" moved there early in 1887. Snow Hall provided rooms for an anatomical museum, an entomological museum, a geological museum, a herbarium, and a zoological museum, as well as classrooms, workshops, and laboratories.

The collection increased through the zeal of Snow and his students, especially Lewis Dyche. By 1884 Snow and Dyche made plans to assemble a special collection that ultimately would include all species of mammals and birds "not only of Kansas, but of the entire Rocky Mountain region."[3] Such a collection would comprise anywhere from 550 to 625 specimens, but Dyche gradually moderated the plan as he began to specialize in the collection and study of large mammals. Although he continued to collect birds, he concentrated his efforts on the collection of large mammals. Even so, he did not attempt to collect all species, and of the species of mammals he collected, he endeavored to include male, female, and young individuals. The collection was thus representative but not all encompassing. After the 1893 World's Columbian Exposition, Dyche expanded the geographic scope of his collection to include the entire North American continent.

The need for a new building to house the expanding collection had long been recognized. The first request for such a building came in 1892, as Dyche's mammals exhibit was being readied for shipment to the World's Columbian Exposition. Chancellor Snow advised the Board of Regents that when the collection returned from Chicago the natural history building would be "taxed to its utmost extent to give it shelter." Snow also intimated that a museum building might well be the price necessary to retain Dyche. "This building," wrote Snow, "should be appropriately planned for the most effective presentation to the students of the University and to the general public of the work of a Kansas boy who has achieved the highest excellence in taxidermic art yet attained in America."[4]

At the Chicago fair, J. M. Dunsmore, Speaker of the Kansas House of Representatives,[5] visited the Panorama of North American Mammals and assured Dyche that the next legislature would appropriate funds for a building to house the impressive collection. Other buildings took precedence, however. Professor Lucien I. Blake had stirred the interest of Kansans with his off-campus lectures on the wonder of the times, electricity, and the legislature appropriated fifty thousand dollars for the construction of a physics and electrical engineering building (named Blake Hall in 1898). The legislature also accepted a bequest from William B. Spooner (Snow's uncle) to construct a library building and a new chancellor's residence. The three buildings were completed by 1895.

In its 1894 biennial report to the governor, the Board of Regents cited the exhibition of North American mammals at the Columbian Exposition as "doubtless the most conspicuous" achievement of the university during the past two years. "The state can do nothing less than provide fireproof shelter for the gifts of her own sons. Nor can the university expect to retain the services of such men as Professors Dyche, Williston[6] and Haworth without furnishing the facilities for the satisfactory prosecution of their work."[7]

By 1895 Chancellor Snow's annual entreaty for a museum building assumed a dollars-and-cents approach. The natural history collections were valued at $107,958.25 (the odd 25 cents were attributable to a specimen in Snow's entomology collection). Dyche evaluated the mammals collection at $51,145. A new, fireproof building was essential if for no other reason than to safeguard university assets. Beyond their monetary value, however, Snow pointed out that the collections embodied "the personal labor of members of the University faculty, who have not only given their time in summer vacations to laborious service for the good of the University without recompense, but have also endangered life and health in visiting regions infested by hostile Indians, by malarial diseases and by pernicious extremes of heat and cold."[8]

Three years later the Board of Regents reiterated Snow's justifications for a new museum building in its eleventh biennial report. Assessing the aggregate monetary value of the collections to be "at least $150,000," it pointed out that the collections were stored in a building "of a dangerously combustible character," and that "on sound business principles" a fireproof structure should be erected.[9] In fact, on one summer evening in 1893 while the mammals exhibit was in Chicago, Professor Williston had discovered and extinguished a fire in the basement of Snow Hall.

Early in 1899 it was suggested that the university's collection of mammals be exhibited at the Paris world's fair, but state legislators decided that funds would be better spent in Kansas, on a museum building. During the 1899 legislative session, the state Senate Ways and Means Committee attached an amendment to a bill allocating $55,000 for a new chemistry building, which would have provided $65,000 for a natural history museum, but the amendment was overwhelmingly defeated in the House. A Jefferson County representative stated that he did not wish to go home and tell his constituents that the state could not provide a suitable place for its destitute insane, but could spend $65,000 "for a building to cover Dyche's dead animals."[10] Buck Dawes, Republican floor leader, also attacked the proposed amendment, declaring, "It's a shame that the professors come up here from that school and neglect their work to lobby for these buildings. We have given enough to that institution already."[11] But the Board of Regents, grateful for Dyche's lobbying efforts to secure the new chemistry building, moved to place a museum building atop its agenda.

By 1900 Chancellor Snow described the need for a museum building as urgent. He pointed out in his twelfth biennial chancellor's report that Snow Hall of Natural History originally encompassed the collections in zoology, botany, entomology, and geology, as well as laboratory and classroom space, at a time when Snow was the only professor of the natural sciences and Dyche was his only assistant. Now, in 1900, Snow Hall was occupied by four separate departments of natural science, six faculty members, and four instructors. Snow wrote, "With the present crowded condition of the museum and storerooms, not more than one-third of this building is available for purposes of instruction, yet every foot of space which it contains is needed for laboratory use. . . . On sound business principles, a fire-proof structure ample for the display and safe-keeping of these collections should be immediately provided. For the erection of such a building $100,000 will be required."[12]

Given the sums appropriated for university buildings to that time, Snow's one-hundred-thousand-dollar request for a museum building was extravagant. The chemistry building had cost fifty-five thousand dollars, Professor Blake's physics and electrical engineering building fifty thousand dollars, and Spooner Library seventy-five thousand dollars. The grand Snow Hall of Natural History had cost fifty thousand dollars in 1885. Nevertheless, the Board of Regents urged the governor to support Snow's request: "Does it need any argument to prove that it is the part of business prudence for the state to spend $100,000 to protect $150,000 worth of property?"[13]

Dyche lobbied vigorously for the building, commuting frequently to Topeka. "It is the Kansas way," he wrote to one member of the legislature, "and it is a good way, to get all she possibly can for her money. It is also a Kansas way, and it is a good way too, to take care of and keep a good thing when she gets it."[14] Dyche advised Regent Charles F. Scott, "It is much easier to interest members of the Legislature and people in general in this part [the mammals collection] of the museum. Other collections may be just as valuable to an educational institution but are not so easily explained or so attractive to the public."[15]

On March 1, 1901, the legislature appropriated funds for a natural history museum. Although the requested sum of one hundred thousand dollars was not achieved, the legislature granted seventy-five thousand dollars for the project. The bill passed both houses unanimously. The Board of Regents instructed Erasmus Haworth, Samuel Williston, and Lewis Dyche to meet with the Board to plan the building.

On the evening of April 18, 1901, the Board of Regents convened at the Eldridge House in Lawrence to view plans and receive bids from five architectural firms. Kansas City's Walter C. Root and George W. Siemens won the award. Walter C. Root was the brother of John Wellborn Root, consulting architect to the Columbian Exposition Committee and the man most responsible for the exposition's overall design. Root and Siemens designed the New England Office Building, the Santa Fe Railroad Office Building, and the Grace Episcopal Cathedral in Topeka; ten buildings at St. Marys College in St. Marys, Kansas; and in Kansas City the Scarrit Office Building, the Postal Telegraph Building, and the General Hospital. The regents decreed that the museum be located across the street and to the west of Spooner Library. And at that meeting Dyche's title was changed to "Professor of Systematic Zoology and Taxidermist for the University."

Bids for construction were opened in August. Henry Bennett of Topeka won the contract. Heating and plumbing were contracted to the Graeber Brothers of Lawrence. Ownership of the university's zoological specimens was established by the resolution: "Whereas Prof. Dyche claims certain specimens of various kinds in the University buildings as his personal property . . . Dyche has offered to accept $1000 in full of all claims against the University to any and all specimens of every kind, whether acquired by him or by purchase . . . ."[16]

Securing funds for a museum building was Francis Huntington Snow's last great achievement as chancellor. He had been unwell for several years, and his poor health, compounded by the death of his son, William Appleton Snow, left him enervated. (Will Snow, who as a boy had accompanied his father on numerous summer collecting expeditions, was working as a reporter for the *San Francisco Chronicle* on October 10, 1899, when he was swept off a small launch greeting a transport ship carrying a Kansas regiment returning from the Spanish-American War. His body never was recovered.) Extended leaves of absence did not improve Snow's health, and in the spring of 1901 he relinquished the chancellorship he had held for eleven years. He was appointed professor of meteorology, entomology, and paleontology. Frank Strong, president of the University of Oregon, was eventually selected as the new chancellor, and he assumed office on August 1, 1902.

Root and Siemens's design for the museum building was based on Dyche's conception. The architects wrote: "The plan as we present it is substantially Professor Dyche's and the arrangement proposed, though unique in our experience, entirely meets with our approval. We think the arrangement has many advantages over the conventional museum scheme." The plan called for the exterior to be built of economical materials. The texture of the rough-hewn limestone, laid in random courses, would complement the building's formal lines. The buff-colored limestone, the same stone used on Spooner Library, could be quarried locally. White limestone would be used for ornamentation, augmented by a mosaic band encircling the exterior. Root and Siemens specified that the mosaic be achieved by contrasting beige stucco and red brick in a stair-step pattern suggesting the shape of the letter "K." The roof would be composed of red clay pantiles, which, like the brickwork, probably were manufactured by the Lawrence Vitrified Brick and Tile Company.

Root and Siemens selected a Romanesque style for the building because of the Romanesque's eclectic, composite nature, because it required less detail work than a classical style and was therefore more economical, and because its ornamental complexion would allow the free use of natural motifs (they pointed out that the Fisheries Building at the World's Columbian Exposition had made such use of natural forms in its ornamentation). "We think the exterior should represent the uses of the building in its detail," the architects wrote.[17]

The entrance portal was modeled after that of the St. Trophime Cathedral in Arles, France, but the iconography of natural history was substituted for the religious icons of St. Trophime. The capitals of the six entrance columns, decorated with mythical animal and intricate plant motifs, support a frieze on which birds and beasts replace the procession of worshippers so prominent in the St. Trophime's frieze. The portal's archivolts (inner curves of an arch) contain animal figures such as the turtle, beetle, flying fish, bat, crane, salamander, elephant, and ox, as well as motifs drawn from classical and Christian iconography, such as the St. John's eagle, the laurel wreath, and *bucrania*. "Natural History Museum" and "1901" are incised in the lintel.

The entrance to the Museum of Natural History, modeled after the portal of the St. Trophime Cathedral of Arles, France. (University of Kansas Archives)

Two aedicules (house-like niches) articulate each side of the building. In classical architecture an aedicule consisted of two columns supporting an entablature and a pediment, and usually housed the statue of a god. Following the classical period, Christian builders placed statues of saints in aedicules. On the natural history museum building, the aedicules are "temples" dedicated to scholars and scientists who contributed to the field of natural history. The aedicule to the south of the entrance portal enshrines the name DARWIN (Charles Robert, 1809–82), the English naturalist famed for his theory of evolution. Aedicules on the south facade carry the names COPE (Edward Drinker, 1840–97), the American naturalist, collector, and editor; and AGASSIZ (Jean Louis Rodolphe, 1807–73), a Swiss-born Harvard professor. An authority on fossils, fish, and glacial geology, Agassiz stimulated the scientific study of nature in the United States. Aedicules on the north facade bear the names of GRAY (Asa, 1810–1888), the American botanist who advocated Darwin's ideas in the United States, and AUDUBON (John James, 1785–851), the famous ornithologist and painter of North American birds.[18] On the front facade to the north of the entrance is the name of the English surgeon and biologist HUXLEY (Thomas Henry, 1825–95), who was such an effective advocate of Darwin's theory that he became known as "Darwin's Bulldog." No names appear in the aedicules of the west (back) facade. Possibly they were intended to accommodate names in the future.

The apse, an important feature of Romanesque ecclesiastical architecture, dominates the museum's west facade and provides space for the Panorama of North American Mammals. Rising above the museum, a tower stands immediately north of the entrance portal. This 111-foot tower, a secular version of a Romanesque belltower, beckons visitors to the museum in the same way a bell would summon worshippers to a church.

The building's only representation of the human figure is a head of Apollo carved on the keystone of the entrance portal's topmost archivolt. Above the head of Apollo, decorating the central corbel supporting the portal roof, a carved owl[19] stares across Jayhawk Boulevard at a red sandstone owl in the Spooner Library gable. The owls engage the two buildings in learned conversation, inviting visitors: Enter Here For Wisdom.

Thirteen-hundred dollars were allocated for the ornamentation of the

building, and sculptor Joseph Frazee was hired for the task. Apparently his son Vitruvius assisted him in the work. Frazee incorporated details of university mythology that were not specified in the architects' working drawings. Oral tradition holds that Frazee allowed two students, Fred Pickett and Antonio Tommasini, to carve a jayhawk for the ornamentation. Robert Taft wrote in *Across the Years on Mount Oread:* "It is the feathered creature—said to be the original representation of the Jayhawk—with wings outspread that stands on a skull placed at the top of one of the four entrance columns of the Museum."[20] But years later Tommasini denied the rumor, reporting that he had merely dressed Frazee's tools and had taken no part in the sculpting.[21]

The first visual representation of the mythical jayhawk? (Photo by Sonya Brock)

Anyone looking for Taft's jayhawk will not find it atop the four entrance columns. There are two birds on a frieze above the north portal column, but there is no skull, and one of the birds is an owl, the other an eagle. Similar birds are depicted elsewhere on the building. However, a bird in the Darwin aedicule does perch on a skull (on the capital of the inside-right column). To the right of the skull the deeply incised letters "KU" guide the viewer's eye to a creature under the bird on the right: It appears to be a big-beaked, round-eyed jayhawk head, carved in a comic style unlike any of the building's other decorations. It is, possibly, the earliest surviving representation of the jayhawk. A popular conceptualization of the K.U. mascot did not fix itself in the public mind for another ten years, when Henry Maloy, a student artist for the *Daily Kansan* and *The Jayhawker,* depicted it as a friendly, large-beaked bird wearing heavy work shoes.

It is fitting that the university yell, originated by members of the Science Club, is prominently carved in the building's decorations, because Lewis Lindsay Dyche was without a doubt the yell's most enthusiastic yeller. In the wilderness he shouted his triumphs out loud, and in his note-books he wrote: "Hurrah for good luck; for Ophelia & Walter; for old K. S. U.; for Prof. Snow and for the regents too!!" After killing six bull walrus off the coast of Greenland, he shouted, "Whoop, Hurrah, Rock Chalk Jayhawk K. U." And when he arrived at the Chicago fairgrounds in 1892, he and his student assistants greeted a welcoming crowd

Henry Maloy's 1912 caricature of the jayhawk. (University of Kansas Archives)

by singing "Stand up for Kansas" and delivering "our old Kansas University yell, which set the crowds to howling and the dogs to barking . . . ." The words to the yell appear on shields held by three chimera-like gargoyles: On the south side of the building a shield reads "Rock Chalk." To the left of the entrance another reads "J Hawk?"[22] And to the right of the entrance the yell is concluded: "K.U."

Although unfinished, on October 17, 1902, the new museum building served as the setting for Frank Strong's installation as chancellor. Lawrence was full of visitors for the event, and throughout town the university colors could be seen. The apse, temporarily cleared of scaffolding, served as an auditorium. William A. Griffith, professor of art, supervised the building's embellishment, and students were granted a three-day holiday to make preparations. At one end of the apse a rostrum was erected, and seats were provided for twenty-five hundred guests. Classes and societies covered the unfinished columns with bunting, drapes, banners, emblems, and autumn foliage. After Strong's inauguration, at eight that evening a thousand guests attended a "luncheon." The apse was lined with tables, and 150 female students dressed in white served. Twelve-hundred incandescent and arc lights, including garlands of electric lamps strung between the pillars, were provided by Professor Blake's electrical-engineering students to illuminate the banquet.

As part of Strong's inauguration, Bailey Hall, which had been in service for about one year, was dedicated. Strong's inauguration in the new museum building seems to have served as its de facto dedication.[23]

When construction was completed, Dyche began work on the interior. The main floor included the mammals exhibit, the grand entrance, a custodian's office, and the guide's room. There was a small library in the bay above the custodian's office. The basement housed the taxidermist's shop, classrooms, storerooms, and a skeleton room. The mezzanine floor overlooked the panorama, and an ornithologi-

Frank Strong's installation as chancellor in the unfinished museum building on October 17, 1902. Drawing by H. Wood, from the Kansas City Star, *October 19, 1902. (University of Kansas Archives)*

cal display was planned for the main room on the second story. A six-foot-wide gallery maximized wall space for cabinets of bird specimens. Paleontological and entomological specimens were displayed on the third floor. Fireproof plasterboard and concrete floors were employed throughout the building.

Dyche's self-education in taxidermic display was extensive. He had visited museums in 1887 and again prior to the *Miranda* cruise in 1894 and his voyage to west Greenland in 1895. He studied the Carnegie Museum in Pittsburgh, the Philadelphia Museum, the Wister Institute of Anatomy in Philadelphia, the American Museum of Natural History in New York, the National Museum in Washington, D.C., the Chicago Academy Museum, and the Field Columbian Museum in Chicago. He sketched exhibits, noting the grouping of animals, groundwork, foliage, and especially the lighting—whether it was natural or artificial—and the proximity of windows and skylights to the exhibits. His specifications for the building were the result of thorough study combined with his original ideas.

He designed the panorama to display the mammals in a "natural" environment. To provide room for a variety of settings (including vertical separation), he called for a main display room (72' x 132') on the first floor to extend into a vaulted apse (72' x 54') on the west end of the building. It was to be lit by natural light, admitted by wells through the higher stories and diffused to minimize fading of specimens.

By the summer of 1903 Dyche was overseeing the installation of the natural history collections into the new building. He was not distracted from the task by an invitation from Dr. Frederick Cook to join an expedition to climb Mount McKinley. "I know that your heart and soul will be in this project," Cook wrote the forty-six-year-old Dyche, "but I fear your health would not permit your going. What do you think about it? You have had so much experience in this kind of work and in this part of Alaska. Are you willing to offer us some suggestions?"[24]

Had Dyche gone with Cook to Mount McKinley in 1903, he would have been disappointed. Cook's party traveled along the base of the mountain, found no climbable route, and gave up. The expedition was marked by petty bickering. Cook tried again in 1906, but again found no access to the peak. The party left him and a packer, Edward Barrill, at the base of the mountain. When Cook returned to civilization a few weeks later he announced that he had reached the summit of Mount McKinley.

Professor Snow took an office on the third floor of the new museum building alongside his entomological collections. Apparently there was friction between Dyche and Snow, perhaps resulting from Snow's physical collapse. Clyde Kenneth Hyder summarized the situation in *Snow of Kansas:* "To imply that during his last years Snow's serenity was unbroken would be to suggest that he was less than human. Nobody could be more generous than Snow in praising his colleagues. Unhappily one of these was inconsiderate in his treatment of Snow. On at least one occasion Snow felt that, through aggressive publicity, a former student was credited with achievements for which he himself was largely responsible."[25]

It seems likely that who would direct the museum was the underlying issue. Although Snow had accepted a professorship after stepping down as chancellor, the Board of Regents stipulated that he "be entirely relieved from regular department work and responsibility."[26] Chancellor Strong attempted to resolve the situation diplomatically by appointing Dyche curator of mammals, birds, and fishes and giving him "virtual charge of all the Museum Building except the upper floor."[27] Clarence McClung was head of the Department of Zoology and curator of the paleontological collections (on the upper floor), and Snow was named curator of the entomological collections (also on the upper floor). But Strong appointed himself ex officio director of the museum.

Dyche hired an advanced student, Leverett A. Adams, to design and construct groundwork for the central portion of the mammals exhibit. For two years Adams built papier-maché mountain steeps and crags and finely detailed sandstone formations. He left in 1905 to become curator of birds and mammals at the State Normal School in Greeley, Colorado. By then Dyche's former assistant, Charles Dean Bunker, had returned to the university after a four-year hiatus as taxidermist at the University of Oklahoma and was put to work on the mammals exhibit.

Two students, Alexander Wetmore and Theodore Rocklund, assisted Dyche and Bunker in building the groundwork and preparing the specimens. As a boy, Wetmore had seen the university's mammal exhibit at the World's Columbian Exposition. He later served as superintendent of the National Zoological Park, and eventually became the sixth Secretary of the Smithsonian Institution and a world-famous ornithologist. Theodore Rocklund worked in the taxidermy shop from 1903 to 1918. Dyche called him "a good, faithful young man."[28] A fellow student referred to him as "Theodore, the boy taxidermist."[29] Rocklund died of pneumonia in France during World War I.

The *Kansan* reported the following early in 1908: "A great amount of work is being done in the Natural History building along the line of making artificial ledges and cliffs. Besides the half circle on the west side of the building the whole north and south ends of the first floor are being devoted to this work. On the west side of the south part of the museum a large chalk cliff, similar to those of Western Kansas, has been built, showing the erosions of both the wind and rain. In the same room two different types of limestone ledges are being built. Photographs were taken of bluffs near Lawrence and these used in making the ledges in the Museum. A gap was made between the two ledges in which a canyon will be painted, extending the cliffs to the background. Scenery will be portrayed upon the walls, and the ceiling painted to represent the sky."[30]

Students working on taxidermy in the basement of Dyche Hall in 1913. Charles Dean Bunker, third from left, supervises. Theodore Rocklund, Dyche's student assistant for several years, is second from right. (University of Kansas Archives)

The groundwork was made by nailing boards together in the general shape of the landscape and then boxing them in. Wire screen was nailed to that rough framework and bent to form rocks, nooks, and crevices, finished off with hundreds of pounds of papier-maché.

A fanciful newspaper story explained the addition of the Kansas chalk cliffs to the panorama. According to the *Topeka Daily Capital,* the university's purchasing agent sent a box of paintings to the museum for display. Seeing the crates of pictures, Dyche told Bunker, "Think of something quick, and then get busy at it. Anything to stop this picture business."[31] For several years the museum building had in fact been used for Professor Griffith's annual art exhibit. By 1909 Dyche was so perturbed at having to contend with "this picture business" that when Chancellor Strong again ordered him to accommodate Professor Griffith's paintings, Dyche instructed Griffith to display them in the museum's basement. A mandate from the Board of Regents compelled Dyche to allow Griffith the use of the second floor.

The groundwork received rocks, logs, and vegetation: bushes, trees, grasses, lichens, and moss appropriate to each section of the panorama. The very log on which the big moose fell when it was killed was incorporated into the display. Real leaves and plants sometimes were used, but Dyche preferred less combustible artificial foliage. He had collected boxes full of bunch grass from the same area where he had shot the mountain sheep, and he had brought barrels of lichens and moss from Greenland. Using that vegetation as models, he created imitations.

Dyche reluctantly continued to teach while working on the panorama and other exhibits. He taught an undergraduate course in "Systematic and Descriptive Zoology," which included lectures and laboratory work. His "Teacher's Course" covered methods of collecting, preserving, and preparing specimens for classroom study, and methodology of teaching zoology. He taught graduate courses by appointment, including "Comparative Anatomy and Osteology," "Museum Work and Methods," and "Advanced Original Work in Systematic and Descriptive Zoology." But he made no secret of his disaffection with classroom teaching. Without a Professor Snow to assume his classes as in former years, Dyche was forced to devote as much of his time to teaching as to the museum, and the exhibits progressed slowly.

"I am just now working out the panorama part of the large mammal exhibit," Dyche wrote Hornaday in 1905. "One entire hall given to North Am. mammals and one to N. Am. birds. I have cut loose from all other branches of natural history work. Have had to remount nearly all the large mammals—a fearful job—almost enough to drive me crazy. The worst of it is over now."

He added, "Mrs. Dyche has not been well for the past week. I have been at home most of the time *cooking* & sending the children . . . to school. . . . Mrs. Dyche is better today and we hope all will be as usual in a very short time."[32] But Ophelia did not improve. Her condition eventually was diagnosed as neuritis, which induced colitis and rheumatism. She stayed intermittently at the university's Bell Memorial Hospital in Rosedale, but mostly she stayed at home on a parlor bed near the stove—for years. With the help of young women from the Haskell Indian College, Dyche managed the household.

Having sold the Massachusetts Street house,[33] the Dyches lived in Walter Roscoe Stubbs's old country estate, nicknamed "The White City" because of its numerous white outbuildings.[34] Dyche hoped to build a new house as soon as Ophelia was well enough to take part in the plans. At middle age Dyche found himself keeping close company with his children, especially the youngest, George. The family tended a cow, horses, rabbits, and fancy poultry (George recalled that he often called on his father to rescue him from game rooster attacks). Dyche's old dog, Collie, and other pet dogs had the run of the estate. Dyche often cooked out of doors using a canvas tent as a smokehouse. He planted large gardens and let George ride the horse as it pulled the plow.

The older children sometimes took meals and boarded with family friends. Lewis Lindsay, Jr. was fond of organizing games. Once he constructed a group sled steered by an ice skate worn by the child on back. He was a studious boy who would become a physician. Dyche tried to secure a position at the museum for Walter, his oldest son, but the Board of Regents deemed it unwise to authorize it.

James R. Mead, Dyche's Wichita friend, arranged for Walter to work for his son's Chicago bicycle company, the Mead Cycle Company. Walter became a Lawrence "rider agent," receiving a free bicycle for himself and a commission on all bicycles that he sold. He was on his way to becoming a mechanic. George would eventually earn a B.S. degree in chemistry from the University of Kansas and establish a prosperous exterminating company in Kansas City. Ruth, pretty and shy, tended to her mother, as she would most of her life.

To complete the panorama, Dyche sought specimens of musk-oxen, Alaskan white (Dall) sheep, and a large male puma. He especially wanted musk-oxen for the collection, having failed to acquire any during his Greenland expeditions. He often told reporters that he intended to go back and get some. "If Mrs. D. was well I would go & get what I wanted," Dyche wrote Hornaday, "but under the present circumstance I cannot think of going."[35] Hornaday wrote to a Norwegian ship's captain describing Dyche's requirements for mountable musk-ox skins, but nothing came of his request. Dyche never saw musk-oxen in the panorama. They were added in 1941, when museum director Henry Higgins Lane bought specimens from a Chicago collection. Lane was gratified to get them, declaring that they were virtually the only large North American mammal missing from the museum.[36]

Ironically, the first musk-ox to visit Kansas was a live specimen. In 1902 a musk-ox calf was brought to Topeka in a boxcar and exhibited by a Chicago furrier. Zoological parks across the country were successfully displaying live animals, and while Dyche labored to create his panorama of taxidermically preserved specimens, many people were actively conserving the living species. William T. Hornaday had become a leader in the wildlife conservation movement.

Hornaday was the driving force in the establishment of the National Zoological Park. In 1896 the New York Zoological Society elected him director and general curator of a proposed zoological park in New York City. Hornaday was instrumental in the foundation of the New York Zoological Park, or Bronx Zoo. In 1905 he became president of the newly incorporated American Bison Society, dedicated to the conservation of the nation's "most conspicuous quadruped."[37] When Hornaday and William Harvey Brown undertook "the last buffalo hunt" in 1886, the extermination of the American bison seemed inevitable, but nineteen years later he was able to contribute significantly to its preservation.

Francis Snow died on September 20, 1908. The previous year he had spent time at a Bonner Springs sanitarium where he recovered sufficiently to go to a cottage by Nagawicka Lake, Wisconsin, with Charles Siler, a recent graduate, as his companion. On the morning of September 20, Snow told Siler, "I don't want any breakfast this morning. This is something different from what I have been feeling."[38] Snow died as Siler tried to help him to a chair on the porch.

Thirty-one years earlier Snow had befriended Dyche and "sent him out to his house with a note to his wife to tog him out with proper clothes and later put him to work for the University." Despite possible differences during their later years, the two men shared a natural affinity. Throughout his career, Dyche recognized how much Snow had done for him. After Snow's death, Dyche honored him in a paper for the Kansas Academy of Science, "Doctor Snow As A Collector, And His Collections,"[39] the first summary of Snow's life work as a scientific collector.

Work continued on the panorama into 1911. The central portion of the exhibit was ready to receive the mammals in 1905, while most of the exhibits were behind glass by 1909. But Dyche, during his lifetime, never declared the exhibits finished. A museum visitor in 1915 saw a display similar to the 1893 world's fair exhibit, although it had been expanded and developed in the groundwork and foliage detail. As in the Chicago exhibit, the bighorn sheep and mountain goats were centered on crags and cliffs. A spring trickled down the mountain, forming a pool in which "fish of various kinds lead a delightful existence immune from the angler's hook."[40] To the left of the sheep and goats there were plains animals: bison, deer, jackrabbits, and a skunk. To the right of the sheep and goats were elk and moose.

For several years Bunker had worked to bring the mammal floor to completion. His Kansas chalk cliffs ran forty feet along the western wall of the panorama. That part of the exhibit included wildcats, coyotes, wolves, badgers, and prairie dogs. Still incomplete was the Arctic portion of the panorama, comprised of groups of walruses, several species of seals, and the sea lions.

"It will be something new and wonderful," Hornaday wrote of Dyche's panorama. "They have lost a good opportunity to do the same thing down at the American Museum in an almost circular hall which they have."[41] Frederic Lucas, a taxidermist who studied at Ward's Natural Science Establishment, described Dyche's panorama as "an amplification of his ideas as shown in 1893 in the Kansas Building at the World's Fair." Dyche's method of display showed various species together in one group rather than the customary grouping of each species separately. Lucas called them synthetic, or life study, groups, "bringing together in one composite picture a number of animals that probably would not be found in so small an area at any one moment of the season depicted, but might all be found there at some moment of the season. Such a group may, or may not, represent a particular spot; it does depict the natural conditions under which the animals are to be found and shows them engaged in the most characteristic and interesting of their varied occupations. In this, the day of moving pictures, we may say that as the moving picture condenses into five minutes' time the events of days or weeks, so these groups depict in a few feet of space the life and happenings of a much larger area."[42]

Lucas became director of the American Museum of Natural History in 1911. While there he confided to Hornaday: "I am somewhat in the position of a chicken tied by one leg for I inherit matters of installation in which I do not believe and yet am expected to carry out. The Museum, as you are aware, is gradually working around to the position we held fifteen or twenty years ago . . . . I sometimes wish that I had made an attempt to get the management of some small museum wherein I could carry out some of my ideas . . . ."[43] A beneficiary of Snow's support, Dyche enjoyed precisely those conditions. Hornaday appreciated the advantages of Dyche's situation, even though on occasion he had urged Dyche to come east. Nearly two decades earlier, in 1891, he had written Dyche, "I often think of you, and how you are building up a great museum with a free hand and in fine style. What worlds of comfort you must take in carrying out your ideals without let or hindrance."[44]

A remarkable museum was built in Kansas, made possible to a large extent by Dyche's geographic isolation. As Hornaday pointed out, Dyche enjoyed "a free hand." He developed concepts he had gleaned from Hornaday and eastern museums, and he was not encumbered by the prevailing conservative thought. Hornaday wrote Dyche, "I am really sorry that your work is so far west that but few can see it, instead of being in a howling big metropolis somewhere East, where millions might see."[45] Yet if Dyche had worked "somewhere East," it is unlikely that his panorama would have been realized.

The museum remained open until November 30, 1932. Because an auditorium ceiling collapsed at the Kansas State Teacher's College in Pittsburg, the state architect inspected all school buildings in the state and found the museum building to be unsafe, and the regents ordered it closed. Builders had used wooden beams to support the slab concrete floors (an acceptable practice at the time), with the floors being reinforced with woven wire instead of iron rods. By 1932 the floors had weakened. Specimens were moved out and stored all over campus. A total of $125,000 gradually was appropriated for the project, but the museum did not reopen until June 7, 1941. The ceiling above the main floor (and the panorama) was lowered from twenty-two to fourteen feet and an additional interior story was added. The heaviest of the museum collections, the fossils, formerly displayed on the top floor, were moved to the basement.

Two years were required to remount and reassemble the panorama animals. A complete renovation of the panorama left it, to the museum visitor, essentially as it had been before the repairs were undertaken. S. T. Dickenson of Lawrence, a housepainter and artist, painted the new backdrop, which continued the landscape created by the groundwork.

Dyche's former student, Alexander Wetmore, spoke at the reopening in 1941. Assistant Secretary (later Secretary) of the Smithsonian Institution in charge of the U.S. National Museum since 1925, Wetmore iterated the importance of the nonpublic elements of the museum:

"We see in the newly opened halls of the Dyche Museum attractive exhibits of many kinds, of mammals, birds, fossils, and other objects where the subjects are presented in interesting and often in lifelike manner. . . .

"But let me impress upon you the very pertinent fact that these displays, attractive though they may be, are not the most important properties of this museum. The exhibitions once installed may be renovated periodically but such changes come only at long intervals. While definitely important as education factors they are in a sense static.

"Behind the scenes in this museum . . . are rows of cases of study specimens of skins and skeletons of birds and mammals, specimens of reptiles and amphibians, and many other creatures, which are used for the training and study of advanced students and are seen only by such visitors who have special interest in them. . . . They form a portion of the valuable properties of our University, and constitute in considerable part the dynamic force of this museum. . . . Their worth increases as they themselves grow and increase. Let me repeat that, while the exhibition halls of this museum are attractive and instructive, behind the scenes in the laboratory collections there is found a most valuable function and one that continues year after year with steadily growing importance."[46]

Lobbying for a museum building in 1900, Dyche articulated his dream to Regent Charles F. Scott: "I want to say that while I am not as old as some people yet I am much older than I used to be. I have done my best for years to build up a good collection of large mammals, and while doing so have gone up against some pretty hard propositions. I want to do one thing more. I want to put the collections I have made in the best possible shape to insure their future preservation. This done I am ready to quit and 'go a fishing' all the rest of the days of my life."[47]

"Prof. L. L. Dyche, 'the man who knows them,' lectures here." From the Topeka State Journal, *October 9, 1909. (University of Kansas Archives)*

12 The Man Who Knew Cook and Peary

. . . hoping you will plant a sunflower on the top of Mt. McKinley.
From a 1909 fan letter to Lewis Dyche

Work on the museum exhibits continued into the fall of 1909. Due to that work, and in consideration of his ailing wife, Dyche had not undertaken an expedition in ten years. But his home-keeping existence was rocked by newspaper reports of a telegram sent by Dr. Frederick A. Cook: "Reached the North Pole April 21, 1908. Discovered land far north. Return to Copenhagen by steamer 'Hans Egede.'" Five days later word was received of another telegram, issued by Robert E. Peary: "Stars and Stripes nailed to the Pole April 6, 1909." The great North Pole controversy had begun.

Frederick Cook had quietly set sail from Gloucester, Massachusetts, in July 1907 on board a hunter's yacht, the *John R. Bradley,* destination unknown. A year later Robert E. Peary, on board his custom-built *Roosevelt* draped in U.S. flags, set sail from New York Harbor to the cheers of thousands of well-wishers, including President Theodore Roosevelt. No word was heard from either explorer until their telegrams were received a few days apart in 1909.

The general excitement caused by the telegrams intensified with Peary's follow-up messages. To the United Press he cabled: "Cook's story shouldn't be taken too seriously. Two Eskimos who accompanied him say he went no distance north and not out of sight of land. Other tribesmen corroborate." To the *New York*

Times he wired: "Do not trouble about Cook's story or attempt to explain any discrepancies in his installments. The affair will settle itself. He has not been to the Pole on April 21st, 1908, or at any other time. He has simply handed the public a gold brick."[1] To the new President, William Howard Taft, he cabled: "Have honor to place North Pole at your disposal." (Taft glibly replied: "Thanks your generous offer. I do not know exactly what to do with it.")[2]

On learning of Peary's claim to the Pole, Cook responded magnanimously: "If Peary says he reached the Pole, I believe him. There is room enough and honor enough for two American flags at the Pole."[3] When Cook arrived in Copenhagen's harbor, a flotilla of boats escorted the *Hans Egede*. Crown Prince Christian met the international hero, and Cook lectured before King Frederick and the Royal Danish Geographical Society. A superficial interview with members of the Royal Geographical Society and professors from the University of Copenhagen resulted in their tentative endorsement of his claim to the Pole. He promised to give them complete records of his journey at a later time.

Peary was furious. He was not about to be cheated of the North Pole prize for which he had worked twenty-three years. But his precipitant attacks on Cook, especially the "gold brick" remark, were contrary to the American sense of fair play, and public opinion swung toward the polite physician.

Before Peary had reached New York or Cook had reached Copenhagen, Lewis Dyche was being asked for his opinion on the controversy. He obliged by putting together a lecture series entitled "Cook and Peary and the Discovery of the North Pole, A Profusely Illustrated Lecture by Prof. L. L. Dyche." He included many of the slides of Greenland he had used in his earlier lectures, as well as maps illustrating the alleged routes of Cook and Peary. Charles Bunker operated the stereopticon projector, with Dyche's son Walter assisting. A Lawrence travel agent served as Dyche's manager, traveling ahead as Eldie Caldwell had done, posting flyers and organizing ticket sales.

Dyche was uniquely qualified to comment on the dispute because he had participated in expeditions with both Cook and Peary. In his lectures he affirmed his faith in both men, but because Cook claimed to have reached the Pole a year earlier than Peary, Dyche was effectively siding with Cook. In Parsons, Kansas, Dyche summarized his position: "I think this trouble and accusations Peary's friends and Peary himself are making are absurd and useless. I cannot understand Peary doing such a thing—it is not at all like him. . . . I believe both men were successful in their quest for the pole. Peary has done a wonderful work in his Arctic explorations. He has been there so many times that besides the knowledge he himself has brought back from the frozen country, he has interested scores of others in the work of exploration. I consider him the greatest Arctic explorer, and I can sympathize with him in seeing another man snatch the prize he had coveted for years just when the victory was in his grasp."[4] Dyche was convinced of the validity of Cook's claim to the Pole. "Dr. Cook has discovered the north pole—no doubt about it," he affirmed in a letter to James R. Mead. "I have known him for 15 years and have every faith in him. He is not a faker nor an advertiser. He is a quiet level headed man of fine disposition & character. His veracity was never before questioned for a second by any one, not even by Peary himself."[5]

Cook, after being lionized by King Frederick, receiving an honorary degree from the University of Copenhagen and a gold medal from the Royal Danish Geographical Society, steamed back to the United States to begin his lecture tour. Peary was already on the Chautauqua circuit. Each man received as much as ten thousand dollars for an appearance.

The North Pole controversy was a debate about each man's honor rather than a trial of hard evidence (such as sextant readings and field diaries). Cook and Peary presented their cases to the public, but neither would provide the data that

would validate his claim to the Pole. The controversy raged, and as it did Dyche's lectures and "character commentaries" proliferated. He frequently defended Cook against Peary's accusations. When asked if there was a chance that Cook had not come near the Pole, Dyche replied: "No, I feel just the same in regard to his story as I did when he gave out his first statement. If Cook says he has discovered the pole—and he does, then he has; for his word is good. I have never known him to ever make any pretense of claiming he had done something he had not. He is as honest as the day is long, to use an old saying."[6]

"Prof. Dyche takes up the club in defense of Cook." From the Topeka State Journal, October 19, 1909. (University of Kansas Archives)

The American public initially sided with the soft-spoken Brooklyn physician. A popularity poll conducted by the Pittsburgh Press showed seventy-three thousand persons siding with Cook and only two thousand backing Peary. It was Cook's heyday. In The North Pole or Bust, Frank Rasky noted that a dahlia at a New York flower show was named for Cook; a copy of Cook's serialized New York Herald account of his polar trek was placed in the cornerstone of a Long Island church; and a "Broadway bar concocted a so-called Cook Cocktail, whose ingredients included a tablespoon of Maraschino and a pony of gin. After imbibing three Cook Cocktails, said the New York Times, drinkers were apt to begin mushing blindly in the direction of the North Pole."[7]

Cook arrived in Kansas City on the morning of October 7, 1909, to deliver a lecture as part of a week-long celebration sponsored by the Priests of Pallas. A delegation had taken a train to St. Louis (where Cook had lectured the previous evening) to escort him to Kansas City in a private railway car. He was given an automobile tour over the boulevards and through the parks of the city, followed by a luncheon at the Evanston Golf Club. He spent the afternoon leading a flower parade. The Kansas City Star reported that Kansas Citians were "Cook crazy." That evening, in his room at the Hotel Baltimore, Cook dined with his old friend Professor Dyche. (Dyche had not seen Cook for several years, but he had written him on several occasions on behalf of Governor Müller of Holsteinborg—Cook owed Müller money and had not repaid the debt.) Ruth Dyche had wished to attend Cook's lecture, but illness kept her home. When Dyche told Dr. Cook this, Cook went into another room, closed the door, and telephoned Ruth in Lawrence.

"Everywhere I went crowds pressed around me," Cook later recounted. "I shook hands until the flesh of one finger was actually worn through to the bone. . . .

I was so busy I could not pause to think, and was conscious only of the rush, the labor, the worry. I no longer slept; indigestion naturally seized me as its victim. A mental depression brought desperate premonitions."[8] He had developed laryngitis early in the lecture tour, and in St. Louis, where he had addressed a crowd of twelve thousand, he could barely raise his voice above a whisper.

About seven thousand persons attended his lecture in Kansas City's Convention Hall. Tickets sold for one, two, and three dollars, and then fifty cents on the day of the show. Preceding the speech a song was sung in honor of the occasion, a two-step titled "The North Pole" ("In the north of the globe/Where the eye had probed/Lay the land of mys-ter-y. . .").[9] Cook delivered his version of the polar dash to a receptive audience, humbly giving most of the credit for his success, in marked contrast to Peary, to the Eskimos who had accompanied him. "They're great fellows, those two Eskimos boys who went to the pole with me," Cook told an interviewer. "I am going to bring them to America and show the people two real heroes. They are about 19 years old each and are bright and active. When I get them here I am going to show them the greatest time that ever an Eskimo had. I suppose they will kill themselves eating candy. They are very fond of it. If it had not been for those two Eskimos I would have been up near the pole in cold storage today."

Reporters begged Cook to show them his field notebooks supposedly containing proof that he had discovered the Pole. "Why don't you tell us what are in them and settle all this dispute?" asked a *Kansas City Star* reporter. "If you have the proofs why not let us have them now?"

"I have explained to you before," replied Cook, "that the records of my astronomical observations are not all the proof. The proofs are all the facts and circumstances of my trip."

"Well let *The Star* have them. *The Star* will print them if it takes the whole newspaper."

Cook laughed. "My original records will go first to the University of Copenhagen," he said. But he estimated that he would not be ready to submit the records for another two months.

"But why should he be asked to prove that he has been there?" Dyche asked the reporters. "He is a reputable man and it is for the doubters to disprove him. The world will believe that he has been there until someone shows that he has not been there—and that time will never come for he has been there just as surely as he has been in Kansas City."[10]

The day before Cook's Kansas City lecture, Peary announced that he had accepted the National Geographic Society's offer to examine his records. The American Geographic Society and the American Museum of Natural History also had offered to examine each man's records, but Cook refused to turn his over to those organizations, pointing out that they had subsidized Peary's expeditions. Cook insisted that he would send his records first to the University of Copenhagen, although he agreed to send copies to the National Geographic Society. Peary refused to submit his records to any European authority. Peary supporters, including the *New York Times,* continued to contend that Cook should submit his records first to the National Geographic Society.

"I fear Peary and his friends have started something they will find hard to stop," Dyche commented in the *Topeka Daily Capital*. "Dr. Cook's word is as good as any man's in the world. He is a gentleman. The Arctic club in Brooklyn is for any American; the Peary club is for Peary. Well, what have we to prove that anyone ever reached any latitude in the far north? Their observations, astronomical records and their word of honor. . . . I am convinced that Dr. Cook was the first man at the pole. His word is good enough for me."[11]

Peary stepped up his campaign against Cook. Through the Peary Arctic Club he released an affidavit to the *New York Times* stating that on his return trip along the Greenland coast he had interrogated the two Eskimos who had supposedly accompanied Cook to the Pole. Peary charged that they told him they had never left sight of land on their journey with Cook. They showed Peary on a map the route they had taken, indicating that they went nowhere near the Pole, having instead circumnavigated Ellesmere Island and Axel Heiberg Land. The *Times* published a map of Cook's route as the Eskimos had described it to Peary.[12]

Cook responded to the charge, stating, "The map published by Commander Peary in itself indicates that the Eskimos have respected their promise made to me that they would not give any information to Peary or his men." Cook argued that it was natural for the Eskimos to be "only too willing to say something that they think will please their questioners."[13] And he argued that the Eskimos did not understand the questions put to them. He vowed to retrieve the two men and bring them to New York where they could substantiate his claim to the Pole.

Dyche, too, rebutted Peary's charge: "Commander Peary's statement . . . to my mind is absolutely incredible. It is based on the testimony of ignorant Eskimos who were incapable of understanding a country to which they had never been before [Ellesmere Island and the Polar pack-ice] well enough to outline such a map as that published today and credited by Mr. Peary to their explanation. Only intelligent white men with instruments could make their way to such a country and be able to report in detail upon it a year after the trip was made." Dyche challenged the "moral character and manhood" of Eskimos, one of whom, quoting Peary's own book *Northward Over the "Great Ice,"* offered to trade his wife and two children for a knife, or of a woman who offered everything she had in exchange for a needle.[14]

The controversy persisted, prompting the *Washington Times* to quip: "England is raising $200,000 to send Captain Scott to the South Pole. About $183,000 of that had better be used to get a good umpire."[15] Dyche's lecture requests increased, and in the pages of Kansas newspapers, he became a hero of mythic proportions. Ignace Mead Jones, daughter of James and Fern Mead, Dyche's close friends in Wichita, remembers attending one of Dyche's matinee lectures for children at the Crawford Theater in Wichita. She recalls that stereopticon slides were shown and that Dyche and his assistants were dressed in Arctic costumes. At one point Dyche left the stage and walked the aisles in snowshoes to show the children things he had brought with him from Greenland.

Governor Stubbs introduced Dyche in Topeka: "I consider him one of the greatest men that has ever been born in Kansas. He devised the ways and means and schemes by which Cook and Peary reached the pole, and if it had not been for him the pole would still be there undisturbed. I am proud of Prof. Dyche as a Kansan who has never seen anything he was afraid to tackle."[16] Dyche promptly set the record straight as to his birthplace: "I ought to be a native Kansan, but I had no control over the fact of my birth. But you will notice that I hiked for Kansas at the earliest opportunity. It was just when Horace Greeley was preaching his 'Go West, Young Man' and I heard the call at a very early age. At the age of three months, I landed with my parents at Lawrence and Kansas has been my home ever since."[17]

Dyche announced his intention to undertake a two-year collecting expedition to Alaska. "This trip will be the crowning feature of my life as a hunter," Dyche told the *Lawrence World,* "and I hope to make it the most successful of the several expeditions that I have made. . . . It would be a rough, dangerous trip, but I have been longing to get back to the north once more."[18] He planned to spend a year in southern Alaska and a year in the northern seas, hunting from a whaler, to add to the university's collection of Arctic animals.

The next skirmish in the Cook-Peary feud concerned Cook's 1906 claim to have climbed the highest peak on the continent, Alaska's Mount McKinley. His illustrated account of the expedition, *To the Top of the Continent,* was published in 1908. Cook claimed that he and Edward Barrill,[19] a Montana guide and packer, had reached the summit after the rest of their expedition had disbanded. Word of Cook's accomplishment came as a surprise to other members of the expedition, especially Herschel Parker (a Columbia University physics professor) and Belmore Browne (an artist and experienced climber), who had left the mountain thinking that Cook merely intended to reconnoiter the area for a future attempt. Cook had wired news of his success to the Explorers Club, and his climb made the front page of the *New York Times* on October 3, 1906. So skeptical were Parker and Browne, however (Browne reportedly had learned that Cook was perpetrating a hoax during a private chat with Barrill), that they asked the Explorers Club to investigate Cook's claim, and on October 7 the *Times* printed a lengthy story titled, "Has Dr. Cook Scaled America's Highest Peak?" Although many members of the Explorers Club (including Robert E. Peary) doubted Cook's account, the gentlemanly clique did not openly challenge it. Mountain climbing did not receive the same attention as polar exploration, either publicly or within the club, and Parker and Browne failed to follow up their accusations. To Peary's subsequent wrath, Parker on at least two occasions attended Explorers Club banquets and passively listened to Cook recount the story of his ascent. Browne and Parker eventually induced the Explorers Club to investigate Cook's claim, but Cook left for the Arctic on the *John R. Bradley* before submitting any evidence of his climb.[20]

In the wake of his disputed claim of the North Pole, Cook's ascent of Mount McKinley came under scrutiny. For several weeks the *Times* published negative opinions and hearsay accounts casting doubt on his McKinley claim. The Explorers Club reopened its investigation of the climb. Then, on October 15, the *Times* published an affidavit issued by the guide, Edward Barrill, stating that Cook had faked the climb. Fred Printz, another Montana guide and packer, substantiated Barrill's story. Barrill stated that he and Cook came no closer than fourteen miles to the peak, and that Cook had ordered him to falsify his field diary. Furthermore, he said that the photograph taken of himself holding the U.S. flag atop the 20,320-foot summit of Mount McKinley (published in Cook's *To the Top of the Continent*) had been taken at an altitude of only 7,000 feet.[21]

Cook survived this stinging attack on his honor amazingly well. He charged that "strong inducements" had been offered to Barrill to issue the affidavit (a charge vehemently denied by the Peary Arctic Club), and he pointed out that Barrill had stood by Cook's account of the climb for three years.[22] Newspapers supportive of Cook also noted that Barrill's belated testimony was suspect. The *Evening Post* commented "that a man who signs a sworn statement that he had been a voluntary participant in the concoction of an elaborate and swindling falsehood cannot be accepted as an unimpeachable witness when he sweared that he lied."[23]

The Massachusetts *Springfield Republican* suggested a straightforward solution to the Mount McKinley controversy: An expedition should be organized to climb the peak and retrieve the metallic tube Cook claimed he left on the summit. The tube was said to contain a record of the ascent and a U.S. flag. "The tube, if found by a party composed of both friends and opponents of the doctor, would dispose of the Mount McKinley controversy for all time, regardless of the affidavit by Barrill," mused the *Republican*.[24]

"*Getting Their Goats*": "*Prof. L. L. Dyche, Explorer and Naturalist, will climb Mt. McKinley after a new species of Mountain Goat.*" *From the* Topeka State Journal, *October 23, 1909. (University of Kansas Archives)*

Cook seized upon the proposal, requesting that Arctic explorer Anthony Fiala head the expedition, and he also invited one of his chief detractors, Herschel Parker, to accompany it. But Parker would have nothing to do with an expedition affiliated with Cook and vowed to mount an expedition of his own. Fiala, too, declined to lead an expedition to McKinley, pointing out that he was not a mountain climber. Cook therefore announced that he would lead the expedition himself. On October 17 Cook appeared before an Explorers Club committee that sought proof he had climbed the mountain, and Cook assured the members, who were surprisingly sympathetic, that he would provide evidence (presumably his field diary) within a month.

In the madcap reasoning that permeated the Cook-Peary controversy, it was presumed that if it were proven that Cook had climbed McKinley, then his North Pole claim would be validated as well. On October 20, Chancellor Frank Strong sent a cable to Dr. Cook: "The University of Kansas offers the services of Prof. L. L. Dyche, the scientist, hunter, and explorer, for an expedition to Mount McKinley."[25] Cook immediately told reporters, "I shall accept Prof. Dyche's services, whether it is to make the expedition with myself or have him go alone. Prof. Dyche is a man whom I should be pleased to trust with any expedition."[26]

"Professor Dyche can climb Mount McKinley if Dr. Cook did," gushed the *Kansas City Journal*. "The Kansas scientist is not quite as spry as he once was, possibly, but he is still full of endurance, pluck, and the benefits of wide and varied experience in exploration. He knows the Arctic region by heart and can almost call the polar bears by their first names."[27]

The Board of Regents granted Dyche a six-month leave of absence without pay to allow him to organize the expedition (tentatively scheduled for the spring of 1910) and to deliver lectures. Dyche maintained that in order to ensure objectivity he would use his own resources, namely the money made from his lectures, to finance the expedition. It was also reported that the university would contribute to expedition expenses.

Dr. Cook meanwhile met the Mount McKinley controversy head on. In an incredibly brazen act (if he did fake the climb), Cook traveled to Hamilton, Montana, hometown of Edward Barrill and Fred Printz, to confront his accusers. Cook rented the town hall and pled his case before Hamilton residents, stating, "My veracity has been attacked by men residing in this community. They have fallen into evil hands, and the temptation was too great. They have sold their birthright for silver, and there probably was more than thirty pieces. I am here to give my version of the Mount McKinley controversy, and then leave my case in the hands of an honest body—the people of the great State of Montana. I will accept their verdict."[28] At first Cook would not allow Barrill to speak since the former had paid for use of the hall, but as the evening wore on what was intended to be a one-man lecture turned into a debate between Cook and his lawyer, Barrill, and the town residents. At the end of the evening a vote was taken: The citizens of Hamilton endorsed Barrill's version of events.

Cook's claim to the ascent of Mount McKinley had become a full-fledged controversy, but the North Pole battle raged as well. It was reported that Peary was preparing his notes and instruments for submission to the National Geographic Society. The Danes meanwhile doggedly maintained their faith in Dr. Cook, although they wondered why it was taking so long for him to prepare his proofs.

On November 4 Dyche traveled to Kansas City accompanied by an entourage of prominent Lawrence citizens, including Mayor Bishop, W. C. Simons of the *Lawrence World*, and J. L. Brady of the *Lawrence Daily Journal*. Dyche was wined and dined, as Cook had been, and he was driven throughout the city in a fourteen-car motorcade. That evening a banquet was held in his honor at the Coates House. The following afternoon, dressed in his Arctic costume, Dyche addressed twelve thousand schoolchildren in Convention Hall. It took twenty patrolmen over two hours to seat the children. A police sergeant remarked, "That was the hardest job I ever tackled. Every time a new bunch of children came into

the hall it was greeted by, 'Hi there, you kids.'"[29] Dyche spoke to the children
mostly of the Eskimo life-style, and ended his lecture with the question, "Would
you like to be an Eskimo?" One replied to Dyche's question by letter: "Would I
like to be an Eskimo? *No, No, No!* I would rather be a cannibal of the Fiji Islands,
where I could have flowers and trees and birds, than in a land where half the year is
in darkness."[30]

The following evening, in what was intended to be his last lecture before
meeting Cook in New York, Dyche spoke to a crowd of fifteen thousand in
Convention Hall. Governor Stubbs, Chancellor Strong, and the Board of Regents
were in attendance. "I can't tell anything about my future plans beyond the fact
that I am going up that mountain if human endurance can achieve it," Dyche
asserted. The *Kansas City Star* reported: "As an explorer he ranks with Cook,
Peary, and Nansen. As a hunter he ranks with Colonel Roosevelt and Daniel
Boone. As a naturalist and practical taxidermist he outranks all of them."[31]

Dyche's notoriety had never been greater. When he told a reporter that he
would give the *Kansas City Star* the first interview following the expedition,
reporters for the *Kansas City Journal* wrote him angry letters. But suddenly there
was nothing to argue about: Dyche did not meet Cook in New York. Quite a lot
happened at once.

On November 16 Governor Stubbs offered Dyche the position of fish and
game warden for the state of Kansas. Chancellor Strong urged Dyche to accept the
post, believing that it would be in the best interest of the university. Strong hoped
that Dyche could maintain his position at the university while serving as warden,
thereby increasing the university's dominion. Accordingly, Dyche accepted the
wardenship, and he did not resign his position at the university.

Having received no further word from Cook, Dyche began to hedge the
Mount McKinley expedition. "I realize that it may be impossible for me to accept
both the wardenship and the opportunity of going to Mt. McKinley with Dr. Cook,"
he told the *Topeka State Journal,* "and it may also be impossible for me to make
the intended hunting trip to Alaska. I must leave it with the university authorities.
It was through them that I was given both positions and it must be through them
that I will lose either of them."[32]

But there was to be no Mount McKinley expedition. As of November 27,
the good Doctor Cook suddenly disappeared. Rumors abounded as to his where-
abouts. His brother first said Cook was resting somewhere near New York, but he
then suggested that the doctor had met with foul play while attempting to take his
North Pole proofs to Copenhagen. His lawyer stated that, fatigued both mentally
and physically by the controversies, Cook had sailed to Europe, but he could not be
found aboard the ship he was said to have sailed on. Cook and his immediate
family simply had vanished.

Two weeks later, on December 9, two men informed the *New York Times*
that they had helped Cook calculate navigational data concerning the North Pole
(one of the men was a graduate of the Navigation College at Bergen, Norway).
Although Cook had not specifically told the men that he wished to use the data to
substantiate his North Pole claim, their testimony weakened his claim, especially
since he was not available to refute their statment. The men had reportedly taken
their story to the *Times* because Cook had failed to pay them for their work.

On December 21 the University of Copenhagen rendered its opinion of the proofs Cook had submitted: insufficient evidence. Cook had offered only a typewritten account of his expedition, similar to serial articles he had published in the *New York Herald*. He had provided no astronomical observations or other hard evidence. Three days later the Explorers Club dismissed Cook from its ranks, citing his failure to furnish facts supporting his claim to having climbed Mount McKinley.[33]

Although Dyche's faith in Cook was shaken, he supported the idea that perhaps Cook was exhausted mentally. "If he really is in a sanitarium it ought to be known," he told the *Kansas City Journal*. "It is no disgrace to go to a sanitarium. Even his brother doesn't know where he is, or if he does won't tell. Unless Cook is broken down mentally and physically there is no reason why he should not have remained on the firing line and faced the music."[34] Dyche found himself in much the same circumstance as in 1894, when, in the dining room of the *Miranda,* he defended Cook in absentia to a horde of mutinous professors. Once again there were few on the side of Dr. Frederick Cook. Weeks later, when asked if he still believed that Cook's records rested at the top of Mount McKinley, Dyche replied, "I guess they are for I haven't heard of anyone bringing them down and I haven't time to go after them myself."[35]

"An Empty Hook." Dyche's years as fish and game warden were filled with controversy, but though he swam in a "sea of malice" he successfully eluded the hooks of his adversaries. From the Wichita Eagle, *October 11, 1913. (University of Kansas Archives)*

13 Fish and Game Warden Dyche

David Leahy,[1] private secretary to Governor Walter Roscoe Stubbs, recounted this story of how Lewis Lindsay Dyche became Kansas fish and game warden:

"I was the only other person present at that conference, merely as a spectator. It lasted not more than ten minutes.

"'Dyche,' said the governor, speaking as he usually did in the imperative mood, 'run down to Pratt at once and report back to me what needs to be done to the fish hatchery to make it serve the purpose for which it was created.'

"Some days later he returned to the governor's office with a report that would have frightened a timid governor. Stubbs, who had become one of the largest railroad building contractors in the Middle West from a small beginning of two mortgaged mules and a capital of thirteen dollars, was not easily scared in the presence of a large project.

"Dyche had submitted a plan for the junking of the hatchery then existing and the rebuilding of a modern one, scientifically constructed, in its stead. The governor reached for his pencil and after figuring for a minute or two reached for the phone and called up Chancellor Frank Strong of the state university.

"'Strong,' he said, 'I want to borrow Professor Dyche for some state work, thanks.'

"Then turning to Dyche he said, 'Go down and do that job and if anyone interferes with you boot him off the place.'"[2]

Leahy's glib reminiscence aside, Dyche was reluctant to exchange his university tenure for a four-year political appointment that until then had routinely been a political gift bestowed upon supporters of the governor. "I'll have to study over that [wardenship]," Dyche told the *Topeka Daily Capital*. "Politicians are forever changing and probably by the time I had become well acquainted with the work there would be a change and out I would go."[3]

Although the fish and game fund had generated sixty-thousand dollars in fines and hunting license fees, the state legislature had failed to release funds for the warden's use, and the office was operating solely from the governor's contingent fund, a total resource of ten thousand dollars. Colonel Thomas Benton Murdock had volunteered to serve as fish and game warden without salary since July, but Stubbs was unhappy with Murdock's management of the meager funds. Their rift was resolved when Murdock died suddenly on November 4, hence Stubbs's offer to Dyche on November 15.

Dyche did not want the position. "The fish and game protection business managed by a few hundred deputy wardens did not look good to us," he later summarized. "It presaged trouble."[4]

William Allen White described in his autobiography how Dyche's predecessor, Colonel Murdock, was offered the position: Thomas Benton Murdock, a loyal Stubbs supporter, had counted on being appointed a state railroad commissioner when Stubbs was elected governor, but Stubbs balked because Murdock had been the "chief fugleman" of George R. Peck, general counsel of the Santa Fe Railroad, "who 'handled' the legislature for the railroads and the other interests which feared reform legislation."[5] Murdock was told, "Bent, Stubbs says he can't make a railroad commissioner out of a man who has been upstairs with every railroad in the state for the last thirty-five or forty years."

According to White, "The tears came into [Murdock's] old rheumy eyes and he cried out like a stuck hog: 'Did Stubbs say that? Did Stubbs say that of me, his friend?' And then he put his arm on the table, laid his head on it, and his body shook in sobs for a moment. Then when his grief and anger were spent, he looked up piteously and said: 'Well, I suppose it's all right. Ask him what else he has got.'"

"It was a terrible story," White wrote. "I have often thought of it. But Stubbs was kind. He made Uncle Bent fish and game commissioner. Stubbs sensed the enchantment of a private [railway] car. The fish and game commissioner had a private car with a fish tank in it which went about the state putting little catfish, bass and carp into the streams and lakes. Back of the fish tank were some berths, a kitchen, a dining room, and a club car. Uncle Bent took it, and his spirit was healed. It was his car. He did not have to share it with two other [railroad] commissioners. It was a bit shabby compared with the shiny office car that the railroad commissioner[s] had, but it was a private car."[6]

The day after Dyche was offered the wardenship, Chancellor Frank Strong sent him a memorandum: "I see that Governor Stubbs has offered you the place of Fish and Game Warden. I hope that you will take it, and especially that you will keep in mind the advantage of the University taking over that work permanently."[7]

Dyche informed Stubbs that he would not accept the wardenship if it meant forfeiting his position at the university. "I have spent 25 of the best years of my life engaged in naturalist work for the university and I could not think of giving it up for this fish and game warden job," Dyche told the *Topeka State Journal*. "I would like to spend my vacations at the fish hatchery and part of the time through the year, if I could direct the work without conflict with the university work."[8]

According to David Leahy, private secretary to Governor Walter Roscoe Stubbs, Dyche "found an unused desk somewhere in the statehouse and moved it into the executive reception room next to mine." This photograph shows Dyche at his desk (in the background) just outside the governor's office. David Leahy sits at his desk in the foreground. (University of Kansas Archives)

Whether or not it was his original intention that Dyche remain attached to the university while serving as fish and game warden, Stubbs embraced the concept: "My idea is to take this department out of politics and put it on a business basis," he asserted. "Instead of having a political machine down there at Pratt I want to have a great industry and I think we are proceeding along the right lines. I believe some arrangement can be made whereby Prof. Dyche will be able to continue his work at the University and direct the fish and game department. As a part of the University the department will be out of politics."[9]

Stubbs, whom Dyche considered to be "a fine man with no rotten spots,"[10] proposed to depoliticize the fish and game wardenship by appointing Dyche to the office. Dyche was well known in the state both as a naturalist and as a university professor, but he had no political affiliations. Although Dyche was a friend of the governor's (Dyche and Stubbs shared a boat dock at the Lake View Fishing and Hunting Club), Dyche belonged to no political party. Stubbs believed that Dyche could improve the dismal fish and game situation in Kansas—despite the fact that Stubbs, in appointing Murdock warden, apparently had been as guilty as any previous governor of using the post as a political reward. Stubbs reasoned that if Dyche accepted the position the fish and game wardenship would fall under the control of the university, ensuring that it would be free from politics in the future. That arrangement also would provide the means for the warden's salary; otherwise, Stubbs would have to wait for the 1911 legislature to release funds for that purpose.

The Board of Regents endorsed the proposition, passing a resolution that Strong sent to Governor Stubbs on November 30: "On account of the lack of appropriations for the fish and game wardenship, and of its great importance to the state, and further because of the desire and duty of the University to do everything in its power for the commonwealth whose name it bears, the Regents of the University of Kansas hereby offer the services of . . . Dyche as fish and game warden for so much of his time as may be necessary to place the fish hatchery and the entire work connected with the position on a thoroughly scientific and economic basis, believing that it may be made of great economic importance to Kansas."[11] Stubbs accepted the regents' offer, and Dyche and the University of Kansas found themselves in the fish and game business.[12]

"The Mt. McKinley business, the Alaskan trip, the lecture business and then the Fish and Game Warden business, all came in quick succession," Dyche wrote James R. Mead. "A two year's trip to Alaska hunting big bears, moose, caribou, sheep, Pacific walrus, seals, etc, etc, would interest me more than all the other things. Would rather take that trip than to own the Fish Hatchery. However I may get some satisfaction in trying to develop the Hatchery and game business in this state."[13] But Mead wrote Dyche, "I would much rather go to Alaska than herd fish in Kansas—it is a hard thankless job. And in your case no pay. There *are* plenty of others who probably could fill the Fish and Game position, but who can take your place in Natural History. Your chosen calling. So you should have gone to Alaska—and gained honor and renown by climbing Mt. McKinley. . . ."[14]

After visiting the state fish hatchery and reviewing the progress of the fish and game department, Dyche realized that the wardenship would require more than his vacations and part-time work. At the warden's office there was no library, no reports from wardens of other states, no systematic bookkeeping, and no laboratory. Dyche moved his personal library and equipment to Pratt, where he improvised a laboratory in an old buggy shed, and began "a careful and systematic study of the state, and collected all information available concerning fish and game and the needs and possibilities in the state of Kansas."[15] His university duties were suspended temporarily.

The state programs for fish and for game had been coordinated under a single agency, the Office of Fish and Game Warden, in 1905. Until then the office had been titled "Fish Warden," and the game laws of the state were "enforced" by constables, marshals, and police officers. But there were few game animals for those officials to protect.

"In former years, when the state of Kansas was new, it might have been considered a game state," Dyche observed. "The prairie lands were covered with herds of buffalos and antelope, and the wooded valleys and hills furnished shelter for many deer and elk.[16] Wild turkeys were quite common in the wooded districts, and prairie chickens were found in great numbers, especially in the eastern part. At present, conditions are changed. Large game animals have completely disappeared. Wild turkeys have likewise become extinct, and prairie chickens are confined to a few counties in the western part of the state and are threatened with extinction. About the only game animal that has held its own is the rabbit, and about the only game bird is the quail. Ducks and geese in former years were very common during the period of migration. Of late years, comparatively, but a very few pass through the country. Kansas can not any longer be counted as a game state."[17]

Consequently the duties of Dyche's office consisted almost entirely of the management of the state's fish resources. But the outlook for fishing in the state was not auspicious either. All rivers and most streams had low-level dams, which disrupted the fish populations. The rivers, streams, lakes, and ponds were overharvested. Fish were illegally dynamited or seined from the water. Dyche soon learned that the most frequent abusers of fishing laws were the deputy wardens he had inherited from the previous administration: In his first three weeks in office, it was reported that not a single arrest was filed with his office, but he received seventy-five complaints about his deputy wardens.

To become a deputy warden, all that was necessary was that a person submit to the state fish and game warden a petition signed by ten taxpayers in his county. The deputy warden received no salary other than his portion of the fines collected, and many deputy wardens found their time better spent illegally hunting or trapping, free from fear of arrest. Some of them were in the business of exporting out of the state game birds they had trapped, but the most common complaint against deputy wardens was seining for fish. Deputy wardens had been given the right to seine for carp, which were considered an undesirable fish, but wardens often were accused of netting bass and catfish under the pretext of seining for carp.

In his first months as fish and game warden, Dyche demonstrated that he would be strict in enforcing the laws and he would cleanse the ranks of his deputies. He solicited such organizations as the Anti-Horse Thief Association to recommend deputy wardens so he would not have to rely solely on ten unfamiliar signatures as the basis for an appointment. He promised, "I will not allow a deputy warden to serve twenty-four hours after I have cause to believe that he has violated the law he has sworn to enforce."[18] Dyche prohibited deputy wardens from seining or trapping fish. And he vowed to hand out an extract of the Kansas fish and game laws with every hunting permit issued.

Dyche also publicized his grand plan for Kansas: a fish pond on every farm. He told the *Duluth Evening Herald,* "Do you know that a farmer can clean up more ready cash on one acre of water, properly stocked with fish, than he can on ten acres of land planted to wheat, corn or alfalfa? That is the history of the fish industry in Germany and other European countries. . . . Now we brag a good deal about the farmer's wife who markets her butter and eggs and secures enough revenue to feed and clothe the whole family. Why not let her also add fish and take that to market, too? Why, the boys on the farm can go out and build a pond during their idle hours and in three years have all the sport they want right at their door catching three-pound black bass or fine, large catfish, and selling them at a good price."[19]

To this end, he learned everything he could about fish culture, making his own investigations of the fish of Kansas and dissecting thousands of fish to determine their feeding habits. By the end of 1911 he had dealt with three or four minor fish epidemics at the hatchery.

In conjunction with his fish studies, Dyche apprised reporters of the qualities of the German carp as a food fish. The carp, popular in Europe, had been introduced throughout the United States by the Federal Bureau of Fisheries beginning in 1877 and had proven itself to be hardy and procreant. But most Kansans disliked the immigrant fish, finding it to be bland, bony, and "rough."

Dyche found the carp to be palatable when cooked properly,[20] and he believed it was the perfect fish for farm ponds, especially since the carp was vegetarian and other popular fish, such as the bass, were "cannibals." Dyche asserted, "Put one hundred bass in a small acre pond and in a couple of years you will have developed about four splendid bass—but that is all you will have, the other ninety-six will have perished."[21] Dyche's rational defense of carp, however, had laid the foundation for a controversy that would plague his entire term of office.

After five months as warden, Dyche received a stormy introduction to Kansas politics in the person of Del W. Travis, who had preceded Colonel Murdock in office, serving as the last fish warden and the first fish and game warden. Governor Stubbs had intimated that Travis was responsible for the legislature not having released funds for the warden's use. Travis accused Stubbs of making a false statement. Then he listed complaints against Dyche's management of fish and game resources. Travis accused Dyche of stocking the rivers and streams of the state with carp, "which means the extinction of the game fish of the state and which will be a detriment to both fish and streams."[22] Travis also charged that carp were driving away migratory birds because they fed on wild rice and celery that those birds sought. He claimed that the Pratt hatchery was being neglected and its ponds were running dry. He accused Dyche of failing to collect fees for game licenses and of not enforcing game laws. Sympathetic to Travis, but contradicting his last indictment, the Kansas State Sportsmen's Association charged that under Dyche's administration they were "game-lawed to death."

"Prof. Dyche reiterates his assertion that the carp is an edible fish." From the Topeka State Journal, *December 24, 1910. (University of Kansas Archives)*

Dyche responded in a letter that newspapers printed throughout the state. He asserted that in the ten months since Travis left office, more money had been collected in license fees than during the entire last year of Travis's term. The water level at the ponds at Pratt was set, he said, so that spring winds would not erode the banks with waves. He said that although carp was a fine food fish, he had not introduced any into Kansas ponds or streams. Carp were raised at Pratt as food for other fish. Whether or not carp fed on wild rice, Dyche observed, wild rice was so rare in Kansas that ducks would not care one way or the other. Dyche also speculated that Travis was angling for the position of fish and game warden himself and that he had ulterior reasons for wanting the job, namely interest in land near the Pratt hatchery. Dyche closed his letter by challenging Travis to a public debate.

The day his letter appeared, Dyche came upon Travis in the lobby of a Pratt hotel. Dyche later summarized the encounter: "When I entered the hotel (the Hupp house) Mr. Travis and a party of gentlemen were reading my article as published in the Topeka Capital. I saluted the crowd with a 'Hello, fellows,' and looking at Mr. Travis said, 'What do you think of it?' Some bystander said, 'Hello, Professor, is that you?' I had to acknowledge that it was. Then I was introduced to the gentlemen in the crowd, most of whom I knew. At this juncture of affairs, Mr. Travis butted in with the remark that I could not run any bluff on him. I addressed my attention to him and asked him what he meant. When I received no answer I told him if he had reference to that article of mine that he had just been reading, that I would stand for it and make good every statement in it. He then tried to start a side issue (an old political trick of his I am told) on the subject of pheasants.[23] The bombastic pheasant talk was cut short when I dared him to show me the birds, finding them with his fine bird dog or in any manner that he claimed existed in great numbers between the Hatchery and the city. He simply remarked that he was no fool. As I did not care to argue that proposition with him, the episode seemed to be closed. At this moment some one of the bystanders suggested that a hall be hired 'so that you fellows can have it out' as some have remarked. I thought it would only be courteous on my part to pay one half the hall rent for the joint debate and offered to do so."[24]

The two men did not carry out their debate in person, instead carrying on their war in the newspapers. Dr. J. W. Schultz, who had served as state fish commissioner from 1897 to 1899, took Dyche's side in the *Wichita Eagle:* "It would seem that Governor Stubbs is the first governor to recognize the importance of the office of state game and fish commissioner. Heretofore the office has been considered as a bon-bon or plum to reward some friend for a political favor. . . . The hatchery, as he [Travis] terms it, is only a stone's throw from his house and it's so convenient when off with his private car taking his mother-in-law to her home in Missouri, the hands that are paid by the state to run the incubators can make hay for Del while they rest. . . . It would seem that Del has learned more of politics than of fish. . . ."[25] Schultz criticized Travis for having given his deputy wardens permission to eradicate carp from Kansas waters, thereby providing them with a pretext to seine out the better varieties of game food fish.

Travis blasted Dyche from the *Topeka State Journal:* "I think it is about time to call the professor's bluff and present him to the state at large for what he really is, namely: a theoretical enthusiast, a sort of pipe dreamer, absolutely devoid of any practical ideas to fish propagation and utterly lacking in any business or common sense method in the administration of his office."[26]

"A man running the hatchery on 'common sense business principles,'" retorted Dyche in the *Topeka Daily Capital,* "would, I presume, be expected to control and utilize the men working for him for political purposes, but not so with a mere 'pipe dreamer' who, by the way, does not use a pipe, drink whiskey or play poker. Of course, in making this last statement, I understand that I am laying myself open to bitter criticism as there are those who may insist that such a 'theoretical enthusiast' does not have 'practical business sense' enough to be able to run the state fish car successfully."[27]

Dyche referred to the Angler No. 1, a magnificent wooden railway car constructed during Travis's administration. Designed as a means of delivering fish throughout the state, the Angler contained twelve two-hundred-gallon fish tanks. Accommodations for passengers included upholstered leather seats that could be made into berths; a desk and bookcase; a dining room with oak dining table, chairs, and built-in china cabinet; an adjoining kitchen fully equipped with gas stove and refrigerator; and a sliding window between the kitchen and dining room so that passengers could be served conveniently. A cook-porter usually accompanied the car. Travis had been accused often of taking joyrides in the Angler with political cronies on hand to play poker and the icebox filled with beer.

The Dyche-Travis newspaper war simmered in ensuing months, although the merits of the carp continued to be a popular topic of discussion. To the sportsmen's complaint that carp were driving away ducks, Dyche replied: "It is the thousands of sportsmen who are out slaughtering the wild ducks every year that is causing their extermination."[28] "Prof. Dyche has not yet defended the sardine," quipped the *Atchison Globe*, "but we expect him to do it most any minute."[29] "Dyche Full of Prunes; Carp Full of Bones," read a headline in the *Topeka Daily Capital*.[30] The *Kansas City Star* sided with Dyche, christening the black bass, due to its "cannibalistic" habits, "the Vandal and the Hun of the fish kingdom."[31] And the following limerick appeared in the *Topeka State Journal:*

A fish and game warden named Dyche
The big German carp doth much lyche
But the people all roar
"We desire him no moar;
We'd rather have black bass and pyche."[32]

By the fall of 1910 Dyche had moved his family to Pratt, although he continued to divide his time between Pratt, Topeka, and Lawrence. (The daughter of James and Fern Mead recalls that Dyche would pause in Wichita during his travels to nap at her parents' house. If no one was at home, he would leave a note on the front door, climb in the porch window, and find a bed upstairs in which to sleep.) In late September he attended a conference of the American Fisheries Society in New York and visited several fish hatcheries and game farms in New England. In November his first fish and game bulletin was published, a comprehensive guide to constructing and maintaining a fish pond. In its introduction he recalled his boyhood days on the Wakarusa River. He encouraged parents to let their boys go fishing: "It does boys good to go fishing. When fishing they are not doing anything else. . . . I have a good notion to throw this paper and pencil away right now and go fishing! What a pity it is that a fellow who is naturally tired and especially hungry for fish has to work on a bright May morning like this when the signs are all favorable, the wind in the west, the very time when fish bite best! What you say, fellows? Let's all quit and go fishing; I am going."[33]

Dyche became fish and game warden at the height of national interest in conservation, stirred by the Theodore Roosevelt administration. Samuel P. Hays depicted the years 1908 to 1910 as being filled with an "intense emotional fervor" for conservation.[34] In *Conservation and the Gospel of Efficiency*, Hays pointed out that "conservation, above all, was a scientific movement, and its role in history arises from the implications of science and technology in modern society. . . . Its essence was rational planning to promote efficient development and use of all natural resources."[35] "Efficiency" is the key word in Hays's analysis of the conservation movement, including the implementation of business methods to utilize the nation's natural resources and the elimination of waste. The appointment of a professor of natural history as Kansas fish and game warden was in keeping with the national sentiment: An expert, a "technician," would decide how the state's natural resources could be utilized most effectively. Dyche's concept of "fish farming" also followed, as Hays termed it, the "Gospel of Efficiency."

Dyche saw the potential for the Kansas state fish and game warden to assume responsibility for conserving *all* of the state's natural resources, not merely game and fish. He devised a proposal to correlate his responsibilities with the conservation of water, the conservation of soil, the checking of floods, the development of a fish industry, the saving of stock water, and the propagation and replenishing of the state with game birds. Related to his plan for a fish pond on every farm was the notion that more rainwater should be saved in ponds, more streams and rivers should be dammed, more lakes built, and less water in general be allowed to drain into the Mississippi River basin. And to stock the farm ponds, the state fish hatchery at Pratt should be expanded extensively. Dyche presented his conservation plan to the state legislature on January 19, 1911. His broadly stated ideas were well received and generally recognized as making "good business sense" for the state. But feathers began to fly when the first stage of Dyche's plan, a comprehensive fish and game bill, was introduced in the Senate.

Dyche had assembled all previous Kansas fish and game laws, revised them, updated them to meet current conditions, and organized them into a single chapter. Although the legislation was introduced by J. D. Myers of Jackson County, it was universally referred to as "The Dyche Bill." As written, the bill would

1. introduce closed hunting seasons for nearly every mammal in the state, including squirrels, muskrats, skunks, minks, raccoons, civet cats, and opossums (owners and legal occupants of land would be allowed to kill animals that destroyed poultry or damaged property);

2. require a hunting license to hunt any animal (rabbit hunters, for instance, previously needed no license);

3. change the open seasons on game birds, making most later in the season and shorter in duration, and reduce bag limits;

4. prohibit the use of pump and automatic shotguns in hunting game birds;

5. prohibit shooting a bird while it was on the ground or water;

6. prohibit shooting waterfowl from motorboats;

7. prohibit shooting birds before sunrise or after sundown;

8. prohibit the use of live birds as decoys;

9. prohibit killing any wild "song or insect-eating" bird and prohibit the selling of the plumage, skin, or body of these birds (bluejays, blackbirds, and crows could be killed if harming crops);

10. prohibit killing any eagle;

11. protect partridges and pheasants for six years;

12. protect quail for five years;

13. protect beavers, otters, deer, and antelope for ten years;

14. require a twenty-five to one hundred dollar fine for the first violation of any of the above, and authorize a twenty-five dollar reward for information leading to an arrest.

Public reaction to the Dyche Bill was hostile. "Why should we let up shooting the ducks when they will only be killed further south anyway?" was a common argument. It was reported that many women suffragists, accustomed to wearing colorful plumage on their hats, opposed the measures in Dyche's bill that would prohibit them from doing so. "It is proposed to prohibit the shooting of ducks on the water," reported the *Lawrence Daily Gazette,* "and also to banish the automatic and the pump gun, although the proposed law does not require that the hunter shall use a flintlock. He may kill the birds with sticks and stones if he prefers. Nor can the hunter use the festive live decoy to inveigle the victim of the air to his blind. He must use the manufactured imitation, a base deception that frequently resembles a real duck as nearly as it resembles an elephant."[36]

Dyche lobbied for his bill during the following weeks, addressing the Senate for over an hour on February 9. "No one was interested in the outcome of the law more than the fish and game warden," Dyche later recorded in his biennial report, referring to himself in third person. "Yet he did not ask a single member of the legislature to vote for a single one of its sections. However, when asked to do so, he gave such information as he was able to concerning certain features of the law."[37] The discussion following Dyche's address to the Senate was filled with merry-making and joking. Passages were ridiculed for their language and their style, jokes were made about the carp, about protecting the skunk, and opposition members referred to one another as "small fry," prompting Dyche to note in his diary: "Senate showed butts when it considered Fish & Game bill."[38]

By late February the Dyche Bill had passed the Senate relatively intact. The most substantial changes to Dyche's proposals involved the duration of open hunting seasons on various game animals. The squirrel season was made four months instead of one, and open seasons on migratory birds were generally longer and further into spring than Dyche wished.[39] Bag limits also were altered. A measure that would have protected quail and prairie chickens for five years failed, but the open seasons on those birds were reduced considerably. One of the most heated Senate arguments concerned a measure banning pump and automatic shotguns. Senator George Hodges, a Democrat, argued in favor of this proposal, calling such weapons "unsportsmanlike," but the measure failed in committee. Nevertheless, Dyche succeeded in pushing through stricter measures for protecting wildlife in Kansas than had existed previously. For example, for the first time in the state's history, nongame "song and insect-eating" birds (such as the robin or the western meadowlark) would be protected.

State fishing laws remained by and large as they had been, with the exception that it became illegal to fish with more than one hook on a line (to reduce the snagging of fish). No dam could be placed on a Kansas stream or river unless a chute or fish ladder also was constructed. One of Dyche's pet ideas had been approved as well: A fisherman now would be allowed to seine for fish (previously illegal) provided he first obtain a permit from the fish and game warden, post a fifty-dollar bond, and use only a seine with a three-inch or larger mesh. Dyche believed that larger fish often ate too many of the smaller ones. A large mesh would remove only the largest fish, thus allowing a fish population to propagate more evenly. Such seining also would allow farmers who did not have time to fish for sport to "harvest" local waters for food fish. Dyche's proposal to require a license for fishing did not pass.

On March 9 the House passed the Dyche Bill seventy-four to thirty-three, without making a single change to the Senate version, and the first stage of Dyche's conservation plan for Kansas was signed into law. A bill also was passed that provided a tax rebate to farmers who constructed a one-acre or larger pond on their farms.

The Dyche Bill formalized the arrangement made between Governor Stubbs and the Board of Regents whereby the fish and game warden was placed under the supervision of the regents.[40] As before, the warden would be appointed by the governor for a term of four years, subject to Senate approval, or until a successor was appointed and qualified, but the wardenship would be administered by the University of Kansas. The warden's salary was set at two thousand dollars per year, an increase of five hundred dollars over Del Travis's salary. In Dyche's case, it was understood that the university would provide an additional one thousand dollars, bringing his total salary to three thousand dollars (thus far, Dyche had received a salary from the university only, no funds having been released by the legislature for the fish and game warden). In a further effort to remove the wardenship from politics, a provision was added that "the fish and game warden shall possess practical knowledge of the qualifications and duties of a fish and game warden."[41]

Governor Stubbs stressed to the legislature that he wished the monies owed the fish and game warden released immediately, and he demanded reimbursement for the $7,258.40 he had paid over the past seventeen months out of his contingent fund for the warden's use. This accomplished, Dyche had the means to manage his office.

The difficulties of enforcing an unpopular law soon became apparent. In Crawford County, a deputy game warden named Doty arrested two men for hunting without licenses, but the local justice of the peace refused to fine them and instead taxed Doty for court costs. When Doty refused to pay, the justice of the peace jailed him. Doty wired Dyche, and Dyche wired Attorney General John S. Dawson to get Doty out of jail and dismiss the justice of the peace for misfeasance in office.

University control of the fish and game wardenship was threatened later that spring. As noted, Dyche was supposed to receive two thousand dollars salary from fish and game funds and one thousand dollars from the university, but the state auditor, W. E. Davis, deemed these to be two separate salaries and held that a man could receive only one salary. The Board of Regents argued that Dyche would receive the fish and game salary for his work as fish and game warden and the university salary for his work "as curator of the Museum of Mammals and Birds and for his services to the Biological Survey"—two salaries for two separate positions. But the auditor held that because the fish and game wardenship was part of the university, it was all one job. Frustrated, the board in its proceedings "resolved that the Board advise Fish and Game Warden Dyche that it refers him to the proper state officers regarding his salary as State Fish and Game Warden, as it is not apparently under the control of this Board."[42] With Dyche threatening to sue Davis for his salary, the board "ordered that a committee . . . take up with the governor the matter of Professor Dyche's salary to see whether the whole matter could be permanently brought under the University."[43] Regent William Allen White wrote Dyche of the board's eventual solution: "Upon my motion we agreed to allow your salary at three thousand dollars out of the University allowance, at least until the possible special session of the Legislature can fix matters otherwise."[44]

It became evident that the new fish and game law would be strictly enforced. In early May, Dyche supported a deputy warden who fined a man twenty-five dollars for shooting an English sparrow (generally considered a pest). Dyche concurred with the deputy warden's opinion that the sparrow was a songbird and therefore protected under the law. "We would suggest that the professor include the mule [as a songbird]," a Beloit newspaper quipped. The *Osborne Farmer* noted, "Prof. Dyche, who wisely announced that the English sparrow is a song bird, is expected to soon come out with the declaration that the mudcatfish is a fur bearing animal."[45] Such criticism had no effect on Dyche, who soon proclaimed the dove an insect-eating bird eligible for the state's protection. As a charter member of the Kansas chapter of the Audubon Society, Dyche's protection of birds was in direct opposition to many hunters. The goals of the Kansas chapter of the Audubon Society were: to discourage the destruction of harmless wild birds and their eggs, to create "a healthy sentiment" against ornamentation with feathers of wild birds, to preserve wild game birds by shortening hunting seasons, and to arouse popular interest in enforcement of laws protecting wild birds and animals.

In Lawrence on May 25, Dyche arrested eleven men who were fishing illegally below the Bowersock Dam. He recounted, "These men were friends of mine, who had caught fish for years for me for laboratory use; but they simply would not quit using unlawful nets until they were arrested. We arrested the whole bunch, took a wagonload of nets and hauled them through the city to the court house."[46] Dyche also vowed to arrest women who wore the plumage of protected birds.

Newspapers reported an argument that took place in the Kansas Supreme

Court chamber: Dyche happened upon a wealthy Shawnee County farmer, Eugene Quinton, who was unhappy about the new game laws. "Is it true that I cannot shoot quail on my own farm until the quail season opens without being liable to arrest?" Quinton asked Dyche.

"That's correct," Dyche replied.

"Well, then I want to tell you," Quinton said, "the state's quail are trespassing on my farm and I demand that you come up there and take every one of them off my place. If you don't remove them I shall drive them off, and I shall use whatever force may be necessary. If I own the quail that are on my farm I have a right to shoot them without being molested by the state, but if the state owns them and I can't shoot them I insist that they be taken off my place."[47]

Newspapers carried the story of a Nemaha County farmer confined to the Topeka State Hospital for the Insane who was caught fishing on the nearby Kansas River with three hooks on one line. A deputy warden was about to lay the "majestic paw of the law" on the man when "he found that a heavier hand had already been placed on his prisoner's head, so he let him go with a severe reprimand." The asylum patient vowed to fish no more, saying, "This country is in bad shape. Any man that will fish with one hook is crazier than I am, and that's a fact. . . . Who is this fellow Dyche, anyway? Why isn't he in here where he belongs?"[48]

Expressing the sentiments of many Kansas sportsmen, Charles Payne, a Maple Hill druggist, wrote Dyche to turn down an appointment as deputy warden: "In my opinion, of all the freak Laws that have encumbered the Statutes of Kansas (and there are a great many), the last Fish and Game Law is easily entitled to first place: some of its provisions being so ridiculous that it would be impossible to enforce them."[49]

In his defense, Dyche pointed out that the hunting seasons and bag limits had been established by the state legislature, not by him. Dyche attempted to depict himself merely as the enforcer of regulations created and passed by legislators. If the hunters disagreed with the law, they should address themselves to the legislature. By assuming that stance, Dyche avoided affiliation with regulations that he thought too lenient. If his recommendations had been fully implemented, most open seasons would have been shorter.

Sportsmen of the state were not only disgruntled, they were organizing. In Coffeyville a justice of the peace dismissed a case against a man arrested for killing a dove when several members of the Kansas State Sportsmen's Association testified that doves were destructive and therefore fair game. In Wichita about fifty hunters formed a state game protective association in affiliation with the Kansas State Sportsmen's Association, the main purpose of which was to repeal Dyche's game law. Fund-raising buttons were sold for fifty cents each.

Dyche did not place sole responsibility for the lack of game on hunters, pointing out in a report to the governor that "practically all the land in Kansas is used for agriculture, horticulture and stock-raising purposes. There are no longer any wild or naturally protected places for game."[50] But Dyche also observed that "all the resident game birds in the state of Kansas could easily be exterminated, and that, too, in a few years, by the methods employed by some hunters who hunt according to law, or what they consider within the bounds of the law. If each farmer in the state of Kansas should allow legal quail hunting for fifteen days each year on his farm, in the course of three or four years there would be few or no quail in the state. . . . The farmer who never allows hunting on his place is the greatest game protector the state has."[51] Dyche held that deer could be reintroduced if hunters would only use "common sense," but he was skeptical that such would be the case.

Unable to hire a network of traveling professional wardens, Dyche relied on the existing system of local deputy wardens but continued to cleanse their ranks, dismissing untrustworthy wardens and introducing new ones (Dyche's former assistant, Charlie Saunders, became a deputy warden in Douglas County). In the last two weeks of November, Dyche revoked the commissions of seven deputy wardens and announced that four wardens who had been arrested for game law violations would be prosecuted.

Given the many years Dyche had hunted animals for the university collections, the vehemence with which he established and enforced the Kansas fish and game law is ironic. Although he imposed his own moral code on his hunting practices, he clearly had violated local game laws at times. In 1891 Dyche wrote Frederic True at the National Museum, "Owing to the various laws which have been passed of late years, collecting has become a hazardous business. For the past two years I have been in mortal terror while operating in the field for fear that I would get into trouble with the powers that be (in the countries where I collected). There is hardly a country (locality) in N. Am. now where a man can go and collect large mammals without violating some law. To say the least this makes the collecting business very unpleasant."[52] E. L. Brown, Dyche's guide on the 1890 moose-hunting trip in Minnesota, wrote Dyche after reading an early draft of *Camp-Fires of a Naturalist,* "Speaking of violating the law in our hunt, I presume it is not from fear of prosecution that you suppress certain parts—these things are not actionable after 60 days."[53]

It is the often-expressed belief of modern-day hunters that sportsmen assumed an active role in the conservation effort because they were the ones who had witnessed the destruction of the nation's natural resources first hand (having also participated in that destruction). Dyche makes a good candidate for such a point of view, as does William Temple Hornaday. Both were master hunter-collectors converted to uncompromising conservationism. But in fighting for measures to protect wild animals, both men found sportsmen to be their principal adversaries. Dyche capitalized on his reputation as a remarkable hunter to introduce and enforce game laws in Kansas.

Most changes to Kansas fish and game law passed by the 1913 legislature reflected Dyche's enforcement of the 1911 regulations. The 1911 measure that had made it illegal to kill, catch, or have in one's possession, living or dead, any wild "song or insect-eating" bird was amended to read "*any* wild bird or birds." In prosecuting game law violators, Dyche's deputy wardens often were challenged to prove that a particular species of bird sang or ate insects; several offenders had used that argument to avoid a fine. Dyche hoped that the new phrasing would eliminate that loophole. However, the English sparrow was specifically excluded from the ranks of protected birds, and the dove was specifically added to the list of game birds. The legislature also allowed that up to twelve live decoys be permitted in hunting waterfowl. The bag limits on snipes, plover, and ducks were increased from twelve to twenty. Despite those compromises, Dyche achieved one important concession: A five-year moratorium was passed on the hunting of quail and prairie chickens. Kansas thus became one of only three states to grant the threatened quail a closed season.

Soon thereafter, the Weeks-McLean Migratory Bird Bill was signed by President Taft. The controversial law, to be administered by the Department of Agriculture, provided that the federal government could enact regulations controlling the killing of migratory birds (game and nongame). Previously, migratory fowl were considered the property of whichever state they were in at any given time. Strong objections were raised throughout the country after the U.S. Biological Survey made public a tentative set of regulations listing which migratory birds could be killed and when. Given the considerable public opposition to the new law, the Secretary of Agriculture decided to appoint an advisory committee of fifteen men prominent in game protection to frame the regulations. Partly to ease the blow of placing migratory birds under federal jurisdiction, men to draft the new regulations were selected from across the country. Dyche and Hornaday were among those chosen. Dyche was in favor of strict federal regulations, and wrote Kansas Senator Joseph Bristow, for one, urging him to vote for appropriations that would support the new law. In September the Advisory Board met in Washington to complete drafting the migratory bird regulations, and on October 1 the regulations took effect.

The constitutionality of the Migratory Bird Law would be argued for years. Many believed that the act declaring migratory birds to be "within the custody and protection" of the federal government was a violation of states' rights. In Kansas and Missouri, hunters organized the Sportsmen's Interstate Protective Association to prove the law unconstitutional and to bring back spring open seasons for migratory birds. Several Kansas City hunters openly violated the law, hoping to be arrested so they could challenge the law's constitutionality. The U.S. Attorney in Kansas City refused to issue a warrant against them, however. Two federal district courts and two state supreme courts, including the Kansas Supreme Court, eventually did rule the statute unconstitutional. The Kansas decision came after a hunter, George L. McCullagh, was arrested for shooting wild ducks from a motorboat. A motion to quash the fine imposed on McCullagh was sustained, with McCullagh winning the decision that the state law for the protection of migratory birds was superseded and nullified by an act of Congress (the Migratory Bird Law). The state appealed the case to the Kansas Supreme Court.

The Kansas Supreme Court overturned the decision, ruling that "Congress has no power to prescribe regulations for the protection of migratory game birds within the boundaries of a state," and "a state law forbidding the shooting of ducks from a motorboat is a valid exercise of the police power, notwithstanding the same act limits the number to be killed by one person in a day."[54] The Court's ruling thus upheld Dyche's game law, but simultaneously it challenged the legitimacy of the regulations that Dyche had helped draft while on the Secretary of Agriculture's advisory board.

The constitutionality question was resolved when the United States ratified the Migratory Bird Treaty with Canada in 1916. A treaty between nations taking precedence over the rights of individual states, the U.S. Supreme Court promptly dropped an Arkansas case that would have determined the constitutionality of the Weeks-McLean Migratory Bird Act.

After the initial implementation of the Migratory Bird Law, Dyche continued to serve on the Advisory Board to the U.S. Biological Survey, helping to frame shooting seasons and bag limits for migratory birds. But most of his energy was dedicated not to the fowl of the air, nor to the beasts of the field, but to the fish of the pond.

A picture postcard of the Warden's residence on the grounds of the state fish hatchery at Pratt, Kansas. (George Dyche)

14 The Fish Farm

Throughout his ongoing battle with Kansas sportsmen, Dyche was concerned primarily with fish: learning all he could about food fish, distributing fish, running the Pratt fish hatchery, and making plans to expand the hatchery. In one year, 1911, Dyche examined the stomach contents of between eleven and twelve hundred carp. As he commented at a meeting of the American Fisheries Society, "We talked fish hatchery to everyone and we talked it all the time."[1] Being attached to the University of Kansas, the Kansas fish and game wardenship became part of the Kansas Biological Survey, and Dyche was instructed to coordinate the activities of the Pratt hatchery with Professor Clarence E. McClung, who headed the Survey.

In a letter to Dyche, Regent William Allen White suggested ways to integrate the Pratt hatchery into university activities: "It seems to me that we might work out some kind of a practical course—a course that would be of practical benefit not only to specializing students, but to the average, every-day young man and woman in Kansas. For instance, I am wondering if we could not give a short course in fish culture, such a course that a Kansas country school teacher could give and by utilizing the work of the big boys, erect a pond on the school grounds and grow the fish, teaching practical fish culture through the country schools. Or might we not give such a short course that the average farmer boy could take it for two or three weeks and learn how to construct dams, how to feed and care for fish, how to know their spawning season and to protect their young, at the same time providing a longer course for those graduate students who desire the more technical study and instruction. I wish you would dictate to me your ideas upon these subjects in clear, untechnical language, such that it might be used in the report of the Committee on Efficiency in the Allied Board of Regents."[2]

Dyche informed White that he had consulted with the heads of the departments of botany, entomology, and zoology, and that they had "expressed a willingness and a desire to avail themselves of any opportunity which might be afforded along the lines suggested. The fish and game department would undertake to give both short and long courses practical in their bearing upon various subjects connected with fish culture. . . . lectures could be adapted to high school students or teachers, to farmers' boys, or to the farmers themselves, the idea being to give that particular information on fish culture and related subjects that would be of value to the people of Kansas." (Dyche later proposed that the hatchery be responsible for supplying high schools and colleges in the state with study specimens of Kansas plant and animal life.) Lobbying for funds, Dyche included in his letter a description of a building he had designed that he hoped would be constructed at the hatchery, at an estimated cost between thirty and fifty thousand dollars. The ground floor would contain an aquarium exhibit for public viewing and student experiments. The second story would contain offices, a library, and laboratory-classrooms. The third story would include an exhibition of "game and fish and such material as might be used by the students in carrying on their investigations."[3] Dyche found himself again undertaking to build a sort of museum. To fellow state fish commissioners, he stressed the building's role as a research laboratory: "The building will be primarily for the students of the University of Kansas, but students from other universities and colleges will be welcomed to carry on certain investigations which should be carried on to clear up a considerable number of problems connected with fish culture . . . ."[4]

The hatchery, three miles east of Pratt, consisted of seventy acres, fourteen of which were water. Consulting with William C. Hoad, professor of civil engineering at the University of Kansas, Dyche called for the hatchery to be expanded to 160 acres, 90 of which would be water. The Board of Regents balked at the price Dyche negotiated for the land, however, and voted instead to have Governor Stubbs initiate condemnation proceedings in order to acquire the property. Legal battles continued for months, and at one point Dyche threatened to build the hatchery in El Dorado, where he was sure it would be welcomed as an addition to the local economy. But eventually the condemnation was successful, and on September 9, 1911, the land was secured, a total of 90.1 acres at a cost of $13,708. The state fish hatchery was thus expanded to about 160 acres, running one mile long and a quarter mile wide, with an additional 10.2 acres about a mile west of the main tract.

Dyche's expansion plan called for the hatchery to be completely rebuilt. Professor Hoad, a specialist in sanitary engineering, found the Ninnescah River water to be contaminated with sewage from Pratt. He and Dyche designed an innovative system, with new water transmitters, gates, drains, and supply pipes. Water would be provided by damming the Ninnescah River with a five-hundred-foot cement dam, creating a lake of about eight acres. Before reaching the supply lake, water would be run through several miles of ground rich in watercress, moss, and other plants in order to aerate the water and to furnish it with plentiful microorganisms. Eighty-three new ponds, each about one acre in size, would be added to the existing 11 ponds, with 17 ponds to be built later for a grand total of 111 ponds. New buildings also would be constructed, including the office and educational building and residences for the warden, assistant warden, and hatchery laborers.

As proposed, the Pratt Hatchery would be the largest freshwater fish hatchery in the world. Its total cost was estimated to be $150,000 (until then, the most extensive federal hatcheries in the country reportedly had been built at a cost of less than $25,000). When Dyche presented his plans, including twenty-two blueprints, to an October meeting of the American Fisheries Society in St. Louis, his colleagues were overwhelmed by the scope of the project. When Dyche finished reading his paper, Daniel B. Fearing of the Board of Inland Fisheries Commissioners told him, "You will be Governor of the state of Kansas in two years."[5] W. T. Thompson of the U.S. Bureau of Fisheries remarked, "Professor Dyche has told us of a number of pamphlets he has written which have been issued by the state. I suggest that he write just one more, on the subject of: 'How I Did It.'"[6]

New ponds at the Pratt fish hatchery. (University of Kansas Archives)

On November 21 the Board of Regents met with Dyche and Hoad in Pratt to accept bids for construction of the new ponds. James A. Green & Company of Chicago drew the low bid at $50,667.22. Sam A. Forter of the Green firm, a former star halfback on the University of Kansas football team, was named civil engineer in charge of construction, and O. C. LeSuer of Lawrence, also a Kansas graduate in civil engineering, was appointed resident engineer to oversee the operation for the state. About three-fifths of the contract money would be expended on labor, most of it local, which prompted the *Pratt Union* to crow, "If there is a knocker left in Pratt County, he should throw away his little hammer or

else move to a place where he will not be so lonesome."[7] Construction of the
ponds began on December 18. Since Pratt was too far from the hatchery for
workers from the U.S. Army Corps of Engineers to travel for their meals, Dyche
cooked for them himself. ("That I did the thing up right is evidenced by the fact
that they are still alive to tell the story," he observed.)[8]

During most of February and March of 1912, and again in July, Dyche was
in Washington, D.C., lobbying for a mining bill for Professor Erasmus Haworth,
attending a convention of the National Association of Game Wardens, and
conferring with George Bowers, Fish Commissioner at the U.S. Bureau of Fisheries. Although eager to receive advice regarding fish propagation, Dyche intended
to follow through with the implementation of the features he and Hoad had
designed for the Pratt Hatchery. While the national trend was for hatchery basins
to be cement-lined (including those at the federal hatcheries), Dyche held that fish
would breed better in a natural pond, with banks sloping to a feather edge and
plenty of shallow water where they could deposit their eggs. To minimize construction costs, Dyche and Hoad allowed the size and shape of each pond to
conform to the nearly level existing terrain alongside the river. The ponds were
built within existing bumps, hollows, and natural depressions. Dyche pointed out
that the irregularity of the ponds was "immaterial for fish-cultural purposes."[9]
Dyche also proposed to distribute fish that were two to three years old: old enough
to spawn, and large enough to avoid being eaten by other fish. Distributing fewer
fish individually capable of survival contrasted with the practice of stocking with
large quantities of fry in the hope that some would survive.

In the spring of 1912, Dyche made extended fish distribution trips aboard the
Angler No. 1 along with Mrs. Dyche and Assistant Game Warden C. W. Myers,
who served as Dyche's personal secretary. They delivered about fifteen thousand
fish to the counties along the northern edge of the state. By June Dyche estimated
that the Pratt hatchery had delivered about two hundred thousand fry and adult fish
in three hundred trips since he had become warden. Dyche and Myers used their
time on the distribution trips to catch up on the considerable paperwork involved
with the hatchery, responding to questions regarding game laws, complaints,
applications for deputy wardenships (on May 1 Dyche approved the application for
the first woman warden of the state, Miss Kate M. King of Shawnee County),[10] and
applications to receive fish, including one from the chairman of the Health Committee at the University of Kansas requesting that Potter Lake be stocked with fish
to combat the fierce mosquito population. Dyche obliged with a shipment of
goldfish. Ever the showman, Dyche arranged for the Angler to be on hand to
display and distribute fish at the Topeka State Fair in September and at the Wichita
State Fair in October.

Construction of the Pratt hatchery ponds, waterways, and dam proceeded
according to schedule. About 125,000 cubic yards of earth were moved to form the
embankments of the new ponds, and 6,875 feet of twenty-one-inch vitrified clay
pipe laid to connect the ponds with the water supply. A concrete receiving
chamber, with bronze and iron sluice gates, connected the piping to the pond
system. Connecting the ponds with one another were 880 feet of twelve-inch pipe,
4,000 feet of ten-inch pipe, and 17,000 feet of eight-inch pipe laid in trenches from
three to nine feet deep. Also built were 94 concrete drain-boxes, 191 bronze and

iron sluice gates, 5 cast-iron floodgates, and 300 wire-mesh screens (copper wire on frames of 3/4-inch wrought-iron pipe). The eighty-three new ponds, combined with the eleven existing ponds, provided about fifteen miles of shoreline.

The back of the newly constructed building at the Pratt hatchery incorporated an apse-like wing similar to that of the Museum of Natural History at the University of Kansas. (University of Kansas Archives)

The Board of Regents determined that "about $41,710.48" was available to fund the construction of buildings at the fish hatchery,[11] and on September 19 the Board once again visited Pratt to accept bids. Stansbury & Hardman of Parsons contracted to build the warden's residence, the superintendent's cottage, three cottages for laborers, fifteen tool houses, and a barn for $9,755.94. A $19,246 contract was awarded to Horner Brothers of Topeka to build a power house and the Kansas State Fish and Game Building. The main part of this three-story brick building was seventy by fifty-two feet. To one side was a sixty-five by forty-two-foot apse, similar in size and shape to that portion of the Museum of Natural History that housed Dyche's panorama of North American mammals. It held twelve large wall tanks for the display of fish. The building was topped by a green tile roof.

Although construction at the hatchery was not completed until November, "FISH DAY!," as flyers proclaimed it, was held on October 29. Between five and six thousand persons attended the festivities. Chancellor Strong opened the valve and water flowed into the new ponds. Speeches were delivered expressing hope that fish cultivation would lower the cost of living and that the hatchery would "do everything in its power by disseminating knowledge of fish."[12] The dedication proceedings were followed by motorcycle races. Schools were let out for Fish Day, with classes competing for trophy flags for best attendance at the ceremonies.

The construction of the Kansas State Fish Hatchery elevated Dyche's prominence among experts in fish culture. In fact, it was rumored in Washington, D.C., that Dyche might be appointed U.S. Commissioner of Fish and Fisheries. A shakeup in the Bureau of Fisheries seemed inevitable following a controversy regarding the killing of fur seals off the coast of Alaska; the Bureau was responsible for the management of these animals. William Temple Hornaday, speaking before the Senate Committee on the Conservation of Natural Resources in 1909, called for a moratorium on killing fur seals in U.S. territory and for treaties to be made with foreign governments banning killing the seals in the open sea. Hornaday believed that he had won the battle, but the following year, Charles Nagel, Secretary of Commerce and Labor, utilized a clause granting him discretionary powers in fur-seal management to allow the Bureau of Fisheries to carry out the annual killing of seals. The ensuing congressional investigation, although outwardly supportive of the administration's handling of the matter, resulted in a law forbidding killing of the seals for five years.

Hornaday sought a man who was firm on the fur-seal question, as well as an expert in fish culture, to impel into the fish commissionership. Dyche, although opposed to an all-inclusive moratorium on the killing of fur seals, had spoken out for measures against pelagic sealing during his visits to Washington, and Hornaday wrote Dyche a letter designated "Private & Confidential": "If you should be offered the position of U.S. Commissioner of Fish and Fisheries (salary $6,000), *I want you to accept it! If* it is offered to you, it will be because some very sincere men regard you as the best man in the United States for that position. It will be because your Country needs you, to lick that Bureau into shape, and put it back on a scientific basis, as it was left by Spencer F. Baird. Just sit tight, keep this request under your hat, and wait. Of course in presidential appointments no man on earth can tell from day to day what will really happen. I do know, however that *just now* the *best man* is being looked for!"[13]

Hornaday did not know that the Washington rumors of an appointment for Dyche were hardly a secret, having been reported in Kansas newspapers for months. Dyche was not appointed, however, and he later claimed that he probably would not have accepted the position had it been offered to him. "The little advertising that it brought me, cannot do me any harm in Kansas since it came after the Legislature adjourned," Dyche wrote Hornaday afterwards. It cannot be considered, even by my enemies as the work of a press agent."[14]

But Hornaday felt that they had both missed a chance. "You know that I like men who have ideas, and who can lead public opinion," he wrote Dyche. "You were, in my estimation, an ideal man for the position. Dr. Field is a good, clean man; but I do not regard him as a strong man, like yourself. Every such position needs a man who can fight and strike hard blows whenever the occasion makes it an imperative duty. In these days, a great many public officers are put under pressure by private interests, and sometimes it takes a man of sand to withstand the pressure, and defy it. I give you notice now that if ever I become President, or Secretary of Commerce and Labor, you will be offered the position of United States Fish Commissioner,—whether you accept it, or not."[15]

On September 12, 1913, while Dyche was out of the state attending meetings of the American Fisheries Society, the National Association of Game Wardens, and the advisory board to the U.S. Biological Survey, the *Topeka State Journal* printed a story that appeared in newspapers throughout the state. It ignited anti-Dyche sentiment. The headline: "IT HAS COST $2 FOR EACH FISH."[16]

The reporter for the *Journal* calculated that between July 1, 1911, and July 1, 1912, a sum of $50,653.41 had been expended to operate the Pratt hatchery, and that during that time about twenty-four thousand fish had been distributed. Therefore, he concluded, it cost the state over two dollars for every fish.

What that reporter neglected in his calculation was that funds were not used merely to distribute fish, but were used to expand the hatchery. The fish distributed that year had been raised in seven ponds (four of the original eleven ponds could not be used for propagation), but the money had been used to build eighty-three more ponds. The *Journal* reporter made it clear that Dyche had not personally benefited from this "misuse" of funds, writing that, while in Topeka, Dyche ate his state-paid meals at the YMCA cafeteria (which cost about twenty-eight cents) and saved the state an additional nickel every meal by serving as his own waiter. Nevertheless, the "two dollars for every fish" charge reinforced the caricature of Dyche as a professorial pipe dreamer who was costing Kansans money with his fantastic "fish farm" scheme. Dyche returned to Kansas to find his job in jeopardy.

The new Democratic governor, George Hodges, had announced that he and members of the state executive council would travel to Pratt in early October to investigate conditions at the hatchery. Dyche issued a statement demonstrating the absurdity of the *State Journal* charges. He outlined how fish and game funds had been expended, emphasizing the costs of the hatchery expansion. He reported how many fish had been distributed and to whom (48,975 fish to 255 recipients). He asserted that he welcomed the official investigation of the Pratt hatchery. But the movement against him had gained momentum while he was out of the state. Further accusations were made charging him with mismanagement and of allowing the ponds to run dry over the summer. "Open Season for Dyche," the *Lawrence Daily Journal-World* announced.

There were two elements opposing Dyche: As always, many hunters in the state and especially the Kansas State Sportsmen's Association were at odds with his game law and with his enforcement of that law. Hunters blamed Dyche for not providing the state with more game, and they were incensed that their license fees had been used to construct the Pratt fish hatchery. "When Prof. Dyche gets his new fish pond in operation," read one letter to the *Fulton Globe,* "we presume carp will be quite plentiful. He should then start a crow hatchery and Kansas would then be a sportsman's paradise."[17]

Likewise, the Democrats were after Dyche. When George Hodges was elected governor, it was rumored that Dyche would be replaced with a Democratic appointee. But Hodges (who in 1911 had argued in favor of the proposal to ban automatic and pump shotguns), announced, "I have come to the conclusion that Professor Dyche knows what he is talking about in connection with this fish and game business."[18] Still, many Democrats kept after Dyche, hoping to give their governor an excuse to dump him in favor of a Democratic warden. The "two dollars for every fish" charge suited their design, since the hatchery was, after all, built during a Republican administration and Hodges could not be blamed for its high cost or its mismanagement.

Although Hodges had agreed to an official investigation of the state fish hatchery, he stood behind Dyche. "As for Professor Dyche himself," Hodges stated, "I regard him as the first fish culturist in the state. It is unfortunate, and also looks bad for the persons back of the stories being sent out about Professor Dyche and the fish hatchery, that they should have chosen a time when he was out of the state with no chance to defend himself."[19] Hodges also pointed out that even though an investigation of the Pratt hatchery would be carried out the following month, none of the charges which had been made against Dyche were official.

With Hodges unlikely to discharge Dyche, it appeared for a while that the controversy had run its course. "Attack on Fish Hatchery Comes to a Sudden End," read one headline in the *Salina Union.* But on September 24, C. T. Rankin of Hutchinson renewed the fight, finally issuing formal charges against the fish and game warden. Filing the complaint with Governor Hodges, Rankin, former secretary of the Kansas State Sportsmen's Association and president of a gun club in Hutchinson, charged that Dyche had:

1. failed to raise and distribute fish in Kansas in 1912 and 1913;
2. permitted thirty thousand fish to freeze in one of the ponds the past winter;
3. built many more ponds than were necessary;
4. failed to enforce fish and game laws in the state, "spending practically all of his time in the office of the Governor and outside of the State of Kansas";
5. expended funds derived from hunter's license fees to travel outside of the state on business not connected with the Fish and Game Wardenship;
6. neglected his duty as warden by not giving enough personal supervision to the hatching and distributing of fish, by failing to propagate game or game birds, and by failing to convict fish and game law violators.

"A merry war undoubtedly will result," reported the *Pratt Union.*[20] "Dyche is considered something of a scrapper, and is ready," asserted the *Topeka Daily Capital.*[21] "Paderewski is a genius in music," quipped the *Mound City Democrat,* "but he would be out of place running a fish hatchery. Dyche has blundered ever since he went into the office which he now holds."[22] In attempting to defend Dyche, several newspapers designated the nonpartisan Dyche "a lifelong Democrat," explaining that "his appointment originally was criticized on that account."[23] The *Lawrence Daily Journal-World* reported, "Gov. Stubbs was severely criticized for appointing Prof. Dyche because the latter was a democrat. Now Gov. Hodges is being criticized for keeping him in office and they charge that Dyche is not a democrat. It is a curious mixup."[24] Curious indeed, especially since during Dyche's early lecture tours Republican newspapers had speculated: "We haven't the faintest idea what Dyche's political ideas are. He is a man of good sense, and so we always supposed he was a republican."[25] The controversy surrounding Dyche's appointment to the wardenship had not centered on the fact that he was a Democrat, since he was not, but that he was *not* a Republican. Similarly, Dyche's difficulties were now attributable to the fact that he was not a Democrat either. Dyche had no party affiliation. While this nonpartisanship had enabled him to walk a tightrope and remain in office during two administrations, it was also a major reason for his stormy career as warden.

Rankin's charges reflected the dissatisfaction of hunters, but the charges also provided the Democrats with ammunition that could force Hodges to replace Dyche. Hodges attempted to disassociate himself from the fracas by pointing out that Rankin's charges should have been filed with Attorney General Dawson, not the governor's office. Hodges then announced that the impending investigation of the hatchery would take the form of an open meeting in Pratt, and he invited all those with complaints against Dyche to attend. Although publicly supportive of Dyche, Hodges had, in effect, made his status as warden a matter open for discussion.

Former governor Stubbs was sufficiently worried about Dyche's fate that he initiated a letter-writing campaign, soliciting testimonials from prominent naturalists and fish and game officials throughout the country. To William Temple Hornaday he wrote: "Will you be kind enough to advise me your opinion of the new Kansas State Fish Hatchery and the methods used for the propagation of our common native fishes . . . ? Also, your opinion of the ability of Prof. L. L. Dyche as a Fish and Game Warden. My reason for asking these questions is that some old-time politicians who formerly ran the Hatchery for political purposes only, are making a fierce attack on Prof. Dyche and his scientific methods of fish culture."[26]

The letters poured in, about twenty-four attestations to Dyche's abilities as fish and game warden. "I have no hesitation in saying," wrote W. T. Thompson of the U.S. Bureau of Fisheries, "that in my estimation they [Dyche's plans for the Pratt hatchery] were the most comprehensive and complete of any pond station in the country. This was the general expression amongst this body of fish culturists. Prof. Dyche is a *live wire*. Energy and enthusiasm, of which he is 'chuck full,' coupled with horse sense, of which I am convinced the Professor has his ample share, will accomplish great things along any lines."[27]

October 9 was the day of reckoning, and Governor Hodges, his executive council, and Attorney General John Dawson traveled to Pratt to examine the hatchery and hold the open meeting. One day earlier, Dyche's old nemesis, Del Travis (who owned land adjoining the hatchery), had built a fence across the road used to transport fish to the railway line, but the episode was evidently ignored by the inspecting committee. Although the summer had been "the driest season known to the oldest inhabitant" of Pratt County,[28] the executive council found the ponds were in satisfactory condition, and accounts of the warden's expenditures were in order. C. T. Rankin did not attend the open meeting. Since the originator of the charges was not present, Attorney General Dawson would not dismiss them officially. However, he did disclose that "so far, there has nothing been presented to me against Prof. Dyche that would make a lawsuit against him that would last ten minutes in any district court before which he might be hauled." In reference to Dyche's accounting for fish and game funds and the cost of the hatchery expansion, Dawson stated, "As to the hatchery itself, it is a good deal like the Panama Canal. A critic of the canal could say that the authorities in charge have been down there for nine years and had spent four hundred million dollars on a canal, and that not one ton of freight had been floated through it yet. The wisdom of the canal can only be vindicated by the future, and the wisdom of the fish hatchery, or lack of it, can only be vindicated by the future."[29]

With the lack of any significant organized opposition to Dyche at the open hearing, and with no evidence presented to back up the charges made against him, Dyche was exonerated. But Governor Hodges was willing to compromise on one of the hunters' complaints: "There is undoubtedly an injustice in the present system of taxing the sportsmen of the state by hunting licenses and using the money exclusively in building and maintaining a fish hatchery," he stated. "It doesn't seem just to tax the sportsmen for a fish hatchery to benefit the fishermen and not make the latter pay a tax. I shall propose a license on fishermen too, the same as on hunters."[30] (The state legislature did not carry out Hodges' proposal, however. Instead, in 1915, the legislature voted that money used for the fish hatchery be limited to a maximum of eighteen thousand dollars per year, and that funds received in excess of that amount be placed in a special fund to be used for game preserves.)

C. T. Rankin meanwhile was telling reporters that he had not attended the open meeting because he had not received an invitation, this despite the fact that Hodges had stated publicly that Rankin had been asked to appear. "Drop the charges, will they?" Rankin roared. "We will push this matter to the limit and get enough signers to petitions to compel Dyche to be brought to trial."[31] But Rankin had missed his chance, and with Hodges pledging to make fishermen bear a portion of the financial burden of the fish hatchery, the latest bid to oust Dyche had lost its momentum.

The 1913 legislature had eliminated the system whereby the University of Kansas, the Emporia State Normal School, and the Agricultural College each had its own Board of Regents. Instead, a single Board of Administration, appointed by the governor, would oversee all three schools. Two of the three persons Hodges appointed to the new Board were, naturally, Democrats. In May 1913 the Board had rescinded the salary increases already approved by the University of Kansas's now defunct Board of Regents, and in keeping with this economy drive the new Board also decided that Dyche's salary should not be drawn entirely from university funds. Once again it was proposed that Dyche be paid one thousand dollars from university funds for his position at the university and two thousand dollars from fish and game funds for the wardenship, and once again State Auditor W. E. Davis disapproved the voucher, ruling that Dyche could not draw two separate salaries.

Through Attorney General Dawson, Dyche requested a mandamus from the Kansas Supreme Court to compel Davis to allow the payment of his full salary. If the Supreme Court failed to uphold his claim, it was presumed that Dyche would be forced to resign the fish and game wardenship, as it would be impractical for him to give up the security of his university position and his retirement pension for the sake of the uncertain wardenship (and it had been particularly uncertain during the past several months). The *Topeka Daily Capital* speculated: "The new method of separating him from his fish and game wardenship—if that is what is going on—is a more subtle way of going at it, and might prove effective, it is admitted."[32]

An opinion was filed by the Kansas Supreme Court the following summer. Auditor Davis argued that the duties of the fish and game warden were "independent of, and incompatible with, the duties of a professor in the University, and that it was the legislative intention that Professor Dyche should devote all his time to the duties of the office." Davis also alleged that there existed a public policy and custom against the payment of two salaries to one person, and "that the plaintiff did not perform any service as professor during the time for which he claimed pay."

The Court ruled against Davis, deciding that "the common law does not prevent one person from holding two offices provided the duties of neither one are incompatible with the duties of the other. . . . It is concluded that there is no rule of public policy that will prevent the state from receiving the plaintiff's services as fish and game warden, and also as a professor in the University, and paying his compensation from the direct appropriation made for his salary as warden, and from the amount provided by the board of administration for his salary as professor." As to whether Dyche had actually performed his duties as professor at the university, the Court questioned "whether it is within the official duty of the auditor to inquire whether, or in what manner, the services were performed . . . ."[33] The Court deemed it unnecessary to rule on that question, however, since it found the positions of fish and game warden and professor of systematic zoology to be clearly compatible.

The spring of 1914 was the first season fish from the new ponds were distributed. The fish were particularly anticipated due to the past dry year the state had suffered. In fact, so many streams and ponds had gone dry that Dyche urged fishermen to refrain from fishing in May and June, the spawning season for Kansas fishes. Throughout that summer, while Austria declared war on Serbia, Dyche made the headlines of small-town newspapers across the state of Kansas for bringing fishes to the masses, "out of the fullness of his heart and fish tanks."[34] The hatchery distributed black bass, crappie, bluegill sunfish, bullhead catfish, and goldfish for ponds. Bullfrog tadpoles also were delivered.

Fish were taken from the hatchery to the Angler in milk tins on horse-drawn wagons and then quickly transported to their destination. Dyche planned to distribute two- to three-year-old fish in the future, but for the time being the fish were fry and large fingerlings, two to seven inches long. Although it would be years before the Pratt hatchery's production reached its capacity, an increase in fish distributed was already evident: 64,320 fish in the spring of 1913; 90,775 fish and 20,000 bullfrog tadpoles in the spring of 1914.

The Angler No. 1, a railway car specially designed to deliver fish throughout Kansas. Fish fry are being loaded onto the car in milk tins. (University of Kansas Archives)

That summer Dyche's third bulletin as fish and game warden was issued, and soon all three bulletins were bound in a single volume, *Ponds, Pond Fish, and Pond Fish Culture,* which served as a guide to building and maintaining a pond as well as how to stock it properly, and it described the characteristics of various fish suitable for ponds. The book was among the first comprehensive manuals on fish ponds published in the United States, and it was sought after not only by the Kansas farmer wishing to build a pond but by fish commissioners, libraries, and universities across the country. It was used as a textbook in some agricultural colleges. The *El Dorado Republican* christened Dyche "the Shakespeare of fish literature."[35] In the five years since he had stepped down from the lecture stage and accepted the wardenship, Dyche had, with his characteristic intensity, molded himself into a leading expert on freshwater fishes and had built the largest freshwater fish hatchery in the world—in the unlikely location of Pratt, Kansas.

Dyche planned to utilize the resources of the expanded hatchery to stock the existing rivers, streams, and lakes of the state, but his vision was to provide fish to individual farm ponds. Raising pond fish was efficient: It takes about seven pounds of grain to produce a pound of beef, and three pounds of grain to produce a pound of poultry, but only about one pound of feed to produce a pound of fish. The concept of pond fish as a cash crop was firmly established in Europe and Asia, but in the United States, with its vast open stretches of land, people were accustomed to beef, pork, and poultry. Newspapers joked about the notion of fish as a regular farm crop. "Ed, milk the cows and feed the fish,"[36] sounded absurd, of course. But times were hard, and the fish were free.

Ponds, as Dyche pointed out, had other advantages: They saved rainwater or stream water for irrigation purposes. They provided drinking water for livestock. Pond ice could be stored to preserve perishable foods. Trees could be planted near the pond, providing a windbreak, shade, and a home for songbirds, "not only enlivening the spot with their songs and bright plumage, but also rearing their young and waging a perpetual war on the injurious insects of the neighborhood."[37] Even if pond fish were not raised as a regular farm crop, they provided recreational fishing. And of course swimming in the local pond, and skating on it in the winter, have become clichés of farm life.

Dyche did not live to see ponds transform the Kansas landscape: Pond construction did not take place on a large scale until the 1930s, the Dust Bowl years, with the advent of the Soil Conservation Service (which helped farmers to build ponds). Nor did "fish farming" emerge as a significant industry in Dyche's day. However, Frank Cross, ichthyologist at the University of Kansas, points out that it was in Dyche's hatchery (at Pratt, and in Pratt "extensions," including research ponds) that the catfish industry was born and bred. Techniques for catfish propagation originated there, and the first private, commercial catfish "farm" was Bus Hartley's, established in the 1950s in Cunningham near Pratt, with the assistance of Seth Way, then chief fish culturist for the Kansas Forestry, Fish and Game Commission.[38] Catfish has since become the biggest fish-farming industry in the United States, with annual harvests exceeding 150 thousand tons.

"The Professor's Dream." The Kansas City Star's *vision of a sleeping Dyche dreaming that his animals have come to life. (The illustration was based on "The Taxidermist's after-dinner dream," published in Hurst and Sons' "Stereoscopic Studies of Natural History," a series of stereoptic photographs.) Redrawn with Dyche's face for the* Kansas City Star, *December 6, 1891. (Donald Lewis Dyche)*

15 The Professor's Dream

Lewis Lindsay Dyche listed three addresses in his 1915 pocket calendar: 1617 Massachusetts, Lawrence, Kansas; the Statehouse, Topeka, Kansas; and the Fish Hatchery, Pratt, Kansas. On any given day he might be in any of the three cities. Dyche had been an energetic traveler much of his life, but he was nearly fifty-eight years old, and a physical examination at the Rosedale hospital late in 1914 revealed that he had an advanced heart condition. Dyche kept that information to himself.

The Lawrence address was a newly built house. For many years Mrs. Dyche had wanted a house on Massachusetts Street, and Dyche had finally put together the funds to have one built to her liking. The new house was completed around Thanksgiving, 1914, but Dyche visited it infrequently. Because he spent a good deal of time at the statehouse, he kept a room in the home of his widowed cousin, Florence Burge, at 407 Woodlawn Avenue in Topeka.

The new year found Dyche's position in jeopardy again. Arthur Capper had been elected governor in November, and it seemed likely that Capper would appoint a new fish and game warden. Dyche's failing health and the pressures of the wardenship were apparent. "Dyche's hair is standing straighter and straighter these days," noted the *Topeka Daily Capital.* "It fairly bristles."[1]

The early January entries in Dyche's pocket diary indicate the extent of his commuting between Topeka and Lawrence (the Pratt hatchery required his attention less during winter months): January 1: "In Topeka 407 Woodlawn and at office in State House." January 2: "Go to Lawrence on 8:00 train." January 3:

"Go to Topeka 6 p.m. train." January 5, 6, 7: "In Topeka abed. Day in office." Dyche does not mention in his diary the exceptional events of January 6.

Accounts vary, but the press reported that while Dyche was showing Governor Hodges and his brother, Frank, a Gila monster, part of the Goss Natural History Collection[2] on display in the statehouse, the reptile bit him. Mrs. B. B. Smythe, custodian of the Goss Collection, described the incident for the newspapers: "Professor Dyche was holding the poor creature's jaws awfully wide open. He, Professor Dyche, had just finished pointing out the poison sacs, when the little fellow grew tired of having his jaws stretched all out of shape. He, the Gila monster, closed his jaws—and took off the end of Professor Dyche's thumb. It bled freely. I bathed it in a permanganate of potash solution, very strong and wrapped it up applying a red cross seal to the bandage. The governor was very much worried."[3] Newspapers reported that Dyche previously had remarked at a meeting of the Kansas Academy of Science that the bite of a Gila monster was not poisonous, but he had since told the governor that it was. Dyche now told a reporter, "I immediately went out and got a volume of the latest government reports to see if the Gila monster really is poisonous. The latest government report says they

"The Reptile that Dared to Bite Prof. Dyche."
This humorous cartoon was grimly ironic: less than two weeks after it appeared, Dyche was dead. From the Wichita Eagle. *January 8, 1915. (University of Kansas Archives)*

are. But you mark my word. The Gila monster is going to be sicker than I am." That last remark was widely reported in the Kansas press.[4]

"I see by this morning's Eagle you have been bitten by a 'Gila' monster," Fern Mead Jordan (widow of James R. Mead) wrote Dyche from Wichita. "Now in the first place I don't believe you would permit any kind of a '*monster*' to bite you, tho' I *have* known of people being '*bit*' without a permit. Really the children and I are uneasy about you—for if this is not a newspaper scare it might be serious & we know how little care you take of yourself."[5]

Preoccupied with his pending battle for reappointment to the wardenship, Dyche paid little notice to the Gila monster bite. He remarked in a letter to Charles Bunker, assistant curator at the natural history museum, "The Fish and Game 'Football' game has been started."[6] The Kansas State Sportsmen's Association was again Dyche's principal opposition. State Senator William M. Price of Lyon County even proposed that the fish and game warden be appointed only on recommendation of the Kansas State Sportsmen's Association. Hunters' complaints against Dyche remained the same: that hunting license fees and fines had been used to build and operate the Pratt fish hatchery, and that Dyche was not providing the state with game animals. Dyche countered those attacks by again proposing to the legislature that a one-dollar license fee for fisherman be levied, although he requested that boys (and presumably girls) under fifteen years of age be allowed to continue to fish for free. As to the call for Kansas game preserves, Dyche was less conciliatory, maintaining that civilization and wild game were incongruous. Game preserves were not cost effective, he asserted, as it was impossible to raise sufficient game for all citizens to have an equal opportunity to hunt. Dyche observed that such preserves in other states catered to the wealthy and to politicians and their cronies. Fishing, on the other hand, was a sport everyone could enjoy.

"The legislature meets next week," reported the *Topeka Daily Capital*. "And the usual assortment of legislators have promised to get the 'goat' of Dyche. Dyche is known as a good scrapper, and so far always has succeeded in holding his own against all comers."[7] The *Wichita Eagle* was less optimistic: "It is from the gunners of the state that Prof. Dyche's firing squad has been recruited. Prof. Dyche knows fish and game, but he does not know politics and man."[8]

The entries in Dyche's pocket diary continue with a January 8 lecture in Auburn, Kansas. On January 9 he returned to Topeka, where he stopped by his room on Woodlawn to pick up some papers, worked at his desk in the capitol until dark, and took the eight o'clock commuter train to Lawrence, arriving in time to attend a young people's party at the Dyches' new home. On January 10 he traveled to Kansas City to visit Dr. Miller, a heart specialist, who confirmed the earlier diagnosis. Dyche revealed nothing to his family other than to comment, "Well, I can't run for any more street cars."[9] In fact, he had been in poor health for at least two months.[10]

Dyche returned to Topeka the following morning to attend the inauguration of the new governor. "Gov. Capper inaugurated at noon," reads the final entry in Dyche's pocket diary. "Fine weather & large crowds." In subsequent days Dyche made a brief trip to Pratt to inspect the hatchery, then returned to Topeka to resume lobbying. On Thursday, January 14, he became too ill to go to his office and was confined to bed at the home of his cousin. A few days later he was admitted to Stormont Hospital. His family was not informed of his deteriorating condition, and it was not until Tuesday, January 19, that word was sent to Ophelia Dyche and the children that he was dying.

Medication had been ineffective. By some accounts, pneumonia had set in. Dyche was in pain, but he was conscious and his mind was clear. He was relieved to have his family with him, and they talked together quietly. He asked Ophelia to bring him a pen and paper and sit near him so they could plan for the family's future. He insisted on outlining his business affairs before he would speak of anything else. Ophelia Dyche could hardly write for weeping at his pained efforts. To his wife Dyche whispered his last words: "And this was your birthday."[11] Then he left his family one final time. Lewis Lindsay Dyche died at 3:15 p.m., January 20, 1915, at Stormont Hospital in Topeka.

The official cause of death was given as dilatation of the heart. Inevitably, with death following the widely publicized Gila monster bite, it was speculated that the bite had caused his death. *Forest and Stream,* among numerous other newspapers and magazines, stated forthrightly that Dyche died from the bite. This perception was aggravated by the fact that the Gila monster was such an exotic, seldom-seen creature, the subject of numerous folk myths.[12]

The governor's brother, Frank Hodges, deplored the misinformation circulating about the Gila monster bite and attempted to squelch the rumors: "It was an incident hardly worth recounting, and it has been given so much prominence that I am afraid the public will gain an incorrect idea from it. For Dyche's sake, I am sorry. He gave his life to ascertaining the truth and now to have a fallacy hooked up with the cause of his death—despite the fact that the true cause of heart disease was faithfully given—is decidedly unfortunate."[13] Despite Hodges's disclaimers, the notion has persisted that Dyche's death was at least partially due to the effects of the Gila monster bite.[14]

Newspapers and organizations paying tribute to Dyche emphasized different aspects of his career. The *Topeka Daily Capital,* a longtime supporter, praised him for his museum work: "It was his unceasing effort and hard work that made the museum the costly and precious collection that it is."[15] Another story, "Dyche Told Peary How to Discover North Pole," recalled Dyche's spirited defiance of Peary's gag order after their return from Greenland: "In retaliation, as soon as the ships arrived in New York, Dyche gave his story to one of the New York papers before Peary could give out an interview."[16] The *Kansas City Globe* proclaimed Dyche's greatest work to have been as Kansas fish and game warden. A resolution of respect passed by the Pratt Commercial Club stated, "At the time of his death he was engaged in the establishment of the largest fish hatchery in the United States as the crowning achievement of his life's work."[17]

Both houses of the state legislature passed resolutions of respect, as did the Board of Administration, which recorded: "In the death of Professor L. L. Dyche the University of Kansas has lost one of the oldest and most devoted members of its faculty and the state has lost one of its most distinguished citizens. Born in poverty, he reached international fame through the exercise of indomitable will power . . . . His exploits as an explorer are the heritage of the state, and the great University Museum, the largest and most unique in the country, the product of his journeys and his skills, is a permanent addition to the wealth of the commonwealth which will be forever cherished as among its richest legacies.

"In recent years he has developed the largest and perhaps the most modern fish hatchery in the United States. He brought to this work the same untiring energy, the same unselfish sacrifice of personal comfort, the same love of nature and the same study and research which characterized him in all his undertakings. His loss is irreparable. This masterful man, the story of whose life would read like a romance was the personification of simplicity in his private life. His life should be an inspiration to every young man in the land."[18]

Chancellor Frank Strong delivered the eulogy at the short service. Praising Dyche for his thirty-eight years of service to the university, Strong closed with the words: "Professor Dyche had in larger degree than most men the creative instinct, the instinct of originality. He had immense persistence and enthusiasm, well attested by his accomplishments against great odds. A mere study of his life is in itself thrilling. . . . He was an extremely likable man, a loyal son of his University, who brought much honor to his alma mater."[19]

A quartet of students sang Dyche's favorite hymns, including "Lead, Kindly

Fish and game warden Dyche. (University of Kansas Archives)

Light." The pallbearers—Governor Arthur Capper, former governor Edward W. Hoch, former U.S. Congressman Justin D. Bowersock, prominent Topeka attorney Thomas F. Doran, university benefactor Thomas J. Sweeney, and Chancellor Frank Strong—bore the casket from the museum for interment at Oak Hill Cemetery.

William Temple Hornaday, Dyche's friend for twenty-seven years, wrote a eulogy that was published in *Recreation,* a sporting magazine, as well as in numerous newspapers across the country: "The state of Kansas has lost one of her most distinguished and also most valuable citizens. Our overwhelming regret at the most untimely taking-off of Prof. Lewis Lindsay Dyche is tempered by one satisfaction. We know that the state of Kansas appreciated him when he lived, we know that he enjoyed the confidence and esteem of the best people of the Sunflower state, and we know that the governor's confidence in his integrity could not be shaken by all the wrathful outpourings of his selfish and mean-spirited enemies.

"The museum of natural history at the Kansas State university is one of Professor Dyche's monuments. It is imposing and imperishable, but it does not represent his greatest work.

"Dyche's most serious and valuable work lay not in the field of pure science and education, but in conservation. . . . As a state fish and game warden, Professor Dyche shone like a good deed in a naughty world. Then he uprose like a colossus, a strong champion of wild life, surrounded by the forces of destruction.

"I regard the measures taken for the increase of the food fishes of Kansas as Professor Dyche's greatest work; because that work is of permanent and practical value to every citizen of Kansas. The wonderful state fish hatchery at Pratt, undoubtedly the finest establishment of its kind in all America, is another monument to his memory. In a larger sense it is also a testimonial of the confidence reposed in him by the people of the Sunflower state, and it is a pleasure to know that he lived to witness its completion.

"The world is far the better because Lewis Lindsay Dyche has lived in it, and where he has gone, no honest man need fear to join him. His loss is upon us all. Peace to his soul."[20]

Hornaday lived to be eighty-two, continuing to write landmark books and articles on natural history and wildlife conservation. In the summer of 1957, twenty years after his death, workmen at the Smithsonian Institution began to dismantle the group of American bison he had collected in 1886 and mounted in 1887. Dyche had observed Hornaday mount a bison cow in this group. Beneath the Smithsonian exhibit the workmen found a metal box containing two copies of *The Cosmopolitan,* dated 1887, which included Hornaday's serialized article on "The Passing of the Buffalo." Across the top of the first installment Hornaday had hand-written the following message:

My Illustrious Successor.

Dear Sir: Enclosed please find a brief and truthful account of the capture of the specimens which compose this group. The Old Bull, the young cow and the yearling calf were killed by yours truly. When I am dust and ashes I beg you to protect these specimens from deterioration & destruction. Of course they are crude productions in comparison with what you produce, but you must remember that at this time (A.D. 1888, March 7.) the American School of Taxidermy has only just been recognized. Therefore give the devil his due, and revile not—

W. T. Hornaday

Chief Taxidermist, U.S. National Museum[21]

In Lawrence, Kansas, two bison collected on that same Smithsonian expedition still stand, as do nearly all of the large mammals Dyche displayed at the 1893 world's fair. Thomas Swearingen, director of exhibits and taxidermist at the Museum of Natural History, believes that, with continued care and maintenance, they may be preserved virtually forever.

A few noted men of science, such as Alexander Wetmore and Leverett Adams, received their training during Lewis Lindsay Dyche's years as curator of the natural history museum. Nevertheless, the first priority of the museum under Dyche's management was not instruction or research, but display—educating students and the public through the accurate and artistic display of specimens of nature. Clarence E. McClung, in recommending Charles Dean Bunker to Chancellor Strong to succeed Dyche as curator, stressed that he "did not wish to do anything that would help perpetuate the old order." Instead, McClung suggested that it would be "a pleasure to learn that the resources of the institution are to be concentrated on teaching and research . . . ."[22] Today still, these three elements—display, teaching, and research—all must be considered when resources are apportioned. An emphasis on public display might strike the modern research scientist or educator as superficial, but it was precisely that emphasis that produced the magnificent museum building.

The Board of Administration formalized Hornaday's sentiment that the museum represented a monument to Dyche when, on January 23, 1915, it resolved "that the building belonging to the University known as the Museum of Natural History be, and the same is hereby named, 'the Dyche Museum of Natural History.'"[23] It was ordered that Dyche's name be carved into the stone arch over the main entrance to the building, but that action was never taken, possibly because the design of the entrance did not lend itself to such alteration. In 1919, however, the words "Dyche Museum" were painted on the glass of the front door and remained there for a few years.

A little over a year before he died, a fatigued and beleaguered Dyche was on board the Angler No. 1, delivering fish. Near Hutchinson, traveling west, he wrote to Fern Ignace Mead: "I had hoped to be in Lawrence or at least in Wichita during Thanksgiving Day, but will eat my dinner and chew my cud out on the plains of Western Kansas. It is just my luck. I was born that way, apparently, and cannot help it. I will just imagine that Mr. Mead is out there eating buffalo hump with me. I always think of him when I am out in this western country, and the hundreds of true stories he told me about it. The times and events he told me about are gone—gone forever. I seem to have been born with a love for wild things and new and untrodden places. But such things are passing away, and I will soon pass with them. This new generation and its ways are almost too much for my spirit and my way of thinking and doing. I was born to think that most things were as they should be and that my fellow beings were honest—at least as honest as the wild men I first knew. How I have been disappointed I would not like to let anyone know, for I hate to give up the natural faith I had in man and men. The day for such men as Mr. Mead and myself seems to have passed."[24]

Epilogue[1]

On a windy night in October 1895, a dashing, mustachioed man stepped aboard the sleeping car of a Santa Fe passenger train a moment before it left the Polk Street Depot in Chicago. With one hand he pressed a new Fedora over his long and shaggy hair. In the other hand he carried the white tusk of an Arctic narwhal.

"Paderewski?" murmured a passenger to her companion.

No sooner had he found a seat than he was joined by newspaper

On October 6, 1895, the New York Herald *depicted Dyche as a dashing Kansan. (University of Kansas Archives)*

reporters. He ran his hand through his mop of dark, crisp hair and smiled. "I'm taking this home to show my wife and babies," he told them. "Everyone else has seen it except them and I think they should see it too. Then it comes off. I haven't seen my babies for six months, and when the crowd leaves and the train starts up I'm going to pull my collar up and my hat down and sneak into a carriage and go

[1]Adapted from "Kansas at the North Pole," *Kansas City Star*, Oct. 31, 1895.

home. Then I'm going to lock the doors and windows and the newspapers will have to commit burglary to get at me. I've told all about the trip in the New York papers, anyway, and it's been telegraphed all over the country. And I'm bound to see that wife and those babies."

A reporter for the *Kansas City Star* wrote, "Professor Dyche is a breezy young man. He abounds in vitality, he is enthusiastic, and he likes to talk."

"When we got back to New York," Dyche told them, "the Peary party tried to muzzle me. But you can't muzzle a Kansas man. It is one of his state rights to talk and write pieces for the papers. They tried to get me to sign a contract to say nothing, but I refused. I wrote seven columns of stuff for the *New York Herald* before Peary had got around to that part of it."

A young bride sitting behind Dyche moved closer in order to hear him speak, and presently was joined by the groom. Soon a small crowd had gathered around Dyche, with a porter hovering at the outskirts.

"They treated me beautifully in New York," Dyche continued. "I was there about thirty days and ate twenty-one dinners given in my honor. I ate dinner twice with Paul du Chaillu, the man who discovered the gorilla and the pygmies in Africa. John Brisbane Walker, editor of *The Cosmopolitan* magazine, entertained me in his home, and the Arctic Club gave me a dinner and a reception. The newspaper men and the artists dined me individually and collectively, as well as other people interested in Arctic exploration and my work. A number of men in New York are talking about outfitting me to find the Pole." He laughed. "A Kansas man may yet accomplish what many brave and wise men have failed to do."

Then, becoming self-conscious, he said, "Say, it's awfully hot in here. I'm not used to steam heat yet." Although it was only seventy degrees in the car, he opened a window while the other passengers backed away. He stuck his head out and let the cool wind blow through his hair.

"I only lack one of having shot every North American mammal, and that one is the musk-ox," he told his audience. "I mean to get that next time. I went ahead of the relief expedition last spring in a little American schooner and was in Holsteinborg in Greenland and had made a collection of arctic birds' eggs before the *Kite* got there. I consider my trip a great success and the honor of it will rebound to the Kansas State University."

One of the reporters asked him for his opinion of Robert E. Peary. "Lieutenant Peary is a fine specimen of American manhood," responded Dyche. "He is reserved and very self-contained, but he was very agreeable to me. He had almost reached the farthest point north when he had to turn back, a terrible disappointment."

Remembering something, Dyche chuckled and reached into his vest pocket to retrieve a letter he had received in St. John's, and showed it to the reporters. Laboriously printed, it read:

Dear Papa—

When are you comeing back from that north pole? Bobs rabbit has seven young ones. Come home from that north pole. --   Walter

Emphatically shaking his head, Dyche told the reporters that coming home was certainly his intention.

So when the Chicago train pulled into the Kansas City depot early the next morning, Dyche jumped off. He crossed the platform and ran to catch the departing local train that would carry him to his family an hour quicker than the regular train. Narwhal tusk in one hand, new hat in the other, he just made it.

PROFESSOR DYCHE.

With his newly purchased New York fedora prominently displayed, Dyche gives his version of the "Peary rescue" to the big city reporters. From the New York Herald, *October 6, 1895.*

NOTES

Chapter 1: Prairie Dreams

[1]In 1860 the county boundary lines were moved, placing the Wakarusa Township, including Ridgeway, in Osage County.

[2]Mary Dyche to Sally Thompson, July 30, 1859, quoted in Mary Dyche Garrett-Haller, *The Dyche Story and Genealogy* (Mercedes, Tex.: 1986), 49–50.

[3]Advertised as "a boy's book," *Camp-Fires of a Naturalist* (Clarence E. Edwords, New York: D. Appleton and Co., 1893) chronicled Dyche's early hunting adventures and campfire discussions on nature. Dyche once jokingly claimed never to have read it, although in fact he had written the rough draft and then hired Clarence Edwords, a newspaper reporter, to complete the project.

[4]Lewis Lindsay Dyche and Clarence Edwords, "Camp-Fires of a Naturalist" TS, Dyche Papers, University of Kansas Archives, Lawrence, Kans., 4.

[5]Discussion recorded in *Transactions of the American Fisheries Society* 41 (1911), p. 281.

[6]E. T. Keim and R. B. Trouslot, "Lewis Lindsey [sic] Dyche, A.M., M.S. Kansas State University, Lawrence, Kans.," *Kansas City Scientist* 5, no. 10 (Oct. 1891):1.

[7]William Allen White et al., *Vernon Kellogg 1867–1937* (Washington, D.C.: Anderson House, 1939), 5–6.

[8]Lewis Lindsay Dyche, *Ponds, Pond Fish, and Pond Fish Culture* (Topeka, Kans.: State Printing Office, 1914), 4–5.

[9]Lewis Lindsay Dyche to James R. Mead, Jan. 18, 1907, Mead Papers, Ablah Library Special Collections, Wichita State University, Wichita, Kans.

[10]"Sick Only a Week of Heart Trouble Prof. Dyche Dies," *Topeka Daily Capital*, Jan. 21, 1915.

[11]"To the Top of the World," *Kansas City Star*, Dec. 22, 1895.

[12]"Silk Tile Made Dyche Famous in a Day," *Topeka Daily Capital*, Jan. 31, 1915.

[13]Ibid.

Chapter 2: The Camp Below the Bluffs

[1]*The Kansas Collegiate,* Mar. 21, 1877, p. 8.

[2]Francis Huntington Snow to Jane Aiken, Feb. 2, 1868, F. H. Snow Papers, University of Kansas Archives.

[3]Clifford S. Griffin, *The University of Kansas; A History* (Lawrence, Kans.: University Press of Kansas, 1974), 88.

[4]Lewis Lindsay Dyche, "Science for a Livelihood," *Science* 8, no. 191 (Oct. 1, 1886):303.

[5]Personal interview with Ronald L. McGregor, Mar. 7, 1986.

[6]R. B. Trouslot to Mrs. Ophelia Dyche, Oct. 1, 1930, Dyche Papers, University of Kansas Archives.

[7]F. H. Snow, "Report of Professor of Natural History," in *Biennial Report of the Board of Regents 1877–78* (Topeka, Kans.: State Printing Office, 1878), 18–19.

[8]Ibid.

[9]Clyde Kenneth Hyder, *Snow of Kansas* (Lawrence, Kans.: University of Kansas Press, 1953), 123.

[10]Lewis Lindsay Dyche, "The University Expedition," *Lawrence Republican Daily Journal.* June 16, 1878, byline; date of publication unknown. (Newsclipping contained in scrapbooks, Dyche Papers, University of Kansas Archives.)

[11]Lewis Lindsay Dyche, "The University Expedition," *Lawrence Republican Daily Journal,* July 3, 1878 (June 28 byline).

[12]Joseph Savage, "On the Bite of the Rattlesnake," *Transactions of the Kansas Academy of Science, 1877 and 1878* 6 (1878):36–38; and Lewis Lindsay Dyche, "Doctor Snow As A Collector, and His Collections," *Transactions of the Kansas Academy of Science* 22 (1909):41.

[13]Francis Huntington Snow to Mrs. Jane Appleton Snow, June 30, 1878, F. H. Snow Papers, University of Kansas Archives, Lawrence, Ks.

[14]Lewis Lindsay Dyche, "The University Expedition," *Lawrence Republican Daily Journal,* July 16, 1878 (July 5 byline).

[15]Lewis Lindsay Dyche, "The University Expedition," *Lawrence Republican Daily Journal,* July 31, 1878 (July 20 byline).

[16]"Record of the Proceedings of the Board of Regents" MS, Jan. 30, 1873, University of Kansas Archives, 129.

[17]"Told of Chancellor Snow," *Kansas City Times,* Apr. 9, 1902.
[18]Lewis Lindsay Dyche, "Camp-fires of a Naturalist" MS, Dyche Papers, University of Kansas Archives.
[19]Clarence E. Edwords, *Camp-Fires of a Naturalist* (New York: D. Appleton and Co., 1893) 28.
[20]Lewis Lindsay Dyche, "Scientific Notes," *University Courier,* Dec. 2, 1882, p. 9.
[21]Dyche, "Camp-fires" MS, 2–3.
[22]Ibid., 11.
[23]Ibid., 20-21.
[24]Edwords, *Camp-Fires,* 108.
[25]See Cohoe, *A Cheyenne Sketchbook,* E. Adamson Hoebel and Karen D. Petersen, eds. (Norman, Okla.: University of Oklahoma Press, 1964).
[26]Dyche, "Camp-fires" MS, 31–32.
[27]Ibid., 33.
[28]Ibid., 37.
[29]Lewis Lindsay Dyche, "Scientific Notes," *University Courier,* Oct. 20, 1882, p. 9.
[30]Ibid.
[31]C. C. Dart, "Editorial," *University Courier,* Feb. 23, 1883, p. 5.
[32]Lewis Lindsay Dyche, "Scientific Notes," *University Courier,* Feb. 6, 1883, p. 9.
[33]"Local," *University Courier,* Sept. 24, 1883, p. 16.
[34]Lewis Lindsay Dyche, "Scientific Notes," *University Courier,* Sept. 24, 1883.
[35]"Personal," *University Courier,* Oct. 10, 1883, p. 56.

Chapter 3: Nimrod

[1]Lewis Lindsay Dyche, "The Last Quarter Century in Science," *The University Review,* Commencement Number (June 1884):11–12.
[2]Hyder, *Snow of Kansas,* 230.
[3]Dyche, "Last Quarter Century."
[4]"Commencement," *Topeka Daily Capital,* June 5, 1884.
[5]In its early years the University of Kansas often was referred to as "Kansas State University."
[6]Few details of Dyche's 1883 expedition are known. Apparently chapters 4 and 5 of Edwords's *Camp-Fires of a Naturalist,* composed from Dyche's recollections nearly ten years later, combine some incidents of the 1883 and 1884 trips.
[7]Dyche, "Camp-fires" MS, 26.
[8]Ibid.
[9]Ibid., 27.
[10]William Harvey Brown, "The Wildcat Division of the K.S.U. Scientific Expedition," *University Courier,* Sept. 12, 1884, p. 3.
[11]Dyche, "Camp-fires" MS, 31.
[12]Brown, "Wildcat Division."
[13]Dyche, "Camp-fires" MS, 35.
[14]Ibid., 37.
[15]Ibid., 39.
[16]Edwords, *Camp-Fires,* 50–51.
[17]Dyche, "Camp-fires" MS, 48.
[18]Edwords, *Camp-Fires,* 53.
[19]"Local," *University Courier,* Sept. 12, 1884, p. 1.
[20]Edwords, *Camp-Fires,* 77.
[21]Dyche, Camp-fires" MS, 100.
[22]Ibid., 102.
[23]Ibid., 100.
[24]Ibid., 104.
[25]For more on Beatty and his mountain cabin, see Elliott S. Barker, *Beatty's Cabin* (Albuquerque: University of New Mexico Press, 1953). Game warden and conservationist, Barker (1886–1988) is best remembered for bringing a singed bear cub rescued from a forest fire to Washington to represent the U.S. Forest Service: Smokey Bear.
[26]"Snow Hall of Natural History at Lawrence, Kan.," *Science,* 10, no. 256 (Dec. 30, 1887):314.
[27]William Temple Hornaday, "The Extermination of the American Bison," in *Report of the United States National Museum Under the Direction of the Smithsonian Institution,1887* (Washington,

D.C.: U.S. Government Printing Office, 1889), 529.

[28]William Temple Hornaday, *A Wild-Animal Round-Up* (New York: Charles Scribner's Sons, 1925), 6.

[29]Hornaday, "Extermination," 541–42.

[30]William Harvey Brown to William Temple Hornaday, Nov. 27, 1898, Hornaday Papers, Manuscript Division, Library of Congress. After graduating from the University of Kansas in 1888, William Harvey Brown worked as an exhibit preparator for the Smithsonian Institution. In 1889 he accompanied a Smithsonian expedition to South Africa, and later joined the British South Africa Company and helped to found the nation of Rhodesia. He married Francis H. Snow's daughter, Martha, and settled in Rhodesia in 1899. For more on Brown, see John M. Peterson's excellent articles, "W. Harvey Brown and K.U.'s First Buffaloes," *Kansas History* 4, no. 4 (Winter 1981):218–26; and "Buffalo Hunting in Montana in 1886," *Montana, the Magazine of Western History* 31, no. 4 (Autumn 1981):2–13; as well as Brown's own book, *On the South African Frontier* (New York: Charles Scribner's Sons, 1898), Reprint, New York: Negro Universities Press, 1970.

[31]"Work in Natural History," *Lawrence Daily Journal,* Jan. 20, 1887, p. 3.

Chapter 4: In a Taxidermy Shop

[1]Montagu Browne, *Practical Taxidermy* (London: L. Upcott Gill, 1884?), 14-15.

[2]Carl Ethan Akeley, *In Brightest Africa* (New York: Garden City Publishing Co., 1925), 14.

[3]William Temple Hornaday to William Harvey Brown, Mar. 16, 1887, quoted in John M. Peterson, "W. Harvey Brown," 222.

[4]Professor Charles E. Bessey, Hornaday's advisor and zoology teacher at the Iowa State College of Agriculture and Mechanical Arts, had nurtured his interest in taxidermy and had arranged for his apprenticeship at Ward's Natural Science Establishment.

[5]Lewis Lindsay Dyche to William T. Hornaday, Mar. 29, 1887 (draft), Dyche Papers, University of Kansas Archives.

[6]William Temple Hornaday, *Taxidermy and Zoological Collecting* (New York: Charles Scribner's Sons, 1909), 112.

[7]For that reason most taxidermists take offense at the term "stuffed": a modern piece of taxidermy is "mounted" around a painstakingly constructed manikin. Hornaday noted, "There are taxidermists who do not like being called anything less than 'sculptors.'"

[8]Lewis and Ophelia Dyche, 1887 diary, Dyche Papers, University of Kansas Archives.

[9]G. Brown Goode, "Report Upon the Condition and Progress of the U.S. National Museum During the Year Ending June 30, 1887," in *Report of the United States National Museum Under the Direction of the Smithsonian Institution, 1887* (Washington, D.C.: U.S. Government Printing Office, 1889), 32.

[10]Lewis Lindsay Dyche, "Taxidermy Notes 1886–87," Dyche Papers, University of Kansas Archives.

[11]Lewis Lindsay Dyche, "Specimens in Museums" 1887 diary, Dyche Papers, University of Kansas Archives, 16.

[12]Hornaday, *Taxidermy,* 230.

[13]Ibid., 222.

[14]Lewis Lindsay Dyche, "Mounting of Large Animals," *Scientific American* 69 (Oct. 7, 1893):234–35.

[15]"Prof. Dyche's Mounted Buffaloes," *Kansas City Times,* Apr. 15, 1888.

[16]Dyche, "Mounting of Large Animals," 234–35.

[17]Ibid.

[18]William T. Hornaday to Lewis Lindsay Dyche, Sept. 22 and 23, 1887, Dyche Papers, University of Kansas Archives.

[19]F. H. Snow, "Department of Natural History," in *Sixth Biennial Report of Regents, Chancellor, and Faculty 1887–8* (Topeka, Kans.: State Printing Office, 1888), 36.

[20]"A Buffalo," *Weekly Capital and Farmer's Journal,* Jan. 26, 1888.

[21]Untitled article, *The Industrialist* [Kansas State Agricultural College newspaper], Apr. 7, 1888.

[22]William T. Hornaday to Lewis Lindsay Dyche, Jan. 31, 1888, Dyche Papers, University of Kansas Archives.

[23]Arthur Lindsay Dyche died in infancy.

[24]William T. Hornaday to Lewis Lindsay Dyche, Apr. 27, 1888, Dyche Papers, University of Kansas Archives.

[25]William T. Hornaday to Lewis Lindsay Dyche, July 12, 1888, Dyche Papers, University of Kansas Archives.

[26]Snow, "Department of Natural History," 37.

Chapter 5: The University Man

[1]Annie Hathaway Williston to her parents, Sept. 29, 1892, quoted in Elizabeth N. Shor, *Fossils and Flies, The Life of a Compleat Scientist, Samuel Wendell Williston (1851–1918)* (Norman, Okla.: University of Oklahoma Press, 1971), 132.

[2]W. H. H. Piatt, "The L. L. Dyche Museum Collection and Zoology Class of 1893," in "Memory Recital of the Gay '90's at K.U." [120-page TS and clippings], Student Activities 1891–96, University of Kansas Archives.

[3]"Legislative Visitors," *The Evening Tribune,* Jan. 20, 1890.

[4]James R. Mead, *Hunting and Trading on the Great Plains, 1859–1875,* Schuyler Jones, ed. (Norman, Okla.: University of Oklahoma Press, 1986), 83.

[5]James R. Mead to Lewis Lindsay Dyche, Mar. 18, 1892, Dyche Papers, University of Kansas Archives.

[6]*The Helianthus* 1 (1889):86–87.

[7]Lewis Lindsay Dyche, report to the Board of Regents, July 1890 MS, Dyche Papers, University of Kansas Archives.

[8]One Rocky Mountain goat was held by the British Museum in London, one at the Leiden Museum in the Netherlands, and a pair at the National Museum in Washington.

[9]The 1886 Winchester was commonly called "Yellow Boy" due to its shiny brass frame. The rifle was relatively light and easily carried. The Remington was a heavier bore sporting rifle used in hunting big game.

[10]Dyche, "Camp-fires" MS, 216.

[11]Ibid., 210.

[12]Hornaday had written an antiliquor book, *Free Rum on the Congo,* published in 1887 by the Women's Temperance Publication Association.

[13]Lewis Lindsay Dyche, 1889 field notebook TS, Dyche Papers, University of Kansas Archives, 7.

[14]Dyche, "Camp-fires" MS, 223.

[15]Dyche, 1889 field notebook TS, 14.

[16]Ibid., 15.

[17]Ibid., 30.

[18]Ibid., 36–37.

[19]Ibid., 41.

[20]Ibid., 42.

[21]Ibid., 59.

[22]Ophelia Dyche to Lewis Lindsay Dyche, Sept. 29, 1889, Dyche Papers, University of Kansas Archives.

[23]Dyche, 1889 field notebook TS, 65.

[24]*The Kansas Telephone* [Manhattan, Kans.], Apr., 1890.

[25]William Temple Hornaday to Lewis Lindsay Dyche, June 4, 1890, Dyche Papers, University of Kansas Archives. The clipping was from *The Naturalist* [Kansas City, Kans.] 4, no. 7 (Feb. 1890):5. R. B. Trouslot indicated in a 1930 letter to Ophelia Dyche that he wrote the piece.

[26]Hornaday to Dyche, June 4, 1890.

[27]*The Helianthus,* 1889, 63.

[28]Eugene W. Caldwell, "My Recollections of the Science Club 'It,'" *Graduate Magazine* (May 1919):232.

[29]Hyder, *Snow of Kansas,* 184.

[30]Caldwell, "My Recollections," 232.

[31]Dyche, 1890 diary TS, Dyche Papers, University of Kansas Archives, 17.

[32]Ibid., 16.

[33]Ibid., 32.

[34]Antlers.

[35]Dyche, 1890 diary TS, 43–44.

[36]The bull stood 85 1/2 inches long and 78 1/2 inches high (not including the head and antlers). It now stands on display in the Panorama of North American Mammals at the Museum of Natural History.

[37]F. H. Snow, "The Museums of Natural History," in *Eighth Biennial Report of the Board of Regents and Officers of the University of Kansas 1891–2* (Topeka, Kans.: State Printing Office, 1892), 16.

[38]Ellen P. Allerton, "Prof. Dyche," *St. Joseph Herald,* June 27, 1891.

[39]Edwords, *Camp-Fires,* 276.

[40]When Comanche was purchased by the Seventh Cavalry in August 1867, his age was approximated as six years. (Reported from I Troop records in "Fort Leavenworth," *Kansas City Times,* Nov. 30, 1891.)

[41]Edward S. Luce, *Keough, Comanche and Custer* (St. Louis: Author, 1939), 65.

[42]Ibid., 67.

[43]Barron Brown, *Comanche* (Kansas City, Mo.: Burton Publishing Co., 1935), 35.

[44]"Record of the Proceedings of the Board of Regents" MS, 1891, University of Kansas Archives, 53.

[45]Lewis Lindsay Dyche to James H. Canfield, Oct. 17, 1892, Dyche Papers, University of Kansas Archives.

[46]C. E. Edwords, "A Naturalist Afield," *Kansas City Journal,* Dec. 13, 1891.

[47]William Temple Hornaday to Lewis Lindsay Dyche, Feb. 7, 1892, Dyche Papers, University of Kansas Archives.

[48]Keim and Trouslot, "Lewis Lindsey Dyche."

[49]William Temple Hornaday to Lewis Lindsay Dyche, Oct. 22, 1892, Dyche Papers, University of Kansas Archives.

[50]William Allen White, *The Autobiography of William Allen White* (New York: Macmillan, 1946), 199.

[51]Charles S. Gleed to Lewis Lindsay Dyche, Aug. 24, 1892, Dyche Papers, University of Kansas Archives.

[52]Edwords, *Camp-Fires,* v.

[53]Ibid., 1–2.

[54]M. H. Stevens, "Camp Fires of a Naturalist," *Kansas City Journal,* Aug. 6, 1893.

[55]Untitled article, *Columbus Ohio Dispatch,* Sept. 16, 1893.

Chapter 6: "The Stuffed Animal State": Kansas in the White City

[1]"Report of the Board of Regents," in *Eighth Biennial Report of the Board of Regents, 1891–92* (Topeka, Kans.: State Printing Office, 1892), 5–6.

[2]*Kansas at the World's Fair, Report of the Kansas Board of Worlds's Fair Managers* (Topeka, Kans.: State Printing Office, 1894), 14.

[3]"Prof. Dyche," *The University Courier* (Christmas edition), Dec. 1891, pp. 7–8.

[4]"University of Kansas' Exhibit at the World's Fair—Prof. Dyche and His Museum," *The University Courier,* June 8, 1892, p. 6.

[5]"Arrived All Right," *Lawrence Daily Journal,* Dec. 13, 1892.

[6]"An Unfair Apportionment," *Topeka Daily Capital,* Dec. 13, 1892.

[7]"The Stuffed Animal State," *Newton Republican,* undated 1893 newsclipping, Dyche Papers, University of Kansas Archives.

[8]Untitled article, *Salina Republican,* undated 1893 newsclipping, Dyche Papers, University of Kansas Archives.

[9]Untitled article, *Kansas City Star,* undated newsclipping, Dyche Papers, University of Kansas Archives.

[10]Untitled article, *Emporia Gazette,* undated 1893 newsclipping, Dyche Papers, University of Kansas Archives.

[11]"Stealing Kansas Thunder," *Students' Journal,* Feb. 2, 1893, p. 2

[12]Louis [sic] Lindsay Dyche, "The Kansas Exhibit," *Denver Times,* Feb. 20, 1893.

[13]Lewis Lindsay Dyche to William Temple Hornaday, Dec. 24, 1892, Hornaday Papers, Manuscript Division, Library of Congress.

[14]Hornaday to Dyche, Oct. 22, 1892.

[15]Hornaday, *Taxidermy,* 221.

[16]Ibid., 222.

[17]Dyche drolly placed a label on the log stating that the log came from the edge of "The Great American Desert."

[18]The number of specimens reported to be in the mammals exhibit varied widely. The actual number was probably about 121.

[19]F. D. Palmer, "The Kansas Exhibit of Mounted Specimens of the Animals of the State," *Scientific*

American 69, no. 3 (July 15, 1893):41–42.

[20]Hubert Howe Bancroft, ed., *The Book of the Fair,* 3 vols. (Chicago: The Bancroft Co., 1893), 631.

[21]"Dyche at Home," *Lawrence Daily Gazette,* Nov. 29, 1893.

[22]Brown, *Comanche,* 108.

[23]Ibid., 72–73.

[24]Comanche's quiescence was further threatened in 1986 by an unlikely assailant: one of his fellow specimens. In the ornithological laboratory directly above Comanche's display case, a large frozen rhea was placed in a sink to thaw prior to being skeletonized. As it thawed the rhea turned in the sink, coming to rest against a faucet handle. The water turned on, and the rhea blocked the drain. Water overflowed the sink, flooding Comanche below. Museum workers found him thoroughly soaked. His face had split open, as had his front lower legs, back, side, and left hind leg. Thomas Swearingen, exhibits director and taxidermist, wrapped the horse in gauze to retard drying and prevent further damage. When he unwrapped Comanche he found that the original water clay had powdered and deteriorated to the extent that, heavy with water, it had settled in the horse's lower legs, splaying apart the hide and ripping out the old stitches. To restore the legs, Swearingen removed Dyche's cotton, excelsior, and clay—down to the metal rods and bone— replacing the clay with a more stable "Critter Clay." Swearingen used "TC 9" tanning cream and wax to repair Comanche's face. The thawed-out rhea was skeletonized and placed in the ornithological collection.

[25]William Temple Hornaday to Lewis Lindsay Dyche, Nov. 1, 1893, Dyche Papers, University of Kansas Archives.

[26]"Report of Board of Regents," in *Ninth Biennial Report of the Board of Regents and Officers of the University of Kansas, 1893–94* (Topeka, Kans.: State Printing Office, 1894), 5–6.

[27]Lewis Lindsay Dyche to Frederic True, Feb. 22, 1894, Smithsonian Institution Archives, Record Unit 189.

Chapter 7: The Last Voyage of the *Miranda*

[1]Too few women applied to join the expedition to warrant making arrangements on the ship for both sexes.

[2]Flier, Dyche Papers, University of Kansas Archives.

[3]Lewis Lindsay Dyche, 1894 diary TS, Dyche Papers, University of Kansas Archives. (All quoted material in this chapter, except where otherwise noted, is taken from this diary.)

[4]Henry Collins Walsh, *The Last Cruise of the Miranda* (New York: Transatlantic Publishing Co., 1896), 16.

[5]"Off for the Polar Seas, Dr. Cook and his Excursionists Sail on the Miranda," *New York Times,* July 8, 1894, p. 9.

[6]Not *all* rats left the ship: Dyche reported that he caught "a rat with a long black tail" on board and "made the skin up for a specimen."

[7]"Was Sad But Funny; Professor Dyche Tells of the Dr. Cook Arctic Expedition," *Chicago Evening News,* Sept. 28, 1894.

[8]William H. Brewer of Yale, noted for his participation in the California Geological Surveys of the 1860s.

[9]"Was Sad But Funny," *Chicago Evening News.*

[10]The Arctic Club's first dinner was held in honor of Captain Dixon on Dec. 27, 1894, at the Hotel Martin in New York City. Dixon himself was unable to attend.

[11]She sank off the coast of Nova Scotia not long thereafter.

[12]"Start and Finish Unlucky," *New York Times,* Sept. 12, 1894, p. 2.

Chapter 8: Greenland, Peary, and the *Kite*

[1]William Herbert Hobbs, *Peary* (New York: Macmillan, 1936), 129.

[2]Lewis Lindsay Dyche, 1895 diary, Dyche Papers, University of Kansas Archives. (All quoted material in this chapter, except where otherwise noted, is taken from the Dyche diaries.)

[3]Lewis Lindsay Dyche, "Walrus Hunting in the Arctic Regions," *The Cosmopolitan* 20, no. 4 (Feb. 1896):357–58.

[4]In later years, after Morris K. Jesup (who as well as being the director of the American Museum of Natural History was also one of the founders of the Young Men's Christian Association and the

Society for the Suppression of Vice for Saint Anthony) had become one of Peary's principal backers, Peary's books contained no more "ethnological" photographs, although Peary continued his Arctic philandering and had a child by Allakasingwah. Henson, too, fathered an Eskimo child.

[5]The word "narwhal" is derived from the Old Norse "nahvalr," or "corpse-whale," so called because its whitish color and size make it resemble a floating human corpse.

[6]Untitled article, *Mercury* [New Bedford, Mass.], Oct. 8, 1895.

[7]"Kansas at the North Pole," *Kansas City Star,* Oct. 31, 1895.

[8]William Wallace to Lewis Lindsay Dyche, June 22, 1895, Dyche Papers, University of Kansas Archives.

[9]"From the Frozen Seas," *New York Times,* Oct. 2, 1895.

[10]"Peary's Trip a Failure," *New York Evening Telegram,* Oct. 1, 1895.

[11]"Home from the Frozen North," *New York Mail and Express,* Oct. 1, 1895.

[12]"Will Never See the Pole," *New York Times,* Oct. 2, 1895.

Chapter 9: An Arctic Paderewski

[1]*American Museum of Natural History Annual Report, 1895* (New York: American Museum of Natural History, 1895), 12.

[2]"Hugh Lee on Dyche," *Meriden [Conn.] Journal,* Jan. 2, 1896.

[3]Robert E. Peary to Lewis Lindsay Dyche, Dec. 12, 1895, Dyche Papers, University of Kansas Archives.

[4]"Dyche Will Go," *Topeka Daily Capital,* Dec. 2, 1895.

[5]"Dyche and the Pole," *Kansas City Journal,* Dec. 2, 1895.

[6]"To the Top of the World, *Kansas City Star,* Dec. 22, 1895, p. 9.

[7]Ibid.

[8]"Dyche Will Go," *Topeka Daily Capital.*

[9]"Dyche's Plan to Reach Pole," *New York Recorder,* Dec. 29, 1895.

[10]"Hugh Lee on Dyche," *Meriden Journal.*

[11]R. Müller to Lewis Lindsay Dyche, Aug. 23, 1896, Dyche Papers, University of Kansas Archives.

[12]Lewis Lindsay Jr. was born Nov. 16, 1895.

[13]Becky Sharp, "Going to the North Pole," *Topeka State Journal,* Feb. 26, 1896.

[14]William Temple Hornaday to Lewis Lindsay Dyche, Mar. 3, 1896, Dyche Papers, University of Kansas Archives.

[15]Sharp, "Going to the North Pole."

[16]"To Head Off Peary?" *Buffalo Commercial,* June 3, 1896.

[17]"Interesting If True," *Cleveland Plain Dealer,* June 4, 1896.

[18]"A Living Mastadon," *Denver Times,* July 16, 1896.

[19]"Dyche Gets White Sheep," *Kansas City Star,* Nov. 29, 1896.

Chapter 10: "Dashing Kansan!" The Magic Lantern Lectures

[1]"University Extension," *Eighth Biennial Report of the Board of Regents and Officers, 1891≠92* (Topeka, Kans.: State Printing Office, 1892), 12–13.

[2]According to the Mar. 14, 1896, *Lawrence Daily Journal,* one of Dyche's eiderdown robes was stolen from a storefront window at Almena, and the sealskin boots were taken from the Eskimo mannequin at Norton Center.

[3]Undated newsclipping, Dyche Papers, University of Kansas Archives.

[4]Neil Graham to E. F. Caldwell, Mar. 25, 1897, Dyche Papers, University of Kansas Archives.

[5]"Lecture on the North Pole," *Kansas City Times,* Jan. 16, 1896.

[6]John J. Ingalls, Kansas senator from 1873–91, was a popular lecturer on the Chautauqua circuit after losing his senate seat.

[7]"He Will Find the Pole," *Emporia Gazette,* Feb. 3, 1896.

[8]Tucker's shop was located at 828 Ohio Street. He was Museum Assistant in Systematic Entomology from 1902 to 1906.

[9]"The Kansas Explorer Receives Generous Treatment Here," *Abilene Reflector,* undated newsclipping, Dyche Papers, University of Kansas Archives.

[10]C. L. Davidson to E. F. Caldwell, Dec. 2, 1896, Dyche Papers, University of Kansas Archives.

[11]"Cold, Cold North," *Topeka Daily Capital,* Jan. 25, 1896.

[12]Lewis Lindsay Dyche, untitled MS, Dyche Papers, University of Kansas Archives.

[13]"Prof. Dyche's Lecture," *Norton Champion,* Jan. 18, 1896.

[14]Esther Haskell to Lewis Lindsay Dyche, Mar. 1, 1896, Dyche Papers, University of Kansas Archives.

[15]Dyche claimed to have been shot five times in his life "through the carelessness of other people." The injuries sustained were apparently all minor, most coming from errant shotgun blasts.

[16]"Poor Boys Would Suffer," *Kansas City Journal,* Feb. 1, 1897, p. 9.

[17]"Dyche to Legislators," *Topeka Daily Capital,* Feb. 23, 1897.

[18]Anonymous letter to Lewis Lindsay Dyche, Feb. 6, 1898, Dyche Papers, University of Kansas Archives.

[19]William Temple Hornaday, *The American Natural History* (New York: Charles Scribner's Sons, 1904), 45–46. See also Hornaday, *Wild Life Conservation in Theory and Practice* (New Haven: Yale University Press, 1914), 126–28.

Chapter 11: Museum Builder

[1]"The Natural History Museum," *Jayhawker,* 1901, University of Kansas Archives, 62.

[2]David H. Robinson, "Reminiscences," *Quarter-Centennial History of the University of Kansas 1866–1891,* Sterling Wilson, ed. (Topeka, Kans.: George W. Crane and Co., 1891), 161–62.

[3]Frank Snow, "Department of Natural History," *Fourth Biennial Report of Regents, Chancellor and Faculty, 1883–4* (Topeka, Kans.: State Printing Office, 1885), 28.

[4]Francis Snow, "Report of the Chancellor," *Eighth Biennial Report of the Board of Regents and Officers, 1891–2* (Topeka, Kans.: State Printing Office, 1892), 16.

[5]Following the 1892 elections, the Kansas House was divided about equally between Republicans and Populists. The Populist Party controlled temporarily, with Dunsmore serving as speaker, until the State Supreme Court gave the Republicans control later in 1893.

[6]In 1902 Samuel W. Williston, Professor of Historical Geology, Vertebrate Anatomy, and Dean of the School of Medicine, left Kansas to head the Department of Paleontology at the University of Chicago. Chancellor Frank Strong lamented, "The inadequate funds of the University of Kansas made it impossible for us to retain him."

[7]*Ninth Biennial Report,* 19.

[8]Francis Snow, "A New Natural History Building," in *Tenth Biennial Report of the Board of Regents and Chancellor, 1895–96* (Topeka, Kans.: State Printing Office, 1896), 23.

[9]Francis Snow, "A Report of the Chancellor," in *Eleventh Biennial Report of the Board of Regents and Chancellor, 1897–8* (Topeka, Kans.: State Printing Office, 1898), 16.

[10]"K.U. Will Not Get Museum," *Kansas City Times,* Mar. 5, 1899.

[11]"No Building for Dyche," *Topeka State Journal,* Mar. 4, 1899.

[12]Francis Snow, "Report of the Chancellor," in *Twelfth Biennial Report of the Board of Regents and the Chancellor of the University of Kansas, 1899–1900* (Topeka, Kans.: State Printing Office, 1900), 16–17.

[13]"Board of Regents' Report," in *Twelfth Biennial Report of the Board of Regents and the Chancellor,* 6.

[14]Lewis Lindsay Dyche, Department of Zoology notes concerning the museum collections (n.d.), Dyche Papers, University of Kansas Archives.

[15]Lewis Lindsay Dyche to Charles F. Scott, Nov. 22, 1900, Dyche Papers, University of Kansas Archives.

[16]"Record of the Proceedings of the Board of Regents" MS, Aug. 6, 1901, University of Kansas Archives, 283–84.

[17]"Building of a Year," *Lawrence Daily Journal,* Jan. 1, 1902.

[18]The aedicules on the north side of the museum were covered by a wing added in 1961.

[19]The blueprints indicate that the museum owl was to have been carved free-standing, perched *atop* the corbel, rather than carved into the corbel's terminal.

[20]Robert Taft, *Across the Years on Mount Oread* (Lawrence: University of Kansas Press, 1941), p. 74.

[21]Antonio Tommasini to Walter Salathiel, Mar. 14, 1941, University Building Files (Dyche Museum), University of Kansas Archives.

[22]A playful hint, perhaps, as to the location of the famous fowl, for it is here that the the humorously carved face can be found.

[23]The *Fort Scott Monitor* reported that the leading feature of the inauguration program was the dedication of the new museum building. Apparently the reporter confused the chemistry building with the museum building because no other accounts substantiate this report. Research has revealed no other dedication or opening ceremony until the museum was reopened in 1941.

[24]Frederick A. Cook to Lewis Lindsay Dyche, Apr. 27, 1903, Dyche Papers, University of Kansas Archives.

[25]Hyder, *Snow of Kansas,* 245.

[26]"Record of the Proceedings of the Board of Regents" MS, Apr. 14, 1903, University of Kansas Archives, 311.

[27]Frank Strong to Lewis Lindsay Dyche, Feb. 23, 1903, Dyche Papers, University of Kansas Archives.

[28]Lewis Lindsay Dyche, draft letter to the Board of Regents, Nov. 4, 1908, Dyche Papers, University of Kansas Archives.

[29]Sam Adams to C. D. Bunker, Dec. 18, 1910, Dyche Papers, University of Kansas Archives.

[30]"Improving the Museum," *Kansan* 4, no. 32 (Feb. 1, 1908):2.

[31]Claud A. Clary, "How Mountains Are Made in Museum at Kansas University," *Topeka Daily Capital,* Nov. 21, 1909.

[32]Lewis Lindsay Dyche to William Temple Hornaday, Jan. 25, 1905, Hornaday Papers, Manuscript Division, Library of Congress.

[33]1611 Massachusetts (still in existence).

[34]1639 Learnard Avenue (no longer exists).

[35]Lewis Lindsay Dyche to William Temple Hornaday, Feb. 27, 1907, Hornaday Papers, Manuscript Division, Library of Congress.

[36]"Dyche Museum's Mammals Now May Be Seen Again After Nine Years," *Kansas City Star,* June 8, 1941.

[37]William Temple Hornaday to Lewis Lindsay Dyche, Jan. 15, 1906, Dyche Papers, University of Kansas Archives.

[38]Hyder, *Snow of Kansas,* 245–47.

[39]Dyche, "Snow As A Collector," 39–45.

[40]Clary, "How Mountains Are Made."

[41]William Temple Hornaday to Lewis Lindsay Dyche, Mar. 5, 1907, Dyche Papers, University of Kansas Archives.

[42]Frederic A. Lucas, *The Story of Museum Groups* (New York: The American Museum of Natural History, 1926), 32.

[43]Frederic A. Lucas to William Temple Hornaday, Sept. 2, 1913, Hornaday Papers, Manuscript Division, Library of Congress.

[44]William Temple Hornaday to Lewis Lindsay Dyche, Dec. 18, 1891, Dyche Papers, University of Kansas Archives.

[45]Ibid.

[46]Alexander Wetmore, address given at reopening of Museum of Natural History, June 6, 1941, TS, Dyche Papers, University of Kansas Archives. Dyche Hall was placed on the National Register of Historic Places on July 14, 1974.

[47]Lewis Lindsay Dyche to Charles F. Scott, Nov. 22, 1900, Dyche Papers, University of Kansas Archives.

Chapter 12: The Man Who Knew Cook and Peary

[1]John Edward Weems, *Race for the Pole* (New York: Henry Holt and Co., 1960), 132–33.

[2]Frank Rasky, *The North Pole or Bust* (Toronto: McGraw Hill Ryerson Ltd., 1977), 350.

[3]Rasky, *North Pole,* 351.

[4]"Most of the Evidence Now Favors Dr. Cook," *Parsons Daily Sun,* Sept. 13, 1909.

[5]Lewis Lindsay Dyche to James R. Mead, Sept. 20, 1909, Mead Papers, Ablah Library Special Collections, Wichita State University, Wichita, Kans.

[6]"Most of the Evidence," *Parsons Daily Sun.*

[7]Rasky, *North Pole,* 351–52.

[8]Frederick Cook, *My Attainment of the Pole* (New York: Mitchell Kennerley, 1913), 496, 504.

[9]Advertisement, *Kansas City Star,* Oct. 9, 1909, p. 9.

[10]"The Arctic Hero Comes," *Kansas City Star,* Oct. 7, 1909, p. 1; and "Cook and Dyche," *Topeka State Journal,* Oct. 8, 1909.

[11]"Dyche on Cook," *Topeka Daily Capital,* Oct. 8, 1909.

[12]"Cook's Route Far From Pole, His Eskimos Say," *New York Times,* Oct. 13, 1909.

[13]"Cook Says Eskimos Kept Pledge To Him," *New York Times,* Oct. 13, 1909.

[14]"Dyche Speaks Up," *Topeka State Journal,* Oct. 13, 1909.

[15]Quoted in Rasky, *North Pole,* 352.

[16]"The Frozen Grail," *Topeka State Journal,* Oct. 19, 1909.

[17]"The Man Dyche," *Hutchinson Daily News,* Oct. 29, 1909.

[18]"Make Trip Into Arctics," *Lawrence World,* Oct. 15, 1909.

[19]Cook spells the name "Barrille" in *To the Top of the Continent* (New York: Doubleday, Page and Co., 1908), and many accounts of the Cook-Peary controversy use this spelling.

[20]It is generally acknowledged that Cook did not ascend Mount McKinley. When Hudson Stuck climbed the peak in 1913 he found no sign of the metallic container Cook claimed he left behind, and photographs that Cook claimed to have taken from that peak actually were taken from sites over fifteen miles away.

[21]"Barrill says Cook Never on M'Kinley's Top," *New York Times,* Oct. 15, 1909.

[22]"Double Search of Mt. M'Kinley," *New York Times,* Oct. 16, 1909.

[23]"Comment of Dr. Cook," *New York Times,* Oct. 16, 1909 (Reprinted from *New York Evening Post*).

[24]"Casts Doubt on Barrill," *New York Times,* Oct. 15, 1909.

[25]"Dyche May Climb Mount M'Kinley For Dr. Cook's Missing Records," *Lawrence Daily Journal,* Oct. 20, 1909.

[26]"Cook Is Delighted," *Topeka State Journal,* Oct. 21, 1909.

[27]"Dyche to Mount M'Kinley," *Kansas City Journal,* Oct. 22, 1909.

[28]"Cook Faces Barrill, But Silences Him," *New York Times,* Oct. 29, 1909.

[29]"Kids Romp 12,000 Strong," *Kansas City Star,* Nov. 5, 1909.

[30]Katrina Baldwin to Lewis Lindsay Dyche, n.d., Dyche Papers, University of Kansas Archives.

[31]"To Prove Cook Is Right," *Kansas City Star,* Nov. 5, 1909.

[32]"Dyche May Give Up Trip," *Topeka State Journal,* Dec. 2, 1909.

[33]Cook's name has since returned to the Explorers Club membership roster.

[34]"Dyche Begins to Doubt Cook's Word," *Kansas City Journal,* Dec. 21, 1909.

[35]"Prof. Dyche and Dr. Cook," *Lawrence Daily Journal-World,* Jan. 2, 1910. The North Pole controversy persevered long after Dyche had withdrawn his participation. Frederick Cook reemerged in the public eye toward the end of 1910 and again began gamely asserting his claim to the discovery of the Pole. Cook attributed his year-long hegira to the unrelenting attacks made on him by the Peary forces. He pointed out that by allowing the Polar fracas to die down he might eventually enjoy the last word. But ultimately neither Cook nor Peary offered substantial proof of their claims to the North Pole. Cook had little to show besides his well-written account of his adventures and photographs that could have been taken virtually anywhere. Peary, on the other hand, while generally recognized as the discoverer of the North Pole, has been increasingly damned by the sloppy evidence he did amass. Although there is some doubt as to whether he was intentionally deceitful, he probably did not come within sixty miles of the Pole—and possibly not even that close. Frederick Cook returned to Kansas in 1925 to serve five years in the federal penitentiary at Leavenworth for his part in a Texas oil stock fraud. He maintained his claim to having reached the North Pole until his death on August 5, 1940.

Chapter 13: Fish and Game Warden Dyche

[1]Not to be confused with the David Leahy who became director of the Kansas Forestry, Fish and Game Commission in 1944.

[2]Dave Leahy, "Vagrant Memories," *Wichita Eagle,* June 15, 1938.

[3]"Governor Offers Dyche Fish and Game Wardenship," *Topeka Daily Capital,* Nov. 16, 1909.

[4]Lewis Lindsay Dyche, "A New and Enlarged Fish Hatchery for the State of Kansas," *Transactions of the American Fisheries Society* 41 (1911):155.

[5]White, *Autobiography,* 184–85.

[6]Ibid., 432.

[7]Frank Strong to Lewis Lindsay Dyche, Nov. 17, 1909, Dyche Papers, University of Kansas Archives.

[8]"Dyche Has A Plan," *Topeka State Journal,* Nov. 19, 1909.

[9]"Dyche Won't Leave State University," *Topeka Daily Capital,* Nov. 20, 1909.

[10]Lewis Lindsay Dyche to James R. Mead, Dec. 29, 1905, Mead Papers, Ablah Library Special

Collections, Wichita State University, Wichita, Kans.

[11]"Record of the Proceedings of the Board of Regents" MS, Nov. 30, 1909, University of Kansas Archives, 119.

[12]Dyche officially received his commission on Dec. 1, 1909. This was a curious arrangement, and Chancellor Strong soon found himself telling the newspapers that although it was true that the university was now responsible for the state fish and game office, university faculty should not be expected to collect hunting license fees or prosecute game law violators.

[13]Lewis Lindsay Dyche to James R. Mead, Dec. 9, 1909, Mead Papers, Ablah Library Special Collections, Wichita State University, Wichita, Kans.

[14]James R. Mead to Lewis Lindsay Dyche, Dec. 12, 1909, Dyche Papers, University of Kansas Archives.

[15]*Biennial Report of the Kansas Fish and Game Warden, for the Fiscal Years ending June 30, 1912,* Bulletin 4 (Topeka, Kans.: State Printing Office, 1912), 7–8.

[16]The white-tailed deer and mule deer had not existed in the state since the mid-1890s; the elk likewise had vanished well before the turn of the century.

[17]*Biennial Report,* Bulletin 4, p. 10.

[18]"To Enforce Kansas Game Laws," *Topeka Daily Capital,* Dec. 21, 1909.

[19]"Fish Pond on Every Farm; Prof. Dyche Proposes to Dedicate His Life to That Work," *Duluth Evening Herald,* Jan. 28, 1910.

[20]Dyche's carp recipe: "First I skin the fish and scrape the fat off its back. Then I make incisions around the fins and pull them out. Then I stuff that fish with a couple of stalks of celery, green ends and all, and sprinkle in a little pepper to hurry the union of flavors. No salt. I soak the fish in salt water an hour or so after I clean it. Then I grease a pan by frying a little bacon in it and place the fish therein with a couple of strips of bacon on the upper side and baste it with ground cracker crumbs and corn meal. I bake the upper side to a doughnut brown then turn it over and treat the under side the same way." From "Prof. Dyche's Recipe for Cooking German Carp," *Topeka Daily Capital,*

[21]"Fish as a Farm Crop of Kansas," *Kansas City Star,* Oct. 23, 1910.

[22]"Prof. Dyche Replies to Del Travis," *Topeka Daily Capital,* May 8, 1910.

[23]Travis had introduced Chinese and Mongolian pheasants into the state during his term as warden.

[24]"Dyche Replies To Travis," *Topeka Daily Capital,* July 4, 1910.

[25]"Attacks Work of Fish Warden," *Wichita Eagle,* June 14, 1910.

[26]"Pipe Dreamer," *Topeka State Journal,* June 13, 1910.

[27]"Dyche Replies To Travis," *Topeka State Journal.*

[28]Untitled article, *Topeka Daily Capital,* Nov. 2, 1910.

[29]Untitled article, *Atchison Globe,* Jan. 12, 1911.

[30]Undated newsclipping, Dyche Papers, University of Kansas Archives.

[31]"Fish as a Farm Crop," *Kansas City Star.*

[32]"By the Way, Limericks; Incident VII.," *Topeka State Journal,* Jan. 11, 1911.

[33]Dyche, *Ponds, Pond Fish, And Pond Fish Culture,* 5-6.

[34]Samuel P. Hays, *Conservation and the Gospel of Efficiency, the Progressive Conservation Movement, 1890–1920,* Harvard Historical Monographs XL (Cambridge, Mass.: Harvard University Press, 1959), 175.

[35]Ibid., 2.

[36]"The New Game Law," *Lawrence Gazette,* Jan. 26, 1911.

[37]*Biennial Report,* Bulletin 4, 14–15.

[38]Lewis Lindsay Dyche, 1911 pocket diary, Feb. 9, 1911, Dyche Papers, University of Kansas Archives.

[39]The open season on geese and ducks was set at Sept. 1 to Apr. 15; plover Aug. 1 to Apr. 30; prairie chickens Oct. 1 to Nov. 1; and quail Nov. 15 to Dec. 1.

[40]This arrangement continued until 1927, although no subsequent wardens were borrowed from the university faculty.

[41]Session Laws of 1911, chap. 198; and "Save Song Birds and Fur Animals," *Topeka Daily Capital,* Jan. 25, 1911.

[42]"Record of the Proceedings of the Board of Regents" MS, Oct. 5, 1911, University of Kansas Archives, 308.

[43]"Record of the Proceedings of the Board of Regents" MS, Oct. 23, 1911, University of Kansas Archives, 319.

[44]William Allen White to Lewis Lindsay Dyche, Nov. 22, 1911, Dyche Papers, University of Kansas Archives.

[45]Untitled article, *Osborne Farmer,* June 8, 1911.
[46]Dyche, "A New and Enlarged Fish Hatchery," 161; and 1911 pocket diary.
[47]"Quails Trespassers," *Concordia Kansan,* Nov. 20, 1911.
[48]"He Fishes No More," *Topeka State Journal,* Aug. 10, 1911.
[49]Charles Payne to Lewis Lindsay Dyche, July 27, 1911, Dyche Papers, University of Kansas Archives.
[50]*Biennial Report,* Bulletin 4, 10.
[51]Ibid., 14.
[52]Lewis Lindsay Dyche to Frederic True, Apr. 10, 1891, Smithsonian Institution Archives, Record Unit 208, Division of Mammals, ca. 1882–1971.
[53]E. L. Brown to Lewis Lindsay Dyche, May 6, 1892, Dyche Papers, University of Kansas Archives.
[54]State of Kansas v. George L. McCullagh, vol. 96 of the *Kansas Reports*(July 1915), 786–90.

Chapter 14: The Fish Farm

[1]Dyche, "New and Enlarged Fish Hatchery," 171.
[2]White to Dyche, Nov. 22, 1911.
[3]Lewis Lindsay Dyche to William Allen White, Nov. 29, 1911, Dyche Papers, University of Kansas Archives.
[4]Discussion recorded in *Transactions of the American Fisheries Society* 41 (1911), p. 317.
[5]Dyche, "New and Enlarged Fish Hatchery," 173.
[6]Ibid., 178.
[7]"State Fish Hatchery," *Pratt Union,* Nov. 23, 1911.
[8]"Dyche in Role of Chef," *Kansas City Journal,* Dec. 21, 1911.
[9]"Dyche's Fish Plan Interests Experts," *Topeka Daily Capital,* Mar. 24, 1912.
[10]"Miss Kate King Deputy Game Warden," *Topeka Daily Capital,* May 1, 1912.
[11]"Record of the Proceedings of the Board of Regents" MS, June 4, 1912, University of Kansas Archives, 381.
[12]"New State Fish Hatchery at Pratt, Opened Yesterday," *Wichita Eagle,* Oct. 30, 1912.
[13]William Temple Hornaday to Lewis Lindsay Dyche, Mar. 12, 1913, Dyche Papers, University of Kansas Archives.
[14]Lewis Lindsay Dyche to William Temple Hornaday, May 17, 1913, Hornaday Papers, Manuscript Division, Library of Congress.
[15]William Temple Hornaday to Lewis Lindsay Dyche, May 23, 1913, Hornaday Papers, Manuscript Division, Library of Congress.
[16]"It Has Cost $2 For Each Fish," *Topeka State Journal,* Sept. 12, 1913.
[17]Mack Cretcher, letter to *Fulton Globe,* Oct. 25, 1912. (In 1923 Cretcher published a novel, *The Kansan,* a "wild west" depiction of early pioneers in Bison City, Kans.)
[18]"Dyche Probably Will Stick," *Atchison Globe,* Feb. 18, 1913.
[19]"Dyche Will Keep His Job," *Lawrence Gazette,* Sept. 16, 1913; and "No Dyche Charges Filed," *Topeka Daily Capital,* Sept. 16, 1913.
[20]"Charges Are Filed Against L.L. Dyche," *Pratt Union,* Oct. ?, 1913.
[21]"Charges Are Filed Against L.L. Dyche," *Topeka Daily Capital,* Sept. 27, 1913.
[22]"Not Fitted for the Place," *Mound City Democrat,* Oct. 10, 1913.
[23]"After Dyche," *Lawrence Daily Journal-World,* Sept. 27, 1913; and "Charges Are Filed," *Pratt Union.*
[24]*Lawrence World,* Oct. 6, 1913.
[25]*Lawrence Daily Journal,* May 12, 1897.
[26]Walter Roscoe Stubbs to William Temple Hornaday, Sept. 30, 1913, Hornaday Papers, Manuscript Division, Library of Congress.
[27]W. T. Thompson to Walter Roscoe Stubbs, Dyche Papers, University of Kansas Archives.
[28]"Commercial Club Resolutions," *Pratt Republican,* Oct. 2, 1913.
[29]"Dawson Exonerates Dyche on Showing," *Hutchinson Gazette,* Oct. 10, 1913.
[30]"Oh, Xou [sic] Fisherman, Pay Up," *Lawrence Gazette,* Oct. 9, 1913.
[31]"Dawson Exonerates Dyche On Showing," *Hutchinson Gazette,* Oct. 10, 1913.
[32]"Find Another Way of Getting Dyche?" *Topeka Daily Capital,* Nov. 22, 1913.
[33]Dyche v. Davis, Kansas State Supreme Court Reports, vol. 92, 971–79.
[34]"State Fish Car Here," *St. John News,* Nov. 27, 1913.
[35]Untitled article, *El Dorado Republican,* Dec. 17, 1914.

[36]"Ed, Milk the Cows and Feed the Fish," *Winfield Free Press,* Nov. 30, 1911.

[37]Dyche, *Ponds, Pond Fish, and Pond Fish Culture,* 11.

[38]Frank Cross, letter to the authors, Mar. 8, 1989.

Chapter 15: The Professor's Dream

[1]"Surviving Gila Monster, Dyche Faces Legislature," *Topeka Daily Capital,* Jan. 8, 1915.

[2]The Goss Natural History Collection was principally an ornithological display of over a thousand birds mounted by Colonel Nathaniel S. Goss.

[3]"Gila Monster Bit Dyche," *Chanute Tribune,* Jan. 8, 1915; and "Gila Monster Bites Off Piece of Dyche's Thumb," *Topeka Daily Capital,* Jan. 7, 1915.

[4]In fact, the bite of a Gila monster can be poisonous. The largest United States lizard, the Gila monster's average length is about nineteen inches. The reptile is found in the desert climates of Arizona, Nevada, New Mexico, and Utah, deriving its name from the Gila River in southern Arizona. Unlike the rattlesnake, the Gila monster has no tubular fangs to inject poison. But it is equipped with sharp, slightly curved teeth, the lower of which are grooved, providing a channel for venom that is released from poison glands in the lower jaw. When the Gila monster bites, clamping its strong jaws onto its victim, the poison mixes with saliva and seeps into the wound, where it can be absorbed into the victim's blood stream (Jay Monaghan, ed., *The Book of the American West,* New York: Bonanza Books, 1963, 492–93). A 1956 study revealed that of thirty-four Gila monster bites on humans, eight deaths occurred, although the deaths could not be attributed with certainty to the effects of the venom in all cases. Recent studies indicate that the lizard does not necessarily expel venom every time it bites (Charles M. Bogert to Peggy Sullivan, Aug. 2, 1986).

[5]Fern Mead Jordan to Lewis Lindsay Dyche, Jan. 7, 1915, Dyche Papers, University of Kansas Archives.

[6]Lewis Lindsay Dyche to C. D. Bunker, Jan. 7, 1915, Dyche Papers, University of Kansas Archives.

[7]"Surviving Gila Monster," *Topeka Daily Capital.*

[8]"The Great Kansas Issues," *Wichita Eagle,* Jan. 8, 1915.

[9]Ruth E. Love, "At 97, Mrs. L. Dyche Recalls Years With Famous Husband," *Lawrence Daily Journal-World,* Jan. 26, 1956; and personal interview with George Dyche, Nov. 2, 1983.

[10]"Prof. L. L. Dyche," *Pratt Kansas Republican,* Jan. 28, 1915.

[11]Love, "At 97."

[12]The Gila monster was the subject of outrageous myths, such as that it spit venom and used its tongue as a stinger; that its breath was deadly; that it had no anus, and therefore regurgitated fecal matter was the source of its poison; and that vapors from its dead body could poison anyone near it.

[13]"The Truth About Dyche," *Lawrence Daily Journal-World,* Jan. 25, 1915.

[14]Based on information provided by newspaper accounts of the incident, Charles M. Bogert, former curator and chairman of the Department of Herpetology at the American Museum of Natural History, believes it unlikely that the Gila monster bite had any immediate relation to Dyche's death: "Had the lizard managed to engage the thumb far enough back of the end, even in the middle of the thumb nail, the lizard would not have been easily or promptly removed. If the soft tissue at the end of the thumb became separated as soon as the Gila monster's front teeth were clamped down on it, there would have been little likelihood that any venom had time to reach the blood stream. . . . Had Dyche received any venom in the wound he would have been painfully aware of it. Symptoms would certainly have been manifest long before he died nearly two weeks later." (Bogert to Sullivan, Aug. 2, 1986).

[15]"Natural History Museum at K.U. Monument to Departed Kansan," *Topeka Daily Capital,* Jan. 21, 1915.

[16]"Dyche Told Peary How To Discover North Pole," *Topeka Daily Capital,* Jan. 21, 1915.

[17]"Resolution of Respect," *Lawrence Daily Journal-World,* Jan. 25, 1915.

[18]"Resolutions of Respect for Professor L. L. Dyche," in "Minutes of the Board of Administration" MS, Jan. 21, 1915, University of Kansas Archives.

[19]Frank Strong, "Lewis Lindsey [sic] Dyche" TS, Dyche Papers, University of Kansas Archives.

[20]"Tribute to the Late L. L. Dyche," *Wichita Beacon,* Feb. 20, 1915.

[21]Quoted in William Bridges, *Gathering of Animals, An Unconventional History of the New York Zoological Society* (New York: Harper and Row, 1974), 22.

[22]Clarence E. McClung to Frank Strong, Mar. 2, 1915, Strong Papers, University of Kansas Archives.

[23]"Minutes of the Board of Administration" MS, Jan. 23, 1915, University of Kansas Archives, 269.
[24]Lewis Lindsay Dyche to Fern Ignace Mead, Nov. 24, 1913, TS, Mead Papers, Ablah Library
    Special Collections, Wichita State University, Wichita, Kans.

The Dyche Family Portrait, cica 1909. From left to right: Lewis Lindsay Dyche, George, Ruth, Lewis Lindsay Jr., Walter, and Mrs. (Ophelia) Dyche.

PUBLICATIONS OF LEWIS LINDSAY DYCHE

"Trade and Profession." *The Kansas Collegiate* 4 no. 4, (Feb. 27, 1878):6.

"The University Expedition." *Lawrence Republican Daily Journal*, July 3, July 5, July 20, 1878. (Series of published letters with bylines dated June 16, June 28, July 5, and July 20, 1878. The publication date for the June 16 letter is uncertain.)

"The Last Quarter Century in Science." *The University Review* (June 1884):11–12.

"The Red Crossbill (*Loxia curvirostra stricklandi*) in Kansas." *Auk* 3 (April 1886):258–61.

"Science for a Livelihood." *Science* 8, no. 191 (Oct. 1, 1886):303.

"The Little Yellow Rail (*Porzana noveboracensis*), in Kansas." *The Ornithologist and Oölogist* 10, no. 11 (Nov. 18, 1886):168.

"Notes on Three Species of Gophers Found at Lawrence, Kas." *Transactions of the Kansas Academy of Science* 12 (1890):29–31.

"'Mammalogy and Mammalian Taxidermy at the World's Columbian Exposition." Paper presented at the Congress on Zoölogy, The World's Congress Auxiliary of the World's Columbian Exposition, Chicago, Aug. 28–Sept. 1, 1893.

"Mounting of Large Animals." *Scientific American* 69 (Oct. 7, 1893):234–35.

"Goal Ahead, Peary Fails." *New York Herald Tribune* sect. 6 (Oct. 6, 1895):2.

"The Kettle River Wilderness." *Recreation* 2 (1895):283–90.

"Walrus Hunting in the Arctic Regions." *The Cosmopolitan* 20, no. 4 (Feb. 1896):347–59.

"The Curious Race of Arctic Highlanders." *The Cosmopolitan* 21, no. 3 (July 1896):228–37.

"Notes on the Food Habits of California Sea-Lions (*Zalophus californianus* Lesson)." *Transactions of the Kansas Academy of Science* 18 (1903):179–82.

"Food Habits of the Common Garden Mole (*Scalopus aquaticus machrinus* Rafinesque)." *Transactions of the Kansas Academy of Science* 18 (1903):183-86.

"'The Creation of the Modern Fowl of Today." *Annual Report of the Kansas State Poultry Association* (1904):10–13.

"The Evolution of Our Domestic Fowl." *The Live Stock Tribune* (July 1904):202.

"The Problem of Heredity." *The Kansas Farmer* 26 (Jan. 1905):94–96.

"The Puma or American Lion (*Felis concolor*. Linnaeus)." *Transactions of the Kansas Academy of Science* 19 (1905):160–63.

"The Golden Eagle (*Aquila chrysaetus*)." *Transactions of the Kansas Academy of Science* 19 (1905):179–81.

"'The Problem of Heredity." *Annual Report of the Kansas State Poultry Association* (1906):5–10.

"The Red Phalarope (*Crymophilus fulicarius* Linn.), A New Bird for the Kansas List." *Transactions of the Kansas Academy of Science* 20 (1906):131–32.

"Some Observations on the Food Habits of the Blue Jay (*Cyanocitta cristata*)." *Transactions of the Kansas Academy of Science* 21 (1908):130–37.

"A Kansas Beaver (*Castor canadensis* Kuhl)." *Transactions of the Kansas Academy of Science* 21 (1908):165–67.

"Observations on the Food Habits of the Blue Jay." *Kansas State Poultry Association Secretary's Report* (1908):6–10.

"Doctor Snow As A Collector and His Collections." *Transactions of the Kansas Academy of Science* 22 (1909):39–45.

"A New Bird for the Kansas List, Taken at Lawrence." *Transactions of the Kansas Academy of Science* 22 (1909):311.

"The Poison-Glands of a Rattlesnake During the Period of Hibernation." *Transactions of the Kansas Academy of Science* 22 (1909):312–13.

"On the Care of Mammal Skins Kept for Museum Purposes." *Transactions of the Kansas Academy of Science* 22 (1909):363–68.

"Stocking a Farm Fish Pond; Varieties Best Suited to the Purpose." *The Farmers Mail and Breeze* 40, no. 23 (Aug. 20, 1910):1, 8.

"Fish Ponds for Kansas Farms; How to Make One and Stock it Properly." *Topeka Daily Capital* (Aug. 21, 1910).

Ponds. Bulletin no. 1 (Nov). Topeka, Kans.: Kansas Department of Fish and
  Game, 1910.
*"Water-Storage Possibilities and Soil Fertility." *Quarterly Report of the Kansas State
  Board of Agriculture* Mar. 1911):21–34.
Pond Fish. Bulletin no. 2 (July). Topeka, Kans.: Kansas Department of Fish and
  Game, 1911.
"A New and Enlarged Fish Hatchery for the State of Kansas." *Transactions of the
  American Fisheries Society*, 41 (1911):155–79.
"Regarding Fishways and Dams." *Transactions of the American Fisheries Society* 41
  (1911):301–306.
"The Kansas Fish Law." *Transactions of the American Fisheries Society* 42 (1912):137–
  38.
"Report on Progress in the Construction at the New Pond-Fish Hatchery in
  Kansas." *Transactions of the American Fisheries Society* 42 (1912):145-46.
"The Relation of Some Game Birds to Horticulture: Ringneck Pheasants and
  Hungarian Partdridges." *Transactions of the Kansas State Horticultural Society* 31
  (1912):37-45.
Biennial Report of the Fish and Game Warden for the Fiscal Years ending June 30, 1912.
  Bulletin no. 4. Topeka, Kans.: Kansas Department of Fish and Game, 1912.
"Kansas" [shooting conditions in different states]. *Forest and Stream* 79, no. 18
  (Nov. 2, 1912):561–62.
"Improved Fish Hatchery at Pratt, Kan." *Forest and Stream* 89, no. 23 (Dec. 7,
  1912):736–38.
"Land Owner, Rabbit Hunter, Game Law," [letter]. *Forest and Stream* 80, no. 3 (Jan.
  18, 1913):77.
"Possibilities of an Acre Fish Pond." *Transactions of the American Fisheries Society* 43
  (1913):67–75.
"One Year's Work at the Kansas State Fish Hatchery." *Transactions of the American
  Fisheries Society* 43 (1913):77–85.
Pond Fish Culture. Bulletin no. 3 (June). Topeka, Kans.: Kansas Department of
  Fish and Game, 1914.
Ponds, Pond Fish, and Pond Fish Culture. (Combined edition of Kansas Department
  of Fish and Game Bulletins 1-3.) Topeka, Kans.: State Printing Office, 1914.
*Biennial Report of the Fish and Game Warden for the Two Fiscal Years ending June 30,
  1913, and June 30, 1914*. Topeka, Kans: Kansas Department of Fish and Game,
  1914.
*"Fur Farming in Kansas." Paper delivered at a meeting of the National
  Association of Game and Fish Commissioners, Oct. 2, 1914.
"Notes on the New Kansas Fish Hatchery and the First Year's Output."
  Transactions of the American Fisheries Society 44, no. 1 (1914–1915):5–12.

'Not seen by the authors.

SELECTED BIBLIOGRAPHY

Akeley, Carl Ethan. *In Brightest Africa.* New York: Garden City Publishing Co., 1925.

Badger, Reid. *The Great American Fair. The World's Columbian Exposition and American Culture.* Chicago: Nelson Hall, 1979.

Bancroft, Hubert Howe, ed. *The Book of the Fair; An Historical and Descriptive Presentation of the World's Science, Art and Industry, as Viewed through the Columbian Exposition at Chicago in 1893.* 3 vols. Chicago: Bancroft Co., 1893.

Barker, Elliott S. *Beatty's Cabin.* Albuquerque: University of New Mexico Press, 1953.

Bridges, William. *Gathering of Animals, An Unconventional History of the New York Zoological Society.* New York: Harper and Row, 1974.

Brown, Barron. *Comanche, The Sole Survivor of all the Forces in Custer's Last Stand, the Battle of the Little Big Horn.* Kansas City, Mo.: Burton Publishing Co., 1935.

Brown, William Harvey. *On the South African Frontier.* 1899. Reprint. New York: Negro Universities Press, 1970.

Browne, Montagu. *Practical Taxidermy.* 2d ed. London: L. Upcott Gill, 1884(?).

Caldwell, Eugene W. "My Recollections of the Science Club 'It.'" *Graduate Magazine* (May 1919):231–34.

Cohoe. *A Cheyenne Sketchbook.* E. Adamson Hoebel and Karen D. Petersen, eds. Norman, Okla.: University of Oklahoma Press, 1964.

Connery, Robert H. *Governmental Problems in Wild Life Conservation.* New York: Columbia University Press, 1935.

Cook, Frederick A. *My Attainment of the Pole.* 3d ed. New York: Mitchell Kennerley, 1913.

— *Return from the Pole.* New York: Pellegrini and Cudahy, 1951.

— *To the Top of the Continent.* New York: Doubleday, Page and Co., 1908.

Davie, Oliver. *Methods in the Art of Taxidermy.* Philadelphia: David McKay, 1900.

Diebitsch-Peary, Josephine. *My Arctic Journal.* New York: Contemporary Publishing Co., 1894.

Dwigans, Cathy M., ed. *A Guide to The Museum of Natural History, The University of Kansas.* Lawrence, Kans.: Museum of Natural History, 1984.

Eames, Hugh. *Winner Lose All, Dr. Cook and the Theft of the North Pole.* Boston: Little, Brown and Co., 1973.

Edwards, Clarence E. *Camp-Fires of a Naturalist.* New York: D. Appleton and Co., 1893.

Fincher, Jack. "George Ferris Jr. and the Great Wheel of Fortune." *Smithsonian* 41, no. 4 (July 1983):108–18.

Forbes, John Ripley. *In the Steps of the Great American Zoologist, William Temple Hornaday.* New York: M. Evans and Co., 1966.

Freeman, Andrew A. *The Case for Doctor Cook.* New York: Coward-McCann, Inc., 1961.

Garrett-Haller, Mary Dyche (Mrs. Rex Garrett). "Alexander B. Dyche." In *Kansas Pioneers,* 188–89. Topeka, Kansas: Topeka Genealogical Society for the Bicentennial, 1976.

— *The Dyche Story and Genealogy.* Mercedes, Tex.: Author, 1986.

— "Ridgeway, Kansas." In *Kansas Pioneers,* 116–18. Topeka, Kans.: Topeka Geneological Society for the Bicentennial, 1976.

Goode, G. Browne. "Report Upon the Condition and Progress of the U.S. National Museum During the Year Ending June 30, 1887." In *Report of the United States National Museum Under the Direction of the Smithsonian Institution 1887.* Washington, D.C.: U.S. Government Printing Office, 1889.

Graham, Frank, Jr. *Man's Dominion, The Story of Conservation in America.* New York: M. Evans and Co., 1971.

Griffin, Clifford S. *The University of Kansas; A History.* Lawrence, Kans.: University Press of Kansas, 1974.

Hall, E. Raymond. *Handbook of Mammals of Kansas*. Misc. publication no. 7. Lawrence, Kans.: Museum of Natural History, 1955.

— *Charles Dean Bunker, 1870–1948*. Misc. publication no. 3. Lawrence, Kans.: Museum of Natural History, 1951.

Harmon, Terry H. "Charles Sumner Gleed: A Western Business Leader 1856–1920." Master's thesis, University of Kansas, 1968.

Hays, Samuel P. *Conservation and the Gospel of Efficiency, the Progressive Conservation Movement, 1890–1920*. Harvard Historical Monographs XL. Cambridge, Mass.: Harvard University Press, 1959.

Heilprin, Angelo. *The Arctic Problem and Narrative of the Peary Relief Expedition*. Philadelphia: Contemporary Publishing Co., 1893.

Henson, Mathew A. *A Black Explorer at the North Pole*. 1912. Reprint. New York: Walker and Company, 1969.

"History, Kansas Forestry, Fish and Game Commission, Pratt, Kansas." TS. Kansas Fish and Game Archives. 1958.

Hobbs, William Herbert. *Peary*. New York: Macmillan, 1936.

Hoig, Stan. *The Peace Chiefs of the Cheyennes*. Norman, Okla.: University of Oklahoma Press, 1980.

Hornaday, William Temple. "'America Leads the World in the Taxidermist's Art' says Professor Wm. T. Hornaday." *New York Herald* sect. 5 (Mar. 24, 1901):9, 16.

— *The American Natural History*. New York: Charles Scribner's Sons, 1904.

— "The Extermination of the American Bison." In *Report of the United States National Museum Under the Direction of the Smithsonian Institution, 1887*, 367–548. Washington, D.C.: U.S. Government Printing Office, 1889.

— "Masterpieces of American Taxidermy," *Scribner's Magazine* 72, no. 1 (July 1922):3–17.

— *Our Vanishing Wildlife, Its Extermination and Preservation*. 1913. Reprint. New York: Arno Press, 1970.

— *Taxidermy and Zoological Collecting*. 9th ed. New York: Charles Scribner's Sons, 1909.

— *Thirty Years War for Wild Life*. New York: Charles Scribner's Sons, 1931.

— *A Wild Animal Round-Up*. New York: Charles Scribner's Sons, 1925.

— *Wild Life Conservation in Theory and Practice*. New Haven, Conn.: Yale University Press, 1914.

Hyder, Clyde Kenneth. *Snow of Kansas*. Lawrence, Kans.: University Press of Kansas, 1953.

Kansas at the World's Fair. Report of the Kansas Board of World's Fair Managers Containing Report of the "Board of Managers, Kansas Exhibit," from April 1892, to March 1893, and transactions of the "Kansas Board of World's Fair Managers," from March 1893, to December 1893, together with illustrations and descriptions in detail of all Kansas exhibits and awards. Topeka, Kans.: State Printing Office, 1894.

Keely, Robert N., and G. G. Davis. *In Arctic Seas, The Voyage of the "Kite" with the Peary Expedition*. Philadelphia: Rufus C. Hartranft, 1893.

Keim, E. T., and R. B. Trouslot. "Lewis Lindsey [sic] Dyche, A.M., M.S., Kansas State University, Lawrence, Kas." *The Kansas City Scientist* 5, no. 10 (Oct. 1891):145–49.

Kersting, Rudolf, ed. *The White World, Life and Adventures Within the Arctic Circle Portrayed by Famous Living Explorers*. 1902. Reprint. New York: AMS Press, 1976.

Lee, Sarah (Wallis) Bowdich. *Taxidermy, or the Art of Collecting, Preparing, and Mounting Objects of Natural History for the Use of Museums and Travelers*. London: Longman, Hurst, Rhees, Orue, and Brown, 1820.

Lewis, Jimmie L. "Bismarck Grove, Lawrence Kansas, 1878–1900." Master's thesis, University of Kansas, 1968.

Lucas, Frederic A. *Meteorites, Meteors and Shooting Stars*. New York: American Museum of National History, 1926.

— *The Story of Museum Groups*. Guide Leaflet Series no. 53. 4th ed. New York: American Museum of National History, 1926.

Luce, Edward S. *Keough, Comanche and Custer*. St. Louis: Author, 1939.

Lunn, Mervel P. "The History and Administration of the Kansas Forestry, Fish and Game Commission." Master's thesis, University of Kansas, 1940.

Mead, James R. *Hunting and Trading on the Great Plains, 1859–1875*. Edited by Schuyler Jones. Norman, Okla.: University of Oklahoma Press, 1986.

Monaghan, Jay ed. *The Book of the American West*. New York: Bonanza Books, 1963.

Nash, Roderick W. *Wilderness and the American Mind*. New Haven: Yale University Press, 1967.

Palmer, F. D. "The Kansas Exhibit of Mounted Specimens of Animals of the State." *Scientific American* 69, no. 3 (July 15, 1893):41–42.

Pearson, Thomas Gilbert. *Adventures in Bird Protection*. New York: D. Appleton-Century Co., 1937.

"The Peary Expedition." *Scientific American* 69, no. 3 (July 15, 1893):43.

Peary, Robert Edwin. *The North Pole, its Discovery in 1909 under the Auspices of the Peary Arctic Club*. New York, 1910; reprint New York: Greenwood Press, 1968.

— *Northward Over the "Great Ice."* 2 vols. New York: Frederick A. Stokes Co., 1898.

— *The Secrets of Polar Travel*. New York: Century Co., 1917.

— "Work in North Greenland in 1894 and 1895." *Bulletin of the American Geographical Society* 28, no. 1 (1896):21–36.

Peterson, John M. "Buffalo Hunting in Montana in 1886." *Montana, The Magazine of Western History* 31, no. 4 (Autumn 1981):2–13.

— "Science in Kansas: The Early Years, 1804-1875." *Kansas History* 10, no. 3 (Autumn 1987):201–40.

— "W. Harvey Brown and K.U.'s First Buffaloes." *Kansas History* 4, no. 4 (Winter 1981):218–26.

Photographs of the World's Fair: An Elaborate Collection of Photographs of the Buildings, Grounds, and Exhibits of the World's Columbian Exposition. Chicago: Werner Co. 1894.

"Prof. Dyche's Arctic Expedition." *The Agora* 5 (Dec. 1895):234–37.

Rasky, Frank. *The North Pole or Bust*. Toronto: McGraw-Hill Ryerson Ltd., 1977.

Rawlins, Dennis. *Peary at the North Pole, Fact or Fiction?* Washington, D.C.: Robert B. Luce, 1973.

Réaumur, René De. "Diverse Means For Preserving From Corruption Dead Birds Intended To Be Sent to Remote Countries, So That They May Arrive There In Good Condition." *Royal Society of London Philosophical Transactions* 45 (1748):304–20.

Savage, Joseph. "On the Bite of the Rattlesnake." *Transactions of the Kansas Academy of Science, 1877–78* 6 (1878):36–38.

Shor, Elizabeth Noble. *Fossils and Flies, The Life of a Compleat Scientist, Samuel Wendell Williston (1851–1918)*. Norman, Okla.: University of Oklahoma Press, 1971.

Shore, Chester K. "How Did the Jayhawk Get This Way?" *Graduate Magazine* 24, no. 3 (Dec. 1925):4.

Stene, Edwin O. *The Development of Wildlife Conservation Policies in Kansas; A Study in Kansas Administrative History*. University of Kansas Governmental Research Series no. 3. Lawrence, Kans.: Bureau of Government Research, 1946.

Sterling, Wilson, ed. *Quarter-Centennial History of the University of Kansas, 1866–1891*. Topeka: George W. Crane and Co., 1891.

Sternberg, Charles H. *The Life of a Fossil Hunter*. New York: Henry Holt and Co., 1909.

Stevens, W. C. "Reminiscences." In *The Fiftieth Anniversary of the Founding of the Kansas Chapter of the Society of the Sigma Xi*. Lawrence, Kans.: University of Kansas, 1941.

Strong, Frank. "Lewis Lindsey [sic] Dyche." *The Graduate Magazine* 13 (Feb. 1915):143-46.

— "Lewis Lindsey [sic] Dyche." *Science* 41, no. 1051 (Feb. 19, 1915):280–82.

Taft, Robert. *Across the Years on Mount Oread*. Lawrence, Kans.: University of Kansas Press, 1941.

Thavis, L. William. "The World's Largest Fish Hatchery." *Popular Mechanics* (June

1912):828.

Walsh, Henry Collins. *The Last Cruise of the Miranda, A Record of Arctic Adventure.* New York: Transantlantic Publishing Co., 1896.

Ward, Roswell Howell. *Henry A. Ward, Museum Builder to America.* New York: Rochester Historical Society, 1948.

Ward, Rowland. *The Sportsman's Handbook to Practical Collecting, Preserving, and Artistic Setting-Up of Trophies and Specimens.* 5th ed. London: Author, 1890.

Weems, John Edward. *Peary, the Explorer and the Man.* Boston: Houghton Mifflin Co., 1967.

— *Race for the Pole.* New York: Henry Holt and Co., 1960.

Wetmore, Alexander. "The Dyche Museum at the University of Kansas." *Science* 94, no. 2452 (Dec. 1941):593–98.

White, William Allen. *The Autobiography of William Allen White.* New York: Macmillan, 1946.

— White, et al. *Vernon Kellogg 1867–1937.* Washington, D.C.: Anderson House, 1939.

Wilson, Guy West. "Necrology. Lewis Lindsay Dyche." *Transactions of the Kansas Academy of Science* 28 (1916–1917):355–62.

Wright, Theon. *The Big Nail, The Story of the Cook-Peary Feud.* New York: John Day Co., 1970.

ACKNOWLEDGMENTS

When Peggy moved from a remote Texas farm to Lawrence in 1974 she found herself longing for the prairie wildlife she had left behind. She spent a good deal of time exploring the Museum of Natural History atop Mount Oread—the Panorama of North American Plants and Animals can be spellbinding with its large mammals collected and mounted a century ago still standing lifelike. In the gift shop she discovered an 1895 lecture poster featuring the museum's namesake, Lewis Lindsay Dyche, posed in Arctic sealskins and throwing harpoons. Intrigued by the images and legacies of this dashing Kansan, Peggy decided to find out more about him. By 1983, after poring over Dyche's letters, scrapbooks, photographs, field diaries, and glass-plate slides in the University Archives, she resolved to write his biography. Bill joined her in that task the following year.

We are indebted to the many books that helped provide a context for Dyche's life, especially Clifford Griffin's *The University of Kansas, A History,* Reid Badger's *The Great American Fair,* and Clyde Kenneth Hyder's *Snow of Kansas* (Professor Hyder also kindly provided us with advice and insight by mail). John Peterson's articles on William Harvey Brown also stand out as being especially informative, and Mary (Dyche) Garrett-Haller's geneaology of the Dyche family provided crucial information about Dyche's early years.

Numerous persons contributed their time and expertise assisting us (although they should be exonerated from responsibility for any shortcomings): Frank Cross, curator of ichthyology at the Museum of Natural History and professor of systematics and ecology, generously read an early draft of the manuscript and tactfully pointed out our transgressions. Thomas Swearingen, the museum's director of exhibits and taxidermist, also provided insight in crucial areas. We are also obliged to Charles M. Bogert, Barbara Stein, Ronald L. McGregor, Ignace Mead Jones, Mrs. Hubert Parker, Donald Lewis Dyche, the late George Dyche, the late Jerry Stannard, Pamela D. Kingsbury, Lou Michel, Linda Thomas, Karl Kabelac of the University of Rochester Library's Department of Rare Books and Special Collections, Susan McClear of the Sitka Historical Society, Sam Daniel of the Prints and Photographs Division of the Library of Congress, James H. Hutson of the Library of Congress Manuscript Division, Harry G. Heiss of the Smithsonian Institution Archives, and the courteous staffs of KU Interlibrary Loan and the Pratt fish hatchery.

Roger Martin, Barbara Watkins, and Donna Butler read and commented on early drafts of the manuscript, for which we are grateful, and Jane Doyle Guthrie capably performed the final edit.

It is doubtful that this book would have been written had the University of Kansas Archives not been such a congenial place to work: We thank Barry Bunch, Ned Kehde, John Nugent, and Thomas C. Ryther for their constant helpfulness and patience.

Herbert and Martha Sharp assisted us in the purchase of a computer, without which it is doubtful the authors could have worked together for the many years the project required. Nancy Matthews kindly provided shelter to Bill while he was conducting research in Washington, D.C.

We are grateful to Philip Humphrey and Cathy Dwigans for their support of this project. And we thank Robert Hoffmann for his foreword to this volume.

Finally, we are forever grateful to Chester Sullivan for his years of good editing, research help, and sound advice.

Index

Adams, Leverett A., 137, 189

Agassiz, Jean Louis Rodolphe, 68, 134

Agassiz Museum, 38

Akeley, Carl, 33-34

Allakasingwah, 100

Allen, J. A., 54, 77

Allerton, Ellen P., 55

American Bison Society, 140

American Fisheries Society, 162, 171, 173, 176

American Geographic Society, 111, 148

American Museum of Natural History: Dyche visits, 38, 136; Dyche corresponds with, 54; Dyche's relationships with, 44, 82; and Peary Relief Expedition, 91-92, 101-102; and Peary North Pole expeditions, 111, 148; mentioned, 33, 141

Amundsen, Roald, 113

Anderson, J. Wylie, 46, 47, 49, 55

"Angler No. 1," 162, 174, 181, 189

Anniversary Lodge, 91, 92, 98-101

Anti-Horse Thief Association, 159

Apache Indians, 12

Arctic Club, 89-90, 105, 111, 149, 192

Auburn, Kansas, 3-5

Audubon, John James, 134

Audubon Society, 166

Axtell, Ophelia. *See* Dyche, Ophelia Axtell

Axtell, Pliny Fiske, 27

Bailey, Edgar H. S., 51

Bailly, Jules, 37

Baird, Spencer Fullerton, xi, xiii

Baker, Lucile. *See* Sharp, Becky

Barrill, Edward, 137, 150, 152

Bartlett, John, 99

Beatty, George, 25, 28-29

Bell, J. T., 57

Bessey, Charles E., 35, 197 *n.* 4.

Bismarck Grove (Lawrence), 38, 117

Bison: hunted by William F. Cody, 5; hunted by James R. Mead, 45; decline of, 12, 46, 158; collected in Montana, xii-xiii, 30-31, 38, 188-89; mounted by Hornaday, xii-xiii, 35-36, 188-89; mounted by Dyche, xii, 34-36, 38-41, 189; at Bismarck Grove, Lawrence, 38; last seen in Kansas, 41; American Bison Society, 140

Blake, Lucien I., 125, 126, 130, 131, 135

Board of Administration, 180, 186, 189

Board of Regents (University of Kansas), 15, 39, 41, 45, 46, 49, 51, 55, 57, 66, 67, 77, 111, 117, 124-25, 129, 130, 131, 137, 138, 139, 152, 158, 165, 166, 171-72, 175, 180

Bonney, Charles C., 74

Borah, William Edgar, 43

Bowers, George, 181

Bowersock, Justin D., 188

Brady, J. L., 152

Brewer, William H., 81, 86, 200 *n.* 8.

Bristow, Joseph, 169

Brown, Barron, 76

Brown, E. L., 52-53, 54, 168

Brown, William Harvey: Smithsonian expedition to Montana, 30-31, 34, 38, 41; collecting expeditions with Dyche, 24-27; work at the University of Kansas, 30, 31, 34, 35, 197 *n.* 30.

Browne, Belmore, 150

Browne, Montagu, 34, 37

Buffalo. *See* bison

Bunker, Charles Dean, 121, 137, 138, 141, 146, 184, 189

Caldwell, Eldie F., 111, 118-19, 120, 121, 146

Caldwell, Eugene W., 51

Campbell, Florence, 114

Canfield, James H., 57

Camp-Fires of a Naturalist, 15, 25, 28, 60, 61, 74, 168, 195 *n.* 3, 196 *n.* 6. *See also* Edwords, Clarence E.

Capper, Arthur, 183, 185, 188

Carp, 160, 162, 171

Case, Francis, 76

Cheyenne Indians, 18-19

ABOUT THE AUTHORS

William Sharp teaches Western Civilization at the University of Kansas in Lawrence, where he is currently pursuing his doctoral degree. He received a Fulbright scholarship to Bonn, West Germany, in 1982–83, and his award-winning short stories have appeared in publications such as *Vanderbilt Review* and *Hawaii Review*. He holds a B.A. in English and German, and an M.A. in Soviet and East European Studies.

Peggy Sullivan, a native Texan, in 1974 came to the University of Kansas where she teaches English and has designed and written English courses for the Division of Continuing Education. Her fiction, book reviews, and essays have been published in scholarly journals. As owner and publisher of Lantana Press, she produced six collections of fiction and poetry in the 1980s and remains an active editor and supporter of writers in diverse fields.